MULTIVIEW:

An Exploration in Information Systems Developme

INFORMATION SYSTEMS SERIES

Consulting Editors

D. E. AVISON
BA, MSc, PhD, FBCS
Professor of Information Systems
Department of Accounting and Management Science,
Southampton University, UK

G. FITZGERALD
BA, MSc, MBCS
Professor of Business Information Systems
Department of Computer Science
Birkbeck College, University of London, UK

This series of student and postgraduate texts covers a wide variety of topics relating to information systems. It is designed to fulfil the needs of the growing number of courses on, and interest in, computing and information systems which do not focus on the purely technological aspects, but seek to relate these to business and organisational context.

INFORMATION SYSTEMS SERIES

MULTIVIEW:
An Exploration in Information
Systems Development

D.E. AVISON BA, MSc, FBCS
Professor of Information Systems
Department of Accounting and Managment Science
University of Southampton

and

A.T. WOOD-HARPER MA, PhD, MBCS
Professor, Information Systems and Computer Science
Department of Mathematics and Computer Science
Salford University, UK

McGRAW-HILL BOOK COMPANY

London · New York · St Louis · San Francisco · Auckland
Bogotá · Caracas · Lisbon · Madrid · Mexico · Milan
Montreal · New Delhi · Panama · Paris · San Juan · São Paulo
Singapore · Sydney · Tokyo · Toronto

British Library
Cataloguing in Publication Data

Avison, D. E.
  Multiview: an exploration of information
  systems development.—(Information
  systems series).
  1. Information systems
  I. Title   II. Wood-Harper, A. T.
  Series
  302 2

ISBN 0-632-03026-7

Library of Congress
Cataloguing in Publication Data

Avison, D. E.
  Multiview: an exploration of information
  systems development/D. E. Avison and
  A. T. Wood-Harper
    p.   cm.
  Includes bibliography references and index.
    ISBN 0-632-03026-7
    1. System design.   2. Information
    storage and retrieval systems.
  I. Wood-Harper, A. T.   II. Title
  III. Series:
  Information systems series (Oxford,
  England)
  QA76.9.S88A922   1990
  004.2'1—dc20

Contents

Foreword

The Blackwell Scientific Publications Series on Information Systems is a series of student texts covering a wide variety of topics relating to information systems. It is designed to fulfil the needs of the growing number of courses on, and interest in, computing and information systems which do not focus on the purely technological aspects, but seek to relate these to the business and organisational context.

Information systems has been defined as the effective design, delivery, use and impact of information technology in organisations and society. Utilising this fairly wide definition, it is clear that the subject area is somewhat interdisciplinary. Thus the series seeks to integrate technological disciplines with management and other disciplines, for example, psychology and philosophy. It is felt that these areas do not have a natural home, they are rarely represented by single departments in polytechnics and universities, and to put such books into a purely computer science or management series restricts potential readership and the benefits that such texts can provide. This series on information systems now provides such a home.

The books will be mainly student texts, although certain topics may be dealt with at a deeper, more research-oriented level.

The series is expected to include the following areas, although this is not an exhaustive list: information systems development methodologies, office information systems, management information systems, decision support systems, information modelling and databases, systems theory, human aspects and the human-computer interface, application systems, technology strategy, planning and control, and expert systems, knowledge acquisition and representation.

A mention of the books so far published in the series gives a 'flavour' of the richness of the information systems world. *Information Systems Development: Methodologies, Techniques and Tools* (D.E. Avison and G. Fitzgerald), looks at many of the areas discussed above in overview form; *Information and Data Modelling* (David Benyon), concerns itself with one very important aspect, the world of data, in some depth; *Structured Systems Analysis and Design Methods* (G. Cutts) looks at one particular information systems development methodology in detail; *Information Systems Research: Issues, Techniques and Practical Guidelines* (R. Galliers, (ed)) provides a collection of papers on key information systems issues; and *Software Engineering for Information Systems* (D. McDermid) discusses software engineering in the context of information systems. There are a number of other titles in preparation.

This new book on Multiview is the result of extensive research by the authors which they have developed into a very useful textbook relevant to all those interested in information systems development. Multiview is a methodology of information systems development which seeks to combine the strengths of a number of different, existing approaches. Many of these approaches are radically different in terms of concepts, philosophy and assumptions, let alone the methods, techniques and tools that they use. The challenge for the researchers was to integrate these approaches and capture the strengths of each approach. The book not only addresses the theory behind the approach but also illustrates the practice and experiences of using the methodology. The authors are refreshingly honest regarding these experiences and discuss the problems and weaknesses that they encountered. They conclude by using these experiences to review the ideas of a methodology and to advocate a more contingency based approach to systems development using Multiview as a framework rather than as a prescriptive tool. Students of systems development, whether they be in the academic world or practitioners, will find this book stimulating. Its title is indeed apposite, this is truly an exploration in information systems development.

Guy Fitzgerald
Joint Consulting Editor
Information Systems Series

Preface

This book looks at both the human and technical aspects of information systems. It also looks at the human and technical aspects of information systems development, for the way in which the analysts carry out their role and attempt to put theory into practice is just as important as the theory itself. The book expounds particular theories about the various aspects of information systems development and, in general terms, shows how these theories can be applied.

The approach adopted in the text has been used by the authors on a number of projects and this book tells the story of some of these as case studies. The book is divided into seven parts and in all but the last of these, where the lessons to be learnt from all the cases are discussed, a case study is presented of Multiview 'in action'. Each case illustrates many of the aspects of Multiview discussed in the chapters preceding the case study, and can therefore be used as useful revision material, but it is also used for illustrative purposes in the chapters following, for instance, to provide examples when explaining some of the techniques used in Multiview.

This aspect of the book is at least as important as the theoretical content and the descriptions of the general application of Multiview. Although the cases are used to illustrate particular techniques, they are not put forward as 'textbook' examples, showing how the application of the Multiview methodology worked perfectly each time. On the contrary, they expose some of the difficulties and practical problems of information systems work. Indeed the authors are concerned to show that information systems development theories should be contingent rather than prescriptive because the skills of different analysts and the situations in which they are constrained to work have always to be taken into account in any project. The realities of the situation will cause departure from the 'ideal methodology' in order to allow for the exigencies of the real world. For this reason, Multiview can be said to be a method for exploring the application area in order to develop an information system.

Information systems development is a hybrid process involving computer specialists, who will build the system, and users, for whom the system is being built. This distinction is sometimes blurred in practice as both are involved in the development process and this book will be of interest to students and practitioners. It will be of particular value to:

- Computer Science students who will already have learnt some computer programming and systems analysis and who will probably have studied some applications of information technology to business and administration. They will now need to consider how they might carry out the process of information systems development.

- Business Studies or Management students who will have been on an introductory course in data processing or systems analysis and have learnt about some of the situations where information technology can be useful. They will now need to consider how a manager or administrator might go about the process of commissioning an information system which will effectively serve the needs of the organisation.

- Practising systems analysts and managers who have had experience in developing information systems or seen them develop. They may now wish to study some recent thinking about the many factors involved in information systems and the way that this theory can be put into practice.

At the end of each chapter are a set of exercises. We have attempted to make these as varied and interesting as possible. Some are 'examination type questions', others require limited practical work, some require some limited research, for example looking at the provisions of a particular application package, and yet others are larger pieces of practical work which require investigation into the reader's own business, polytechnic, university, library or some other organisation.

As stated above, the book is divided into seven parts. Each of these parts may contain one or more chapters. The first part gives an overview of the Multiview methodology and places it in the context of information systems theory and practice. The next five parts cover the five stages of Multiview. Part seven reviews the theory and practice, drawing some lessons and conclusions about Multiview and its application in the case studies.

The five stages of Multiview are as follows:
- Analysis of human activity
- Information analysis
- Analysis and Design of the socio-technical aspects
- Design of the human-computer interface
- Design of the technical aspects.

They incorporate five different views which are appropriate to the progressive development of an analysis and design project so as to form a system which is complete in both technical and human terms. The five stages move from the general to the specific, from the conceptual to hard fact and from issue to task. Outputs of each stage either become inputs to following stages or are major outputs of the methodology. Although this does imply order, projects using the Multiview methodology do not always develop from stage 1 through to stage 5. As we shall see in the case studies, the methodology can be used flexibly, as appropriate to each situation.

The first stage looks at the organisation - its main purpose, problem themes, and the creation of a statement about what the information system will be and what it will do. The second stage is to analyse the entities and functions of the system described in stage one. This is carried out independently of how the system will develop. A number of diagrammatic aids are discussed which are used in this process.

The philosophy behind the third stage is that people have a basic right to control their own destinies and that if they are allowed to participate in the analysis and design of the systems that they will be using, then implementation, acceptance and operation of the system will be enhanced. This stage emphasises the choice between alternative systems, according to important social and technical considerations. The fourth stage is concerned with the technical requirements of the user interface. The design of specific dialogues will depend on the background and experience of the people who are going to use the system, as well as their information needs.

Finally, the design of the technical subsystem concerns the specific technical requirements of the system to be designed, and therefore such aspects as computers, databases, control and maintenance. Although the methodology is concerned with the computer only in the latter stages, it is assumed that a computer system will normally form at least part of the information system. However, we do not argue that the final system will necessarily run on a large mainframe computer (as is the case for many information systems development methodologies). This is just one solution - in fact many systems, including some of those described in the case studies discussed in the text, are implemented on a microcomputer.

We would like to acknowledge the co-operation of all those people - too many to mention individually - who were involved in the six case studies presented in the text. In addition, we wish to thank Simon Bell, Niels Bjørn-Andersen, Alan Booth, Paul Catchpole, Steve Corder, Bill Cotterman, Guy Fitzgerald, Paul Gardner, Paul Golder, Julie Horton, Kuldeep Kumar, Agneta Olerup, Jim Senn, Hanifa Shah, Sam Waters and Bernard Williams who have all made a valuable contribution. Comments and criticisms from Peter Checkland, Frank Land and Enid Mumford have been especially helpful in the development of the Multiview methodology.

Most of all we wish to thank and acknowledge the contribution of Lyn Antill, an independent consultant, now with Shell (UK), who was one of the co-authors of the original text on the methodology - *Information Systems Definition: The Multiview Approach* (A.T. Wood-Harper, Lyn Antill and D.E. Avison, 1985), who has contributed much to the methodology and also played a major part in the Polytechnic Distance Learning Project discussed in Part Two of this text. This case is developed further in that original book.

PART ONE

MULTIVIEW:

AN INTRODUCTION

Chapter 1
Information Systems Development

In this chapter we will discuss in outline what we mean by the term 'information system' and what is involved in the development of such a system. We will look in particular at the logical specification of the design rather than at the software or hardware engineering required to build the system. We will also look at the reasons why we have put forward the 'Multiview' approach as being a more complete solution to the problems of information systems analysis and design than many of the methods currently taught in polytechnics and universities or practised in industry.

1.1 INFORMATION SYSTEMS IN PERSPECTIVE

An **information system** can be defined as:

'a system to collect, process, store, transmit, and display information'.

This gives a very wide interpretation of an information system, and this book offers narrower terms of reference. For example, informal information systems such as the 'old boy network' or the 'grapevine' could both be included within this definition. But we would not normally talk about 'setting up a grapevine'. This book concerns itself with the development of **formal** information systems.

One of the 'founding fathers' of the modern discipline defines an information system as:

'an integrated man/machine system for providing information to support the operations, management and decision making functions in an organization. The system uses computer hardware, software, manual procedures, management and decision models and a data base.' (Davis 1974)

Davis (1983) looks at the individual components of this definition:
* *Man/machine system*: this consists of information technology and people's activities in preparing and using information.
* *Support, operations management and decision making functions*: this gives the context of information systems in organisations.

- *Computer hardware and software*: this gives the facilities by which information systems give more useful and interesting information.
- *Manual procedures*: this gives the design of user procedures which are vital for the success of the operation of computer-based information systems.
- *Management and decision models*: this gives a gamut of models which support the decisions from highly structured to unstructured situations and from the operation level to strategic decisions (see also Keen & Scott Morton 1978).
- *Data bases*: these are based on the concept of data as an organisational resource, and this view is made viable by data base (now more usually written as *database*) technology.

As we see in Figure 1.1, data, which are the raw facts available, act as the 'building blocks' of information, a major constituent of the information system which supports the activities in an organisation.

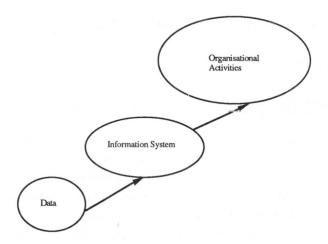

Fig. 1.1. The relationship between data, the information system and the activities of the organisation

We follow Davis's lead and further limit the area of interest covered by the book in that we are *primarily* concerned with computerised information systems. There are circumstances when it is not advisable to use a computer system, but the main interests of the book are towards defining information systems which will be computerised in some way, that is, **computer-based information systems**.

Another recent definition (Buckingham *et al*, 1987) broadens the area and highlights the fact that although information technology is normally used, it is not necessary for information systems:

'An Information System is any system which assembles, stores, processes and delivers information relevant to an organisation (or to society), in such a way that information is accessible and useful to those who wish to use it, including managers, staff, clients and citizens. An Information System is a human activity (social) system which may or may not involve the use of computer systems.'

As described previously, this is a broader definition than that used in this book, but the reader should be aware of the societal implications of the information systems issues that are discussed, and also that the term 'information systems' does not *necessarily* imply 'computer information systems'.

There is a great deal of academic research concerned with classifying information systems. This book is not a contribution to this particular debate. However, it might be helpful to give examples of the types of information systems that, for the purposes of this book, could be regarded as 'typical'. These include:

- Accounting
- Personnel and payroll records
- Sales order processing
- Stock control
- Banking records
- Reservations
- Decision support systems
- Office automation
- Point of sale systems
- Public information systems
- Library information retrieval systems.

Computer information systems are changing and evolving at a great pace. The systems that are being developed in the 'eighties and 'nineties are very different from those of the 'sixties and 'seventies. This atmosphere of change is both exciting and confusing, and this applies to users and computer experts alike. Indeed, in a market where there are new products every week and where products are announced long before they are ready (and arrive with different specifications), it might be dishonest to claim to be an expert at all.

In this atmosphere of change, the computer professional has two major options. The first is to select a particular product range and get to know this range and its developments thoroughly. This technical knowledge will be valuable to potential clients or employers. The other approach is to stand back and look more carefully at the whole process of designing information systems with the aim of finding a more intelligent and flexible approach which copes with changes in the market as they occur. This is the option that the authors of Multiview have taken.

There is another reason for this choice: different ranges of 'solutions' will be appropriate to different companies, different departments of the same company, different users and user groups and different agents of change, that is, programmers, systems analysts, operators, and so on. A more flexible approach is likely to be appropriate under these circumstances.

1.2   APPROACHES TO INFORMATION SYSTEMS DEVELOPMENT

The process of information systems development has been under study by practitioners and theoreticians since the 'fifties and there are many schools of thought about the methods that should be employed. These are all based on different views of the issues at stake. Some authors are concerned primarily with the **technical problems**, others with the **strategic implications** of information systems for the organisation, others with **reducing costs** and yet others with the changes in the nature and content of **clerical work**. All of these views may be appropriate when taken in context. However a more complete view of the whole process of information systems development requires that these different viewpoints are identified and the relationships between them set out.

In order to gain a better understanding of the various aspects of information systems development, we shall look at the **systems life cycle**. This covers all the steps that a system is thought to go through from the time that the users decide that they have a problem which needs to be tackled to the point where the system is live and running. This could be said to be the 'classic' view of the way that information systems develop from the definition phase, through to the development phase, towards installation and operation. We do not say that all systems go through the same stages. They certainly do not. It may not even be appropriate to say that they all ought to go through the same stages, although it is frequently argued that they should.

The systems life cycle charted in Figure 1.2 shows the three main stages: **Definition, Development** and **Installation and Operation**. The cycle normally starts at the point where someone in authority decides that they have a problem which is to do with the processing of information, and that something ought to be done about it. This means that some form of **study** has to be carried out in order to investigate the problem and to suggest possible ways of dealing with that problem.

In a small organisation it could be that the person who carries out the study also makes the decisions. The study could, for example, consist of a review of microcomputers and lead to the decision to purchase an office microcomputer.

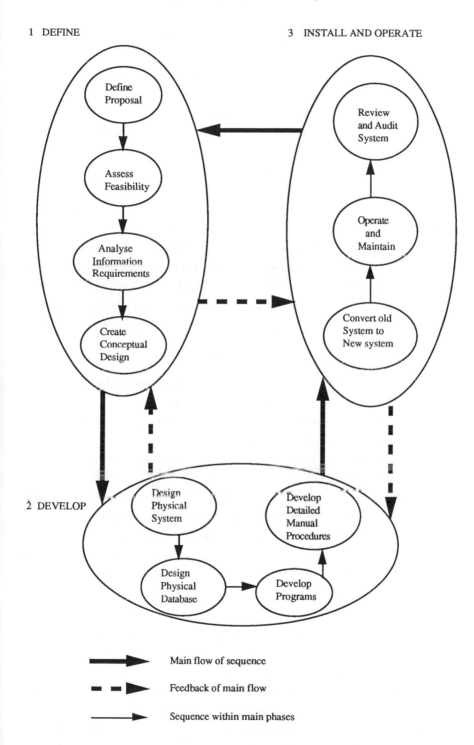

1 DEFINE

3 INSTALL AND OPERATE

Define
Proposal

Review
and Audit
System

Assess
Feasibility

Operate
and
Maintain

Analyse
Information
Requirements

Create
Conceptual
Design

Convert old
System to
New system

2 DEVELOP

Design
Physical
System

Develop
Detailed
Manual
Procedures

Design
Physical
Database

Develop
Programs

Main flow of sequence

Feedback of main flow

Sequence within main phases

Fig. 1.2. Life cycle of an application to depict the 'logical' flow of the phases

Alternatively, an external consultant could be called in. In larger firms a request may be made to the 'data processing department', 'computer department' or 'information centre'. Where external consultants or data processing personnel have been called in, it is usual to set **terms of reference** for the 'project' (sometimes called its scope) to the systems analyst or systems analysts concerned and:

- Identify the problem area (placing boundaries around it) and its main features
- Identify the people who have a stake in the project
- Identify the need for the project from the point of view of the organisation, and
- Allocate the resources to carry out the project.

The analyst then investigates the feasibility of various approaches to the problem. The terms of reference may set out various 'degrees of freedom' to the analyst in the area under investigation. It may be that the analyst has been called in to **computerise** a particular function so that the feasibility study is limited to an investigation of whether computerisation is possible and what the costs and benefits would be. At the other end of the scale, the analyst may be asked: "Are there any suggestions which might help us in our work generally?". The investigation then becomes a major part of the project rather than merely a preliminary to it.

The **feasibility study** will include:

- A high level description (or overview) of the proposed information system(s). This is essentially a statement about what the system will **do**.
- The time scale and manpower requirements of the project. This is essentially a statement about what the project will **involve**.
- A cost-benefit analysis. This is essentially a statement about what the project will **cost** and what it will be **worth**.
- An evaluation of the feasibility of the project from the technical, human, and operational viewpoints. This is essentially a statement of how **difficult** the project will be, and how **satisfactory** and how **usable** the results.

Once it has been concluded that a particular area of work would benefit from an alternative way of processing or an alternative information system, most likely involving computerisation, the next stage is to study the work in detail so as to create a complete analysis of the information requirements. This will include a specification of all the data that has to be kept by the system and the functions that the system is to perform. This is the stage of the project that has been traditionally regarded as **systems analysis**.

In order to create a successful **design**, the analyst also has to give some thought to the way in which a new computer system might be used in the day to day work of the organisation. The users themselves may be quite capable of stating their requirements in this area. However, there are many cases where it is not so simple. For example, they may not be able to see what all the alternatives are until someone points out different ways in which the same job could be performed. It is increasingly the case that changes likely to be brought about by a new system would have considerable effects on the nature and content of people's jobs, so that there is considerable likelihood of industrial relations problems and/or poor operator performance if this aspect of the work is not also analysed. The phase defines the:

- Activities of the users
- Reports to be generated
- Queries to be answered
- Function and data models, and
- User interface requirements.

Once these requirements have been analysed, the analyst has to **design** a conceptual system that would meet these requirements. This phase includes the detailed logical specification of the computer system.

> All the stages so far discussed come under the heading of
> SYSTEMS DEFINITION
>
> MULTIVIEW largely addresses problems associated with the ANALYSIS and DESIGN activities of INFORMATION SYSTEMS DEFINITION
>
> MULTIVIEW is a methodology to STRUCTURE THE TASKS for the ANALYSTS and USERS during these analysis and design activities

Fig. 1.3. Information Systems Definition

Before looking more closely at Multiview, which mainly addresses the 'definition' phase of the life-cycle (see Figure 1.3), we briefly mention the phases which follow definition in the life-cycle. The main activities are seen in Figure 1.2. Once a definition has been completed and a computer solution to the problem suggested, the work is handed over to the software and sometimes hardware engineers who will develop the information system. Equipment is selected and configured. Software is purchased and/or written. This is known as the **systems development phase**. The third phase is the **installation and operation** of the completed system. The system will continue to be operated and maintained until someone in authority decides that there is a new problem that needs to be investigated. It is then that the **cycle** starts over again.

1.3 MULTIVIEW

This book presents an approach to systems analysis and design and to the evaluation of potential solutions to information processing problems. It draws on several important threads in recent research. The analysis of **human activity systems** (Checkland 1984 and Wilson 1984) and **socio-technical systems** (Mumford 1981 and Land & Hirschheim 1983) has been wedded to the more conventional work on **data analysis** (Rock-Evans 1981 and Shave 1981) and **structured analysis** (Gane & Sarson 1979 and de Marco 1979) so as to create a theoretical framework for tackling computer systems design which attempts to take account of the different points of view of all the people involved in using a computer system.

However, these earlier works have been interpreted in a particular way (indeed, the original authors may not agree with our interpretation) and since the publication of the original text on Multiview (Wood-Harper *et al*, 1985) other work has been assimilated into the framework.

We have seen that there are theoretical and academic antecedents, as well as those based on commercial experience. However, the methods described in the book are, above all, of practical value. We use these methods for our own consultancy work, and Multiview has changed considerably as a result of this experience. The case studies (introduced in Section 1.7) describe some of that experience.

Multiview helps in providing answers to the following questions:

1 How is the information system supposed to further the aims of the organisation using it?

2 How can it be fitted into the working lives of the people in the organisation who are going to use it?

3 How can the individuals concerned best relate to the computer in terms of operating it and using the output from it?

4 What information processing function is the system to perform?

5 What is the technical specification of a system that will come close enough to doing the things that you have written down in the answers to the other four questions?

Most computer scientists, programmers and technical analysts are primarily interested in *question 5*. It is their interest in the technology that probably brought them into computing in the first place. Most people working on large systems have developed a great interest in *question 4*. This is because untangling the logic of all the different records that need to be kept provides considerable intellectual satisfaction.

The interest of computer people in these two questions is reflected in the fact that there are large numbers of books on the technical aspects of computer hardware and programming, and an increasing number about the techniques of information modelling, that is determining the flow of information through the system and the way it has to be processed and stored. Most teaching in academic computer science departments has centred around these two aspects of information systems design, and it may be entirely appropriate for computer scientists to specialise in these areas. However, good answers to these two questions are not sufficient to ensure successful information systems.

Question 3 relates to the **human-computer interface** (also called the user interface or man-machine interface). This book looks at this aspect of information systems at length. Trade unions have taken an interest in *question 2*, even though British and American unions have been behind their Scandinavian counterparts (who have had legislation to back them). *Question 1* is what the managing director has been asking all along. Unfortunately too many senior managers have had trouble with the answers. Either they did not understand the jargon in which proposals from would-be suppliers were couched or bitter experience convinced them that the answers contained more sales talk than substance. All too often managers themselves have not had the right training or advice on how to harness information technology to the needs of their operations.

Information systems are often seen as technical systems which have behavioural and social consequences. This is a rather narrow view. They are better seen as social systems which rely to an increasing extent on information technology. The technology is only a component. This wider perspective of information systems requires that a number of **stakeholders** in an information systems project are identified. These will include the individuals or group who request the new system and authorise the work to go ahead; the managers, who are responsible for the organisational functions in which the system is embedded; clerical staff and others, who operate the system; computer staff, who create and maintain the system; and external users of the system, such as customers or claimants, who receive the computer-produced invoices and forms. One major objective of Multiview is to help them to communicate with each other about what is needed and what is proposed. This may not be easy, because they may be looking at the system in different ways. One group may think in economic terms, another in terms of status and responsibilities, another in terms of job satisfaction, and yet another in terms of the nature of contact with the organisation.

1.4   MULTIVIEW IN OPERATION

We have looked at the questions which Multiview is intended to help answer. These will be explained more formally in the second chapter and discussed in detail throughout the book. Before doing that, we will look briefly at the way in which the methodology can be operated in a practical situation.

A common occurrence is the situation where a senior consultant sits down with senior management of the organisation in order to settle the terms of reference of the project. Of particular concern is the way in which the project is to be managed. In this frame of mind, and with much talk of 'policy implications' and 'business strategy', they work out answers to question 1 (in Section 1.3). What, in terms that are meaningful to both parties, does the organisation hope to gain from its investment in Information Technology? Are they trying to cut down in paperwork, speed up information processing, reduce staffing and other costs, enable more informed decision making, or what?

A decision will be taken at this stage as to whether these objectives are feasible, and also whether a computer-based system is likely to be the best way of achieving them. Alternative solutions could include rethinking the objectives, setting up improved manual operations, and continuing the computerisation study (and there may be many alternative computer solutions). Indeed, it might be recommended that the existing system is improved at the same time as, or even before, computerisation.

Following this, the analyst needs to find out what information needs to be collected and processed, and what function the system is to perform. Decisions also need to be taken about the feasibility of computerisation as difficulties are encountered.

Only after all of these stages have been completed is there a call for knowledge of specific computers, database management systems, software packages, and so on. Now the analyst can go to the suppliers with a clear statement of what is required, and can challenge them to supply a system that is adequate from a human and technical point of view to do the job, and is available, suitably priced and supported. Where a company has its own data processing department, the analyst's specification of the user requirements may be used by the technical analysts and programmers in the organisation to build a suitable system. It may be necessary to go through some of the stages again if there are difficulties in buying or building such a system.

But Multiview in operation differs widely according to the particular situation. It is a contingency approach. Projects follow various courses depending on such issues as to whether the objectives are clear and stable, the degree of user involvement that is practicable, working practices, the complexity of the situation, and the type and views of management (Andersen *et al*, 1990). For this reason, the use of Multiview can be said to be an *exploration* in information systems development. The six case studies described in this text provide an opportunity to see Multiview in operation in a number of situations.

1.5   MULTIVIEW: A CONTINGENCY APPROACH

Davis (1982) advocates the contingency approach to information systems development where the methodology chosen will depend on the particular circumstances where it is to be applied. In other words, different methodologies will be used for different situations, a kind of 'horses-for-courses' approach. He suggests that the level of uncertainty in a situation is critical in this choice, and argues that four components of the overall system affect the total level of uncertainty:

• The complexity and ill-structuredness of the system
• Its current state of flux
• The number of users affected, skills needed and skills possessed, and
• The level of experience and skill of the analysts.

The approach adopted therefore will be contingent on the particular situation, according to the complexity of the problem and the levels of user and analyst competence.

Other writers such as Burns & Dennis (1985), Capper (1984), Episkopou & Wood-Harper (1986), Land & Somogyi (1986) and Markus (1984) have either extended Davis's work on uncertainty or offered other factors which will affect methodology choice.

The implication here is that organisations will avoid standardising on one chosen methodology because there will be circumstances where it is not particularly suitable. For each particular situation they will have available a number of different information systems development methodologies from which they choose one. As Avison & Fitzgerald (1988) show, there are a large number of information systems development methodologies from which to choose.

Iivari (1987) presents a different contingency framework which emphasises contingent approaches *within* the methodology rather than *between* methodologies. This is the type of contingency approach suggested in this text. Multiview is a flexible framework which provides an alternative to choosing between different methodologies. The techniques and tools available within the Multiview framework are chosen and adjusted according to the particular problem situation. Multiview is a blended methodology drawing from a number of major methodologies already in use or proposed. However, it provides a significant contrast to many methodologies in common use, such as SSADM in the UK (see Downs *et al*, 1988), where the steps are prescribed in great detail and are expected to be followed rigorously in all situations.

1.6   THE PROJECT TEAM

We have deliberately avoided being prescriptive about the way in which the project team should be selected and managed. Multiview can be used equally by large teams working on complex systems and by an individual working on a microcomputer system. Of course the way in which the project is managed will be different.

There is much discussion about whether the sort of person who can comprehend the problems of the manager running an organisation is also capable of understanding the details of a technical process such as data analysis. The fact is that different people have different skills and backgrounds to bring into a project. Some can cover the wide range of human and technical problems and others are better at specialising in one or other aspect. Different situations call for different combinations of skills. Some systems analysis and design problems are primarily technical, others are primarily human. Problems come in various sizes, small, medium, large, and super-large. Size brings with it complexity. However, even a small problem may be complex in that it has many threads. There may, therefore, be more than one type of analyst (and more than one of each type) involved in the project. There will be both technically oriented analysts and human/socially oriented analysts.

As we have already commented, much will depend on the particular problem situation. For example, the project team may consist of business systems analysts at the early stage and later include technically oriented analysts, programmers and operators. However, in some situations users and other interested parties (a trade union representative or member of the personnel department, for instance) may be added to the project team. It is difficult to be prescriptive in information systems work, but there is certainly the need for input from users (whether as part of the project team or working cooperatively with it) as the users' experience will be vital.

We tend to use the term 'users' as a homogeneous group, but they are not. Their requirements will depend on the type of system and type of user, amongst other criteria. A minimum distinction between users would be:

- **Professional users**, that is, data processing people who will use the computer system to develop programs and systems.
- **Regular users**, that is clerical and secretarial staff who may access the computer system daily to input data or to process text. They are frequently referred to as the operators of the system. Assuming that steps have been taken to ensure their cooperation, they are likely to be willing to train in the use of the computer so that they can use the system. These inducements may mean tangible things, like salary increases, and less tangible things, such as improved status, job interest and security. When regular users are familiar with the system, they may be put off by

the level of help given to the casual user. Regular users may find this unnecessary and irritating and it may also slow down the running of the system.

- **Casual users**, who are frequently middle managers or top managers. They might have had little previous experience of computing and their use of the new equipment may be very varied. They are unlikely to have the time or inclination to train to use each computer system thoroughly, and the enquiries they make each day could be related to different applications or different parts of the same application. The human-computer interface for casual users must therefore be particularly helpful. Some computer systems have two or three types of interface which can be selected according to the experience of the user.

Thus the organisation of the project team will depend on many factors. With the present shortage of skills, the availability of staff might be a major constraining factor.

1.7 THE CASE STUDIES

Live projects in systems analysis, design and implementation form a major thread running through this book. At least one of the authors was involved in each of these projects. The case studies are used to illustrate the topics described in each of the first six of the seven 'Parts' of the text, but they have another purpose as well. They are there to serve as commentary on the theory of analysis expounded in the book. In other words, they are there to address the question: 'does it work in practice?'. The case studies are told as stories because systems development *is* a story. They are stories of human endeavour: of real people using their technical, intellectual and social skills grappling with 'messy' reality.

We cannot design a series of 'scientific' experiments to test out whether our theories are right. To evaluate a methodology it is necessary to see it working in different situations and being used by different analysts. It is also important that the process of analysis and its results should be looked at from different viewpoints. What looks good to the analysts may not be so impressive to the user. The case studies presented here form part of our on-going work of methodology evaluation (see Episkopou & Wood-Harper 1984 and Avison & Wood-Harper 1986).

We have not chosen the case studies because they are 'classic examples of how systems analysis should be done'. In a practical discipline one must always distinguish between the **ideal methodology** as taught in text books, and the realities of any situation which causes departure from the ideal in order to allow for the exigencies of the real world. The case studies expose the difference between what we would *like* to be in an ideal world and what *is* in the real world. Many design methodologies are prescriptive not only of what must be done but of the order in which it has to be done. In the real world, decisions are often made before all the facts have been gathered. Frequently this is due to time or cost constraints. This is just as true of the systems designer as of the general or the entrepreneur. No one could pretend that this is the ideal way of decision making, but it is a fact of life and Multiview can help to make decisions which are supportable even in these situations.

The first case, described at the end of Part 1, concerns a professional association and provides an example of an organisation which is having problems with its clerical systems. The case highlights some of the political, social, and organisational aspects of information systems work which concern the human rather than the technical dimension. At the end of Part 2 the polytechnic distance learning unit case is presented. This describes the early phases involved in creating a computerised system related to learning materials for students taking a vocational course at a distance from a polytechnic. The users here had experience with computers. This case study is developed fully in Wood-Harper *et al* (1985). The third case study concerns a freight import agency situated at a small airport. Systems requirements and possible solutions are suggested. A major feature of the problem situation is uncertainty. At the end of Part 4 a case is described involving a small computer consulting company. The last two cases (at the end of Parts 5 and 6) are rather larger in scope and take place in larger organisations. The fifth case study involves the development of a prototype computer system for a district health authority. It provides an example where Multiview was adapted significantly for the particular problem situation. User reactions to the prototype information system for community health workers are discussed. The final case, described at the end of Part 6, concerns a fully integrated information system for an academic department. It provides a full example of the application of Multiview. In the final chapter (Part 7), these cases are examined as a whole and lessons learnt are discussed.

These cases were all real examples of Multiview in use. Multiview has been developed in the tradition of **action research**, where there is a close interaction between theory and practice, the framework changing frequently according to the experience gained in using it. Readers of Wood-Harper *et al* (1985) will note a number of changes in the framework developed since that time and also see differences in emphasis when reading this present text.

1.8 THE SOCIAL AND POLITICAL ENVIRONMENT OF INFORMATION SYSTEMS

When an analyst looks at an organisation, the most obvious aspects are those related to the **functional system**, in other words, what people there **do**. Activities within the functional system include making things, processing information, and making decisions. This is of primary interest to the analysts. However, there are other systems at work which may or may not parallel the functional systems. Notable amongst these are the **social system** and the **political system**. To misunderstand these systems may lead to strikes, non-cooperation, or too much power being placed in the hands of the technologists.

The social system is concerned with values. These are the sorts of things that people think are good or bad, right or wrong. To give one example found in many British companies: senior staff eat in the 'staff dining room' whilst manual staff eat in a 'workers' canteen'. The Japanese in particular may find this a surprising vestige of the British class system and regard it as quite wrong. The social system also includes things like the way in which certain groups of people talk to each other and whether, and to what degree, the decision-making process is democratic (see Section 1.9).

The political system is about people's interests. This includes obvious things like the relationships between trade unions and management, and between different unions. It also includes things like career structures, because the political interests of individuals may only partly coincide with their functional position. For example, it may be functionally appropriate for work to be changed and staff to be redeployed, but it may not be in the interests of an individual manager, whose empire is reduced, or the individual worker, who loses job prospects. The computer-based information system is likely to lead to considerable organisational change which will affect working practices and people in the organisation may view these changes positively or negatively.

1.9 LEVELS AND STYLES OF MANAGEMENT

There are different levels of management in organisations. The managers at each level may be making decisions about the implementation of information systems. At the top or **strategic** level of management, decisions are made about where the company should be going. An example of this sort of decision is provided where management decides to take advantage of the advances in telecommunications in order to decentralise the company's operations. This could permit salesmen to keep in closer contact with their customers whilst having instant access to computerised information held in the company's database.

Middle management tend to be concerned with how to organise work so as to achieve the long term strategy defined by top management. They might be particularly interested in planning aids such as spreadsheets, which can, for example, be used to answer questions related to sales forecasting and budgeting. The use of such tools enables middle management to estimate the likely effectiveness of particular tactics. They are also likely to want exception reports from the computer when things do not appear to be on target.

The lowest level of management is the **operational** or supervisory level. They may have some freedom to implement their own information systems, but they are more likely to be in charge of the day to day operation of the system chosen by the middle manager or strategic management, represented by a decision of the Board of Directors.

These management levels are, of course, generalisations, but it is necessary for analysts to have some idea of the level of management of the people that they are dealing with at any time, their likely concerns, and the freedom of action that they have in making decisions.

It is also necessary for the analyst to have some idea of the degree of flexibility of the organisation. Some organisations are **rigid** and **bureaucratic**. At the other end of the scale are organisations which can be described as **organic**. These firms are composed of individuals willing and able to adapt to changing circumstances. No organisation will be at one end of the scale, but the British Civil Service provides an example of an organisation nearer the bureaucratic end of the scale and the new technology companies provide examples of those companies nearer the organic end of the scale (otherwise they are likely to go out of business).

Another sort of polarity is between **democratic** and **autocratic** organisations. This distinction concerns the way in which decisions are made in the organisation. Decisions can be imposed or reached after consultation or negotiation.

Systems analysis, design and implementation is a long-term and complex process affecting the whole organisation. It may take place over some years. Indeed it is often better thought of as the continuing process of the design and redesign of information systems as organisations attempt to cope with changing needs. Information systems **emerge** as a result of negotiation between managers, operators, analysts and suppliers, and as a result of the interplay of the functional, social and political systems. Different types of management decisions are made at various stages in the systems life cycle and this is achieved in ways which depend on the style of management and the type of organisation.

1.10 SUMMARY

Although information systems include informal and clerical systems, we concentrate in this text on formal systems which are likely to be computer-based in part. However, we are aware that all problem situations will have social and political aspects which are at least as important as the technical. Multiview includes stages which relate to this human and social dimension as well as the technical aspect which is emphasised only in the latter part of the framework. It attempts to address questions related to the organisation as a whole, the people working in the organisation, the particular aspect of human-computer interaction, the various functions that the information system is to carry out and the technical specification for performing those functions. It is a contingency approach, which means that the techniques and tools described in the framework which are chosen in a particular problem situation will depend on the particular circumstances where it is applied. Each application of Multiview can be said to be an exploration in information systems development.

1.11 EXERCISES

1   What activities make up the systems development process, and what roles do the systems analysts and users play in this process?

2   For an organisation with which you are familiar, for example the department in the organisation in which you work, or university or polytechnic department in which you are studying, outline the formal and informal systems that exist.

3   Define the various level of management of organisations and attempt to put names to the three levels of management, defining their roles, for an organisation with which you are familiar. If you had difficulties in doing this 'neatly', what were the reasons?

4   For a particular application area, such as a bank or a hospital, identify the stakeholders and discuss how each group should influence the decision-making process related to the development of a computer-based information system.

Chapter 2
A Framework for Information Systems Definition

In this chapter we describe the logical framework of Multiview. We include in this discussion the relationship between the methodology, the analyst, and the situation in which the analysis is being carried out.

2.1   AN OVERVIEW OF MULTIVIEW

Systems analysis and design is concerned with understanding what is needed from an information system and creating a specification of an information system that will meet those requirements. In order to do this systematically, it is necessary to have a **methodology**. Modifying Checkland (1983) and Lyytinen (1987), an information systems methodology may be defined as:

> 'a coherent collection of concepts, beliefs, values and principles supported by resources to help a problem-solving group to perceive, generate, assess and carry out in a non-random way changes to the information situation.'

This is more than just a set of methods for tackling the different problems involved. It also implies that there is a sound theoretical basis, in other words, that the analyst understands **why** a particular method is used in a particular situation.

The chase for the perfect methodology is somewhat illusory, because different methodologies represent different views of the world. These differences may stem from the way in which the problem is perceived. Information systems design could be seen as a logical, technical or people problem. Different analysts have adopted different methods because they have taken a different view of the situation. There are also differences in the systems analysis and design approaches used which are caused by differences in the situation in which the analyst is working. Approaches that may be successful in a large bureaucratic organisation may well be different to those which work in a small fast moving company.

In this book we describe an approach to information systems development which combines important aspects of some of the major methodologies into a more coherent and flexible approach, and thus offers the student and practitioner a broad understanding of the whole process of systems analysis and design. The methodology covers five different stages of systems analysis and design, each with its own appropriate view of the problem, and each with the best available methods for tackling that aspect of the problem.

There exists in actual systems analysis and design practice a three-way relationship between the analyst, the methodology and the situation, shown in Figure 2.1, but parts of the relationship are missing in many texts and expositions of information systems development methodologies. For example, many methodologies assume - though the assumption is not stated - that each situation is essentially the same and that analysts are similar in background and experience.

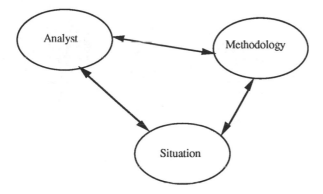

Fig. 2.1. The interaction between the analyst, the problem situation and the methodology

The stages of the Multiview methodology and the inter-relationships between them are shown in Figure 2.2. The boxes refer to the analysis stages and the circles to the design stages. The arrows between them describe the inter-relationships. Some of the outputs of one stage will be used in a following stage. The dotted arrows show other major outputs. The five stages are:

1   Analysis of human activity

2   Analysis of information (sometimes called information modelling)

3   Analysis and design of socio-technical aspects

4   Design of the human-computer interface

5   Design of technical aspects.

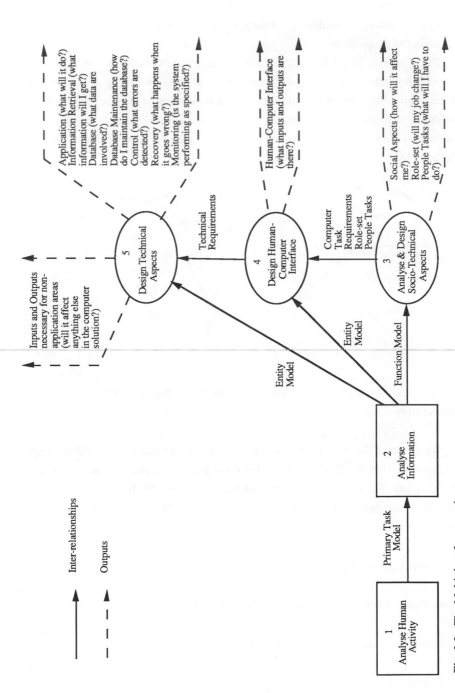

Fig. 2.2. The Multiview framework

They incorporate five different views which are appropriate to the progressive development of an analysis and design project, covering all aspects required to answer the vital questions of users. These five views are necessary to form a system which is complete in both technical and human terms. The outputs of the methodology, shown as dotted arrows in Figure 2.2, are listed in Figure 2.3, together with the information that they provide and the questions that they answer.

Because it *is* a multi-view approach, it covers computer-related questions and also matters relating to people and business functions. It is part **issue-related** and part **task-related**. An issue-related question is: "What do we hope to achieve for the company as a result of installing a computer?". A task-related question is: "What jobs is the computer going to have to do?".

Outputs	Information
Social Aspects	How will it affect me?
Role-set	Will my job change? In what way?
People Tasks	What will I have to do?
Human-Computer Interface	How will I work with the computer? What inputs and outputs are there?
Database	What data are involved?
Database Maintenance	How will I maintain the integrity of data?
Recovery	What happens when it goes wrong?
Monitoring	Is the system performing to specification?
Control	How is security and privacy dealt with? What errors are detected?
Information Retrieval	What information will I get?
Application	What will the system do?
Inputs and Outputs necessary for non-Application Areas	Will it affect anything else on the computer subsystem?

Fig. 2.3. Methodology outputs

The distinction between issue and task is important because it is too easy to concentrate on tasks when computerising, and to overlook important issues which need to be resolved. Too often, issues are ignored in the rush to 'computerise'. But, you cannot solve a problem until you know what the problem is! Issue-related aspects, in particular those occurring at stage 1 of Multiview, are concerned with **debate** on the definition of system requirements in the broadest sense, that is 'what real world problems is the system to solve?'. On the other hand, task-related aspects, in particular stages 2-5, work towards **forming** the system that has been defined with appropriate emphasis on complete technical and human views. The system, once created, is not just a computer system, it is also composed of people performing jobs.

Another representation of the methodology, rather more simplistic, but useful in providing an overview for discussion, is shown in Figure 2.4. Working from the middle outwards we see a widening of focus and an increase in understanding the problem situation and its related technical and human characteristics and needs. Working from the outside in, we see an increasing concentration of focus, an increase in structure and the progressive development of an information system. Each stage addresses one of the five questions posed in Section 1.3.

The rest of this chapter outlines the five related views of the Multiview methodology. You are advised to consult Figure 2.2 frequently whilst reading the rest of the chapter. The five views are covered in more detail in the rest of the book and illustrated with discussions on the methodology in practice which stem from the various case studies described in the book.

2.2   STAGE 1 - ANALYSIS OF HUMAN ACTIVITY

This stage is based on the work of Professor Peter Checkland at Lancaster University. He has carried out extensive studies, both theoretical and practical, on systems analysis using the concept 'human activity system' (Checkland and Griffin 1970 and Checkland 1981 and 1984). The very general term **human activity** is used to cover any sort of organisation. This could be, for example, an individual, a company, a department within a larger organisation, a club, or a voluntary body. They may all consider using a computer for some of their information systems.

The central focus of this stage of the analysis is to search for a particular view (or views). This **Weltanschauung** (sometimes also called 'Assumptions' or 'World View') will form the basis for describing the systems requirements and will be carried forward to further stages in the methodology. This world view is extracted from the problem situation through debate on the **main purpose** of the organisation concerned, sometimes described using the terms 'raison d'etre', 'attitudes', 'personality' and so on. Examples of world view might be: "This is a business aimed at producing

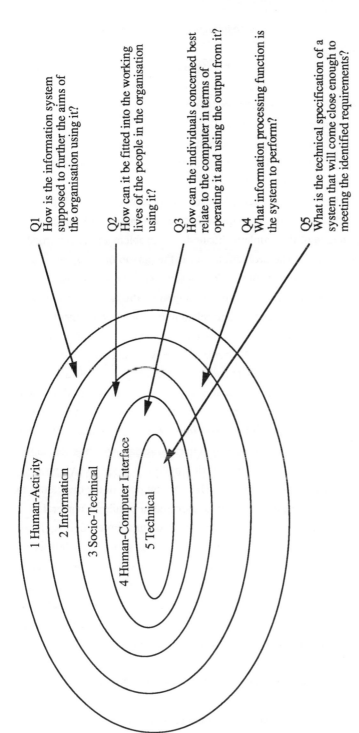

Q1
How is the information system supposed to further the aims of the organisation using it?

Q2
How can it be fitted into the working lives of the people in the organisation using it?

Q3
How can the individuals concerned best relate to the computer in terms of operating it and using the output from it?

Q4
What information processing function is the system to perform?

Q5
What is the technical specification of a system that will come close enough to meeting the identified requirements?

1 Human-Activity

2 Information

3 Socio-Technical

4 Human-Computer Interface

5 Technical

Fig. 2.4. The Multiview methodology

maximum long term profits" or "This is a hospital dedicated to maintaining the highest standards of patient care".

The phases within the methodology of this stage are shown in Figure 2.5. These substages can be grouped into four main ones:

1 Perceiving the problem situation (substages 1-3)
2 Constructing systems models (substages 4-7)
3 Comparing the systems models to perceived reality (substage 8)
4 Deciding on the comparison and then implementing the consequences of these decisions (substages 9 and 10).

This is a simplification because there are several iterations not appearing in the diagram. Firstly, the problem solver, perhaps with extensive help from the problem owner, forms a **rich picture** of the problem situation. The problem solver is normally the analyst or the project team. The problem owner is the person or group on whose behalf the analysis has been commissioned. The 'picture' represents a subjective and objective perception of the problem situation in diagrammatic and pictorial form, showing the structures of the processes and their relation to each other. Elements of the rich picture will include the clients of the system, the people taking part in it, the task being performed, the environment, and the owner of the system. This picture can be used to help the problem solver better understand the problem situation. It is also a very useful tool from which to stimulate debate, and it can be used as an aid to discussion between the problem solver and the problem owner. There are usually a number of iterations made during this process until the 'final' form of the rich picture is decided. The process here consists of gathering, sifting and interpreting data which is sometimes called 'appreciating the situation'. Drawing the rich picture is a subjective process. There is no such thing as a 'correct' rich picture. The main purpose of the diagram is to capture a holistic summary of the situation. This is discussed in detail in Chapter 4.

From the rich picture the problem solver extracts **problem themes**, that is, things noticed in the picture that are, or may be, causing problems and/or it is felt worth looking at in more detail. The picture may show conflicts between two departments, absences of communication lines, shortages of supply, and so on.

Taking these problem themes, the problem solver imagines and names **relevant systems** that may help to relieve the problem theme. By relevant, we mean a way of looking at the problem which provides a useful insight, for example:

Problem theme   =   conflicts between two departments

Relevant systems   =   conflict resolution system or
                                    system for redefining departmental boundaries.

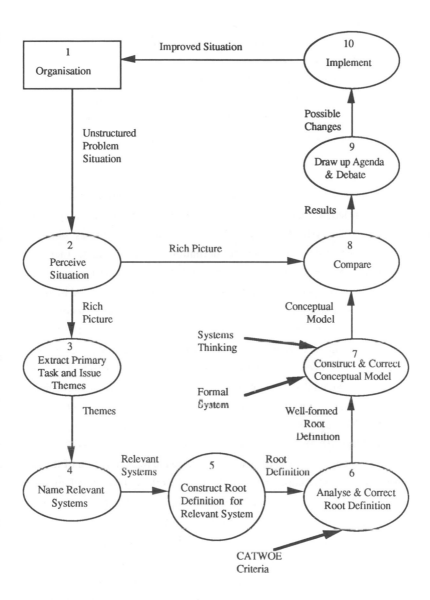

Fig. 2.5. Analysis of human activity systems to depict processes and products

Several different relevant systems should be explored to see which is the most useful. It is at this stage that debate is most important. The problem solver and the problem owner must decide on which view to focus, that is how to describe their relevant system. For example, will the conflict resolution system be 'a system to impose rigid rules of behaviour and decision-making in order to integrate decisions and minimise conflict' or will it be 'a system to integrate decisions of actors through increased communication and understanding between departments' or even 'an arbitration system to minimise conflict between departments by focussing disagreements towards a central body'?

Once a particular view or **root definition** has been decided upon, it can be developed and refined. Thus, by using a checklist technique called the **CATWOE** criteria, discussed fully in Chapter 5, the root definition can be analysed by checking that all necessary elements have been included. For example, have we identified the owner of the system? all the actors involved? the victims/beneficiaries of the system? and so on.

When the problem owner and the problem solver are satisfied that the root definition is well formed, a **conceptual model** (or activity model) of the system is constructed by listing the "MINIMUM list of verbs covering the activities which are NECESSARY in a system defined in the root definition....". At this stage, therefore, we have a description in words of **what** the system will **be** (the root definition) and an inference diagram of the activities of **what** the system will **do** (the conceptual model).

Aids to forming the conceptual model include the checklist technique of comparing the system described against a formal systems model. This is a compilation of features which have to be present if a set of activities is to comprise a system capable of purposeful activity. This checking process ensures that no vital elements have been excluded. (Note that provided that the root definition has been well formed according to the CATWOE criteria, it is unlikely that discrepancies will occur at this stage.) Other aspects of systems thinking can also be used to ensure that the conceptual model is adequate (see Checkland 1984).

The completed conceptual model is then compared to the representation of the 'real world' in the rich picture. Differences between the actual world and the model are noted and discussed with the problem owner. Possible changes are debated, agendas are drawn up and changes are implemented to improve the problem situation.

In some cases the output of this stage is an improved human activity system and the problem owner and the problem solver may feel that the further stages in the Multiview methodology are unnecessary. In many cases, however, this is not enough. In order to go on to a more formal systems design exercise, the output of this stage should be a well formulated and refined root definition to map out the **universe of discourse**, that is the area of interest or concern. It could be a conceptual model which can be carried on to stage 2 - the analysis of entities, functions and events.

2.3 STAGE 2 - ANALYSIS OF INFORMATION (ENTITIES AND FUNCTIONS)

The purpose of this stage, which is also known as **information modelling**, is to analyse the entities and functions of the system described, independent of any consideration of how the system will eventually develop. Its input will be the root definition/conceptual model of the proposed system which was established in stage 1 of the process.

Two phases are involved: (a) the development of the functional model (discussed fully in Chapter 8), and (b) the development of an entity model (discussed fully in Chapter 9).

(a) *Development of a functional model*

The first step in developing the functional model is to identify the *main* function. This is always clear in a well formed root definition. This main function is then broken down progressively into subfunctions, until a sufficiently comprehensive level is achieved. This occurs when the analyst feels that the functions cannot be usefully broken down further. This is normally achieved after about four or five subfunction levels, depending on the complexity of the situation.

This idea of **functional decomposition** will be familiar to readers who have studied or practiced structured programming and is a feature of a number of methodologies for information systems development. As an example, if the main function of an accounts department is to 'provide financial information', it can be broken down into the subfunctions 'keeping books' and 'providing reports'. These are further broken down. A series of **data flow diagrams**, each showing the sequence of events, are developed from this hierarchical model. The hierarchical model and data flow diagrams are the major inputs into stage 3 of the methodology, the next stage, which is the analysis and design of the socio-technical system.

(b) *Development of an entity model*

In developing an entity model, the problem solver extracts and names entities from the area of concern. An **entity** is anything that you want to keep records about. For example, depending on the problem situation, entities could include customers, sales, patients, hospital beds, and hotel reservations. Relationships between entities are also established, such as 'patients occupy beds' and 'doctors treat patients'. The processes of forming entities and relationships can be very subjective. A good model will require a good understanding of the problem situation in order to decide which entities and relationships are important. The preceding stage in the methodology - analysis of the human activity systems - should have already given this necessary understanding and have laid a good foundation for this second stage.

An **entity model** can then be constructed. An entity model is a chart with entities shown in boxes and relationships indicated by lines and arrows between the entities. Examples will be shown in Chapter 9. The entity model, following further refinement, becomes a useful input into stages 4 and 5 of the Multiview methodology.

2.4   STAGE 3 - ANALYSIS AND DESIGN OF THE SOCIO-TECHNICAL ASPECTS

The philosophy behind this stage is that people have a basic right to control their own destinies and that, if they are allowed to participate in the analysis and design of the systems that they will be using, then the implementation, acceptance and operation of the system will be enhanced. It takes the view therefore that human considerations, such as job satisfaction, task definition, morale and so on, are just as important as technical considerations. The task for the problem solver is to produce a 'good fit' design, taking into account people and their needs and the working environment on the one hand, and the organisational structure, computer systems and the necessary work tasks on the other. Some readers may be surprised at this explicit statement of the analyst's values, and be tempted to argue that the analyst should be 'objective'. However, as we shall see in Chapter 11, objectivity, that is non-involvement, is just as value-laden a stance as insistence on the democratic process.

An outline of this stage, largely based on the work of Professor Enid Mumford of the Manchester Business School, is shown in Figure 2.6. The central concern at this stage is the identification of alternatives: alternative social arrangements to meet social objectives and alternative technical arrangements to meet technical objectives. All the social and technical alternatives are brought together to produce socio-technical alternatives. These are ranked, firstly in terms of their fulfilment of the above objectives, and secondly in terms of costs, resources and constraints - again both social and technical - associated with each objective. In this way, the 'best' socio-technical solution can be selected and the corresponding computer tasks, role-sets and people tasks can be defined.

The emphasis of this stage is therefore *not* on development, but on a **statement** of alternative systems and **choice** between the alternatives, according to important social and technical considerations.

It is also clear that, in order to be successful in defining alternatives, the groundwork in the earlier stages of the methodology is necessary and, in order to

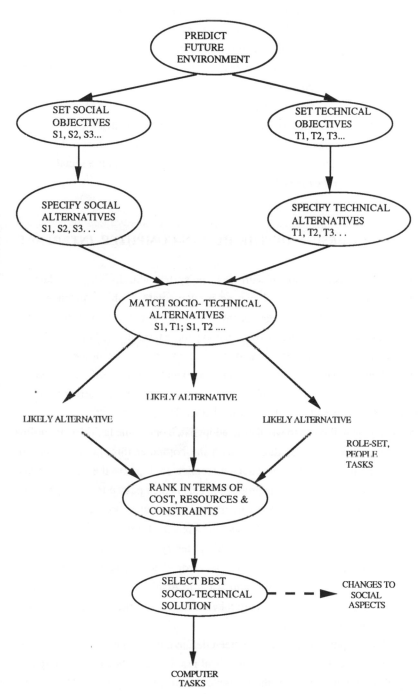

Fig. 2.6. Outline of socio-technical analysis and design (adapted from Mumford 1983, Wood-Harper *et al*, 1985 and Wood-Harper, 1989)

develop and implement the chosen system, we must continue to the subsequent stages.

An important technique applicable to this stage is **future analysis**, which owes much to the work of Professor Frank Land of the London Business School. This aids the analyst and user to predict the future environment so that they are better able to define and rank their socio-technical alternatives.

The outputs of this stage are the computer task requirements, the role-set, the people tasks, and the social aspects. The computer task requirements, the role-set and the people tasks become inputs to the next stage of the methodology, that is the design of the human-computer interface. The role-set, the people tasks, and the social aspects are also major outputs of the methodology.

2.5   STAGE 4 - DESIGN OF THE HUMAN-COMPUTER INTERFACE

Up to now, we have been concerned with what the system will do. Stage 4 relates to how, in general terms, we might achieve an implementation which matches these requirements. The inputs to this stage are the entity model derived in stage 2 of the methodology, and the computer tasks, role-set and people tasks derived in stage 3. This stage is concerned with the technical design of the human-computer interface (sometimes called the man-machine or user interface) and makes specific decisions on the technical system alternatives. The ways in which users will interact with the computer will have an important influence on whether the user accepts the system.

A broad decision will relate to whether to adopt batch or on-line facilities. In on-line systems, the user communicates directly with the computer through a terminal or workstation. In a batch system, transactions are collected, input to the computer, and processed together when the output is produced. This is then passed to the appropriate user. Considerable time may elapse between original input and response.

Decisions must then be taken on the specific conversations and interactions that particular types of user will have with the computer system, and on the necessary inputs and outputs and related issues, such as error checking and minimising the number of key strokes. There are different ways to display the information and to generate user responses. The decisions are taken according to the information gained during stages 1 and 2 of Multiview.

Once human-computer interfaces have been defined, the technical requirements to fulfil these can also be designed. These technical requirements become the output of this stage and the input to stage 5, the design of technical subsystems. The human-computer interface definition becomes a major output of the methodology. This is discussed fully in Chapter 13.

2.6 STAGE 5 - DESIGN OF THE TECHNICAL ASPECTS

The inputs to this stage are the entity model from stage 2 and the technical requirements from stage 4. The former describes the entities and relationships for the whole area of concern, whereas the latter describes the specific technical requirements of the system to be designed.

After working through the first stages of Multiview, the technical requirements have been formulated with both social and technical objectives in mind and also after consideration of an appropriate human-computer interface. Therefore, necessary human considerations are already both integrated and interfaced with the forthcoming technical subsystems.

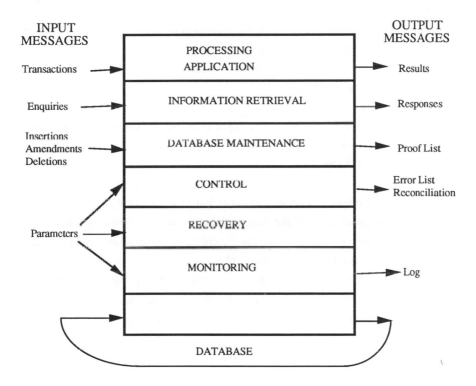

Fig. 2.7. Outline of the requirements for the technical specification

At this stage, therefore, a largely technical view can be taken so that the analyst can concentrate on efficient design and the production of a full systems specification. Many technical criteria are analysed and technical decisions made which will take into account all the previous analysis and design stages. The final major outputs of the methodology are shown in Figure 2.7. These are the application, and information retrieval, database

maintenance, control, recovery and monitoring aspects, and the database. The inputs
and outputs necessary to support these are also defined. This is illustrated in Figure 2.7
and discussed in detail in Chapter 16 (see also Waters 1979a and 1979b).

2.7   SUMMARY

To summarise, the methodology exhibits five different views, all of which can be
emphasised, reduced in scale, or even omitted, according to (or contingent on) the
circumstances.

The stages are:
- The analysis of human activity;
- The analysis of information (entities, functions and events);
- The analysis and design of socio-technical aspects;
- The design of the human-computer interface; and
- The design of technical aspects.

Following this framework, during the length of the project, we move from the
general to the specific, from the **conceptual to hard fact**, and from **issue to
task**. Outputs of each stage either become inputs to following stages or are major
outputs of the methodology.

The final outputs of the methodology are the social systems, the role-set and people
tasks, the human-computer interface and the technical specification, and the necessary
inputs and outputs to support the non-application system. These include all the
necessary information to design, implement, operate and maintain a more complete
information system in both human and technical terms. Each of the five stages in
Multiview is supported by tools and techniques. These are fully described in the text at
the appropriate Part. Information systems definition comprises analysts and users who
are dealing with a problem, and they are using the methodology to elicit the information
requirements and provide a technical specification to meet these requirements.

2.8   EXERCISES

1   Compare the Multiview framework with that of an alternative information systems
    development methodology.
2   For an application area with which you are familiar, identify the main activities and
    problems that exist in carrying out these activities to best effect.
3   Show how the concerns of the systems analyst might change as an information

systems project develops from the initial stage to implementation. Do you think that one person could cope with each of these stages?

4 For an information system, such as a library system, suggest social and technical alternatives.

Chapter 3
Case Study 1: The Professional Association

Work at a professional association constituted the first application of the methodology in the practical world. The work had three phases: an initial study, a full requirements analysis and finally the development of some of the computer applications, including a computer system which handled routines associated with the Association's examinations. In this section we discuss aspects of the initial study and the full requirements analysis, and in the text of the chapters in Part 2 we will use all three phases to serve as illustrations of the use of some of the techniques discussed in these chapters.

The purpose of this case study is to illustrate the possible background to information systems projects, and to highlight some of the political, social, and organisational aspects which concern the human rather than the technical dimension of information systems work. The description here represents the personal views of the analysts involved, and in no way represents an 'objective' study (Wood-Harper, 1989).

The initial study was requested in correspondence from the secretary of the Association. This was a top post in the organisation. She felt that many of the systems ought to be computerised and she wished to know the type of computerisation that would be appropriate for the situation, and whether the Association should establish its own computer system or go to a service bureau. She identified four objectives for the study:

- Identify relevant computer applications
- Provide a broad outline of a computer based system
- Identify, in general terms, appropriate hardware for relevant applications and make purchasing recommendations
- Produce a full written report of the findings.

She served as the champion for the new system and, as such, was a major actor in the situation. She had been with the organisation from its beginning, possessed considerable administrative experience and had considerable influence.

The Professional Association is a professional body initiated for people working in or attempting to enter a particular profession. It was founded in the 1970s in response to the growing number of people working in the field, and the increasing importance of that field in the world at large. The Association is thus a recently established organisation and one that experienced rapid growth. The current administrative system was purely manual and depended on the skill and efficiency of those participating. The system had worked well on this basis in the past and there was little evidence of errors or inaccuracies. All the functions were under the control of the secretary. The education subsystem was administered by an education secretary and, at the time of the initial study, there was a vacancy for an office manager to remove some of the administrative workload from the secretary. The workload at the time featured peaks and troughs throughout the year. These were coped with by the flexible use of the employees across all the various functions, which included:

- Membership administration, such as payments and accounting
- Service record administration for service performed by and offered to the Association
- Examination administration for examinations run by the Association
- Tuition administration, such as information about subjects, tutors and fees
- Retired members' appointments register, including a list of members prepared to accept employment
- Company file administration
- Employment agency register
- Production of the year-book
- Production of tuition books
- Production of the handbook
- Production of the glossary
- Production of conference papers
- Production of minutes, forms and notices
- Production of the accounts and analyses, and
- Mailing list administration.

The following problems were identified:

1 Work load at peak times of the year was becoming too demanding. In particular, examinations produced major peaks of work three times a year. These peaks required all of the full time staff plus temporary help.
2 Membership was growing particularly rapidly. There was an estimated 10% growth per annum which put increasing strain on the workload.
3 Administration and accounts occupied much of the time of the senior management, particularly the secretary. This reduced the time available for promotion of the Association to the outside world. The appointment of an office manager was felt to be a way of relieving this pressure.
4 The number of examinations was to increase from three to nine.
5 Student membership was also growing rapidly. This, together with the increase in

the number of papers, would increase the examination administration workload substantially.

6   There was little spare capacity to undertake new functions and general expansion.

7   The production of the year-book consumed large resources in both time and staff.

The Association was heavily dependent on its small numbers of staff, and the departure of key staff would have had a considerable effect. Therefore, at the time when the analysts were called in, the Association was at a crossroads. In order to be able to accommodate its future growth and maintain efficiency and credibility, some action needed to be taken. There existed a number of alternatives, one of which was the computerisation of some or all aspects of the Association's administration.

Two major forces were in existence at the time of the study. Some key staff, already identified as important for the continued smooth operation of the Association, were worried about computerisation and its impact. The second major group, whose influence could be felt, comprised the members of the professional association themselves. The Association, because of its limited capacity, was not providing the desired services as well as expected. The issue of upgrading their current approach might well influence whether or not the Association continued to receive its membership fees.

The consultants felt that they were, to some extent at least, involved to provide an expert opinion 'validating' the secretary's initial requirements. This was, in part, because the Association was a committee-run organisation, with the committees composed of many people from many different organisations. The committee members were not on the staff of the Association. This particular organisational characteristic made user participation difficult.

The structure of the organisation also influenced the choice of university academics to conduct the survey, in particular the desire to avoid the bias of a particular vendor-related consultant. There was an element also of a person not so much concerned with the absence of bias, but who wanted to employ a team to validate her own views about the proposed system. This was a sort of 'hidden agenda' concerned with her wish to relocate to central London. This is not unusual in analysis work, the analysts are frequently expected to recommend the proposal favoured by the actors with the greatest political strength or who called for the study in the first place.

Personal conflict and political issues were very evident in this study. Some staff wished to move to the centre of the capital city. General staffing would be more difficult, but they argued that the computerised system would reduce the staff requirements, thus making the move a more viable option. This is a prime example of political manipulation, with the development of a computer system serving as the power lever. Markus (1984) describes a similar case in her book.

In the second phase of the case study, which consisted of a more detailed study and requirements analysis, there were more opportunities to interview the committee members. The treasurer, who was chairman of the finance committee, also became an important actor. He occupied a significant position of influence within a large local government authority and wished to use his experience in this application area.

The question of hardware now became a political issue. Since many of those involved in the Association were also involved with other large organisations, they had already developed a hardware bias. That bias was more to do with their own feelings of security with a familiar computer system, than with the requirements of the situation. Pettigrew (1983) also reports this effect.

A major problem area exposed in the first phase, that of the examination system, was by now becoming untenable. The clerical load became intolerable and this was particularly urgent as the present three examinations per year were increased to nine. These examinations were to be taken at over one hundred examination centres. The education secretary became another important actor. Indeed, he threatened to resign if a computerised information system was not provided within six months. Aspects relating to developing this information system further are discussed in Part Two of this text.

An important lesson learned from these issues was that the information systems definition process should identify and isolate interested parties, that is, the stakeholders in the organisation and their possible or probable impact upon the system development process. It was felt also that conventional systems analysis and design methodologies, which concentrate on technical decisions and require all these human and social issues to be already resolved (or assume that they are not there), did not help in this type of problem situation. Some of the ideas and techniques in Multiview that were developed during and since the lifetime of the case study are directed at these political problems.

PART TWO

MULTIVIEW STAGE 1:
ANALYSIS OF HUMAN ACTIVITY

Chapter 4
The Human Activity System:
Forming the Rich Picture

4.1 DRAWING THE BOUNDARIES OF THE SYSTEM

An information system is not an end in itself, though it may be the end of the analyst's work. People commission information systems in order to pursue some other activity for which the information is needed. The purpose may be a straightforward short term one, for example putting accounts processing on to the computer in order to enable better reporting and monitoring of the company's financial activity. The purpose may also be oriented towards helping strategic levels of management. Top management of a company may see their competitors making use of information technology and want to keep pace with them, or they may have spotted an opportunity for improved business which can be achieved with better information processing. They may feel that "Information Technology is the future" and would like to be involved in its development.

The starting point for an analysis of information systems requirements is a consideration of what the organisation is trying to achieve - what it is **for**. The term **human activity system** is a concept which is an aid to thinking and understanding, in the most general way possible, the organisation in which the information system is to operate. This may be a one-man firm, a few individuals, a department, or a company. The activity could be commercial, scientific, administrative, or academic. In fact there are so many possible permutations, that it is really very important to be quite sure which people engaged in what activities are the subject of the investigation.

This is usually quite straightforward where, for example, a small company is looking at its accounts system. However, in a large organisation or a small department in a large organisation, the whole situation is usually much more complex. It is necessary to exercise care in drawing the boundary around the organisation and around the groups within it.

It could be that the organisation which will be served by the information system is new or has not matured into the form that it will take when the system is operational. Ideally, the information system will be planned to be set up at the same time as the new department or company. This means that planning the system goes alongside planning the organisation. The human activity system will also be changed to some extent by the creation of the information system so that there is always some element of redesign.

At the start of the systems design exercise, people wanting to buy a computer system may only have a fuzzy idea about what they want to achieve by its use. Even when the proposed objectives have been sorted out, they still need to be formulated in such a way that they can be explained to analysts and suppliers and therefore do not have any in-built assumptions about the business.

Research has shown that there are several recurrent themes among the organisational objectives that people have claimed they were trying to achieve by installing computer systems. These reasons include the following:

- To save money by more efficient processing of the same work
- To get better access to their own information
- To provide an improved customer service (and hence bring in more business)
- To improve control over their activities
- To keep more accurate and therefore more useful records
- To increase the job satisfaction of their workers
- To be able to take on new kinds of work
- To handle an increased volume of work with the same staff
- To replace the present system before it collapses, and
- To try out new technology.

The most popular of these has been to cut costs, although only in the most labour intensive activities has this been achieved. Improved processing and reporting comes a close second. Surprisingly, perhaps, the third most popular objective is simply to try out the new technology. "Perhaps my business would benefit from a microcomputer" seems to be a popular thought. One or more of these objectives might well be in the rich picture. But the rich picture may include no mention at all of any prospective use of information technology, for its real purpose is to expose the problems, issues, conflicts, and people, amongst other things, which are of concern in the problem situation.

4.2   RICH PICTURES

The techniques that Multiview uses here have been developed largely from the insight of Professor Checkland at Lancaster University in the UK. He specialises in solving problems where the managers of the organisation are unclear about their objectives. This is usually caused by change. A company may have grown (or shrunk) beyond recognition or changed its activities or have been affected by changes in the operating environment. Alternatively, people may want to think in advance about a new organisation that they are setting up.

The first technique used in Multiview for analysing human activity systems is to draw the rich picture. This is a pictorial caricature of an organisation and is an invaluable tool for helping to explain what the organisation is about. It should be self-explanatory and easy to understand.

One may start to construct a rich picture by looking for elements of **structure** in the problem area. This includes things like departmental boundaries, activity types, physical or geographical layout and product types.

Having looked for elements of structure, the next stage is to look for elements of **process**, that is, 'what is going on'. These include the fast-changing aspects of the situation: the information flow, flow of goods, and so on.

The relationship between structure and process represents the **climate** of the situation. Very often an organisational problem can be tracked down to a mismatch between an established structure and new processes formed in response to new events and pressures.

The rich picture should include all the important **hard** 'facts' of the organisational situation, and the examples given have been of this nature. However, these are not the only important facts. There are many **soft** or subjective 'facts' which should also be represented, and the process of creating the rich picture serves to tease out the concerns of the people in the situation. These soft facts include the sorts of things that the people in the problem area are worried about, the social roles which the people within the situation think are important, and the sort of behaviour which is expected of people in these roles.

There is a temptation at this point for many analysts to represent the situation in terms of systems needed. A 'system' in this sense is not about hardware and software but is a perceived grouping of people, objects and activities which it is meaningful to talk about together. Representing the situation in terms of 'information systems needed' should be discouraged at this stage. These should come once the analysis has been carried out. The question to be tackled is: 'what systems can be described in the situation?', as opposed to 'what systems does the manager think exist?', and only then to 'what information systems are actually needed?'.

Typically, a rich picture is constructed first by putting the name of the organisation that is the concern of the analyst into a large 'bubble', perhaps at the centre of the page. Other symbols are sketched to represent the people and things that inter-relate within and outside that organisation. Arrows are included to show these relationships. Other important aspects of the human activity system can be incorporated. Crossed-swords indicate conflict and the 'think' bubbles indicate the worries of the major characters.

In some situations it is not possible to represent the organisation in one rich picture.

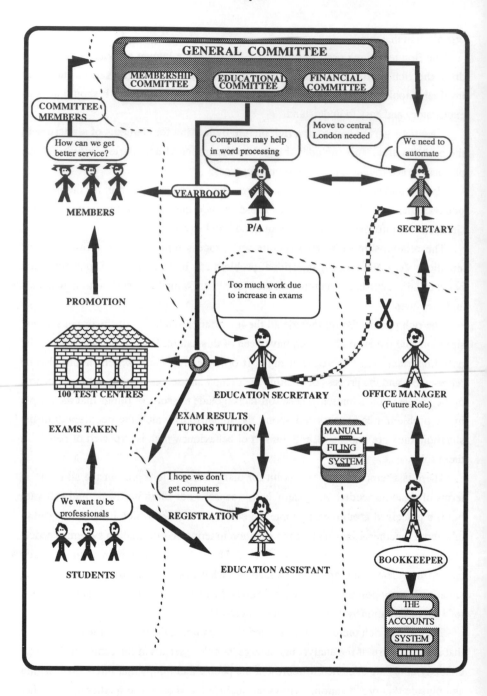

Fig. 4.1. Part of the rich picture of the Professional Association

In this case, further detail can be shown on separate sheets. The perceived relative importance of people and things should be reflected by the size of the symbols on any one rich picture.

Figure 4.1 represents a rich picture for the professional association described in Chapter 3. It represents an early draft of part of the rich picture of this human activity. If it has been well drawn, you should get a good idea of who and what is central to the organisation and what are the important relationships. You may like to re-read the case study and alter the rich picture so that other facts are included. Bear in mind that there is no such thing as a 'correct' rich picture. Drawing the rich picture is a subjective process. A second rich picture is shown as Figure 7.1.

The act of drawing a rich picture is useful in itself because:

- Lack of space on the paper forces decisions on what is really important (and what are side issues or points of detail for further layers of rich pictures);
- It helps people to visualise and discuss their own role in the organisation;
- It can be used to define the aspects of the organisation which are intended to be covered by the information system; and
- It can be used to show up the worries of individuals and potential conflicts.

Differences of opinion can be exposed, and sometimes resolved, by pointing at the picture and trying to get it changed so that it more accurately reflects people's perceptions of the organisation and their role in it.

Once the rich picture has been drawn, it is useful in identifying two main aspects of the human activity system. The first is to identify the **primary tasks**. These are the tasks that the organisation was created to perform, or which it must perform if it is to survive. Searching for primary tasks is a way of posing and answering the question 'What is really central to the problem setting?'. For example, it could be argued that the Professional Association aims to increase standards in its profession. Everything else is carried out to achieve that end. Primary tasks are central to the creation of information systems, because the information system is normally set up to achieve or support that primary task. The next stages of the Multiview methodology concentrate on the primary tasks.

The second way that the rich picture is of particular value is in identifying **issues**. These are topics or matters which are of concern. They may be the subject of dispute. They represent the (often unstated) question marks hanging over the situation. In the Professional Association, they might include 'what do we hope to achieve by installing a computer system?'. This was a major issue when the systems analysis was done, indeed it was the issue that brought in the consultants. This process of identifying the issues will lead to some debate on possible changes. It might be possible for these issues to be resolved at this stage, but it is essential that they are understood. Issues are important features, as the behaviour resulting from them could cause the formal information system to fail. Unless at least some of them have been resolved, the information system will have little chance of success. In some situations, the issues can be more important than the tasks. In the Professional Association, the issue of whether to move to central London was also particularly important. It seemed to the analysts that they served as ammunition for the person requesting the study. The secretary wanted to relocate, and this was felt to have a bearing on her desire to establish computerisation at the Association.

4.3   PROBLEMS AND PROBLEM SITUATIONS

The analyst starts by looking at an unstructured **problem situation**. This emphasis on the 'problem situation' as opposed to the 'problem' is important. By looking at the problem, rather than the whole situation, it will be difficult to be able to tell whether the diagnosis of the problem is correct. All too often a client will say "I am having a problem with X", when the problem is actually being caused by something else. A problem with stock control may be caused by a weak stock records system or a lack of time in the shop to update records as items are sold or by the fact that there is a lot of pilfering. If the analysts are limited to the official statement of the problem, then these 'real' causes may never be uncovered. It is therefore necessary for analysts to keep eyes, ears and minds open and avoid jumping to early conclusions about the 'problem'.

There are a number of ways in which analysts get drawn into the problem situation and a number of roles that they may be called on to play. It is important that their role and their relationship with other people in the problem situation have been well defined and well explained. Whether an external consultant, a member of the data processing department, a representative of the supplier, or a friend giving free advice, it is important to think about the roles of the client, problem owner and problem solver.

The client, sometimes referred to as the customer, is the person who is paying the analyst. The client may be the problem owner, though frequently the client is a senior manager who has called in the analyst to look at a problem in one area of his domain. In this case the problem owner will be the manager of that work area. Sometimes there is no one obvious problem owner: two departments could have developed a partial response to a changing situation and have different ideas about how to tackle it. The problem solver is normally the analyst, but frequently the problem owner is also trying to solve the problem. In this case it is important that the two roles are differentiated at any one time.

The rich picture can help the owners of the problem sort out the fundamentals of the situation, both to clarify their own thinking and decision making and also to explain these fundamentals to all the interested parties. The rich picture becomes a summary of all that is known about the situation. An analysis of the rich picture will help in the process of moving from 'thinking about the problem situation' to 'thinking about what can be done about the problem situation'.

4.4   DRAWING THE EXAMPLE RICH PICTURE

The problem owner in the Professional Association shown in the rich picture is the general committee of the Association. As we saw in the description provided in Chapter 3, there was conflict between the secretary, who was the client, and the committee for whom she acted, on how best to serve the organisation in its overall goal of improving the standards of the profession. The secretary who was the client, was expected to become the system user.

As the study was further under way, the role of the education secretary became more important. He is responsible for the examinations, and this system became the focal point of later analysis. There was a real conflict between the secretary and the education secretary regarding how and what to automate (hence the crossed swords in the rich picture). As the education secretary became a more powerful stakeholder and the analysts homed in on the examination system, he became the client. Hence he is central in the rich picture shown as Figure 4.1. At the time of the first part of the investigation, it was the secretary who was central.

The building shape in the left of the picture represents the one hundred test centres. It is important to draw attention to the difficulties of handling the examinations. The role of 'students', on the bottom left of the picture, changes from the 'think bubble' - "we want to be professionals" to 'members' who ask "how can we get better service" once they have passed the examination at the test centre and have entered the profession.

Other stakeholders are also included in the rich picture. Developing further the theme of computerisation, some actors are less positive about the prospect. The education assistant, an important actor in the examination system, had not used computers before and the think bubble contains "I hope we don't get computers". In retrospect, more attention should have been paid to her views. As one of the main persons involved, her misapprehension about the 'system' should have been considered more fully.

We have included the accounting system. The bookkeeper, bottom right of the picture, was presently satisfied with this system but it would be looked at in the future.

In drawing the rich picture, some things have been left out which are understood by the participants but which would not be assumed by an outsider. One of these is the social roles of the people in the Association and the sort of behaviour which is expected of people in these roles. Sometimes footnotes are useful to describe or list these. A second aspect is in the level of detail. The complexity of the marking system and other regulations for admission to the Association, with which the stakeholders were familiar and well understood, could not be gleaned by an outsider looking at the rich picture. A second rich picture, drawn at a greater level of detail, would help here. Rich pictures can be 'decomposed' into others of greater detail.

With the analysts coming in as outside consultants, it was important that these 'assumptions' are drawn out. The approach adopted here was for the analyst to ask the users for a detailed explanation of a complex situation. Where a team of analysts is available, they can be divided so that different sorts of questions can be asked - those relating to management strategy, those relating to data, and those relating to people's roles. The rich picture, once drawn up, proved a very useful communication tool in this situation and was refined according to new information. No thought is given at this stage to possible solutions. The methodology avoids 'design before analysis'.

The simplicity of the final rich picture is achieved by pruning the answers so that there is as much agreement as possible and so that the final picture really does represent the important people, activities and issues of the problem situation.

4.5   SUMMARY

The first stage of the analysis is to draw up a rich picture of the organisation in order that the analyst, client and problem owner agree on the starting point. The picture should show all the major people, activities, tasks, and issues, and should reveal major worries and potential conflicts.

The picture is achieved by getting hold of as much background information as possible from all sources. We have concentrated on interviewing all major parties, but other sources of information include published material and observation. It is essential to draw up this picture because otherwise there could be too large a discrepancy between the perception of the client about the problem to be solved and those of the analyst. Indeed there are often very large differences in the assumptions made between various individuals in the client organisation. This can be caused by differences in education, experience, interests, and so on.

The picture should include elements of structure and process and the relationship between them (the climate). The picture should include both hard facts and soft facts. The latter include subjective information about worries and interests. The social roles of the people in the picture should be clear, as should the role of the analysts and the rest of the 'actors'. The picture should yield both the primary tasks of the situation and the issues which surround those tasks.

4.6 EXERCISES

1 Alter the rich picture given as Figure 4.1 to reflect your interpretation of the case study described in Chapter 3.
2 Distinguish between the problem owner, clients and actors for an organisation with which you are familiar. Identify the primary tasks and issues. Draw a rich picture of the problem situation. Distinguish between 'hard' and 'soft' facts represented in the picture. Identify the stakeholders in the problem situation. Are they all represented in the picture?
3 Describe using narrative only, the problem situation shown in the rich picture of the distance learning unit (Figure 7.1). Why is there no mention of computer systems?

Chapter 5
The Human Activity System:
Constructing the Root Definition

5.1 THE IMPORTANCE OF DEFINITION

In Chapter 4 we looked at the use of rich pictures which help everyone concerned to understand the nature of the human activity system that the information system is to serve. But getting a feel for what is going on is not enough. Critical aspects of the organisation and its objectives need to be defined in order to prevent any possibility of misunderstanding. These definitions also serve as touchstones against which to test new ideas. It will be possible to assess whether each proposed solution furthers the objectives that have been defined.

Most people when asked what the information system is for will give a vague answer, such as "to help with stock control" or "to do accounts". This is not an adequate basis for further development work. Furthermore, it is not an adequate specification against which to judge the final system. Many disputes between users and suppliers relating to computer information systems, for example, are caused because each had a different impression of what was to be done. Such disputes cannot be resolved without recourse to an agreed statement of requirements. With such a statement, the dispute would probably never have occurred. A stock control system may have been implemented which 'works', but it may not give the help that the user thought was needed. So many times we have heard systems analysts say that 'the system works' but the users are saying that 'the system is useless'. What has happened is that the technologist has implemented successfully a system according to his or her specification. But this was not what the user wanted.

Multiview uses the technique of **root definition** proposed by Checkland to address this problem. For our purposes the root definition is the root from which the information system should grow. The root definition can also be used to start a debate on major issues, although this book will concentrate on information systems aspects. The next section looks at some of the processes which lead up to the construction of the root definition.

5.2   RELEVANT SYSTEMS

A system is a grouping of people, objects and activities. The significant thing about a system is that the 'whole is greater than the sum of the parts'; in other words, the grouping of these elements adds something to the overall picture. This is sometimes described as a **holistic** view of systems.

Systems need to have **boundaries** drawn around them. A given object can be considered as part of several overlapping systems. A filing cabinet, for example, might be part of the records system and it is also part of the office system. In different situations a particular system boundary can be more or less useful, and this question of usefulness is crucial, particularly when deciding where the boundary is to be drawn round the future information system. A further consideration is that of 'systems within systems'; for example a registering system for candidates exists within the examinations system in the Professional Association case study.

Systems are abstract concepts, and it is difficult to separate them from the multitude of human activities. Some organisational activities can be considered as quite **systemic** in the sense of being organised to achieve a clear purpose. This term is used rather than 'systematic' which is sometimes used to describe behaviour that is very formalised, to the extent that it can mean following the rule book - however out of date or irrelevant it happens to be. By systemic, we mean 'organised into systems with clear inputs and outputs'. The rich picture helped to represent the situation pictorially. The situation now has to be viewed systemically. By this term we do not mean, for example, 'start at the top left-hand corner', but 'look at the most significant groupings of people, objects and activities' and consider how they relate to achieve the outputs.

We have to extract **relevant systems** from our rich picture. In other words, we need to decide which systems we want to examine further. We talk about a 'relevant' system, because it is a system which is relevant to the problem situation. By relevant, we mean that it will yield insight into the situation when the system is described more fully. For the Professional Association case, we started by trying to talk about a 'system for improving the standards of a profession' because that was what it was there for. In fact the relevant system became the examination system, although this was not identified in the early stages of the work. This process is one of negotiation between problem owner and problem solver, perhaps through the client. The question of negotiation is an important one, and perhaps alien to scientists who expect precision. With human activity systems there is no one 'right' answer. Problem owner and problem solver have to talk round and through the problem situation trying to get at the essence of the relevant system and to define its boundaries in a way that is useful.

Once we have thought more about our system 'to examine students for entering the profession', it will help us to understand the information handling that is required. This will, in turn, help us to solve the problem in hand, that is, create an appropriate information system. It will help in other ways as well, because we are concerned with more than this, such as the ways in which the Association may improve services to its members. However, such issues are an aside to the relevant system, which must be relevant to the process of improving the problem situation, and our situation is one of handling the information processing aspects of the examinations system.

5.3   ROOT DEFINITIONS

Root definitions can be used to define two things that are otherwise both vague and difficult. These are **problems** and **systems**. It is essential for the systems analyst to know precisely what human activity system he is to deal with and what problem he is to tackle.

The root definition is a concise verbal description of the system which captures its essential nature. Each description will derive from a particular view of reality. To ensure that each root definition is *well-formed*, it is checked for the presence of six characteristics. Put into plain English, these are **who** is doing **what** for **whom**, and to whom are they **answerable**, what **assumptions** are being made, and in what **environment** is this happening? If these questions are answered carefully, they should tell us all we need to know.

There are technical terms for each of the six parts, the first letter of each forming the mnemonic **CATWOE**. We will change the order in which they appeared in our explanation to fit this mnemonic:

- **C**ustomer is the 'whom'
- **A**ctor is the 'who'
- **T**ransformation is the 'what'
- **W**eltanschauung is the 'assumptions'
- **O**wner is the 'answerable'
- **E**nvironment (or environmental constraints) is kept as the 'environment'.

The word Weltanschauung may be new to many readers. It is a German word that has no real English equivalent. It means something like 'world view' or 'all the things that you take for granted'.

The first stage of creating the definition is to write down headings for each of the six CATWOE categories and try to fill them in. This is not always easy because we often get caught up in activities without thinking about who is really supposed to benefit or who is actually 'calling the tune'. We may question our assumptions and look around the environment even more rarely.

Even so, the difficulty for the individual creating a root definition is less than the difficulty in getting all the individuals involved to agree on the definition to be used. Only experience of such an exercise can reveal how different are the views of individuals about the situation in which they are working together.

When we were trying to create the root definition for the Professional Association's examination system, we went through the following process. First we picked out what we thought were the issues and primary tasks. These represented the things that the users were concerned about:

- Efficient administration and management of the examinations system;
- Choosing a solution which would not mitigate against the Association's other systems, such as membership records management and accounting; and
- Building up a good reputation for the Association.

Within this, we isolated three major components which we call the relevant systems. We concluded that these issues and primary tasks could largely be resolved by the following relevant systems:

- Administration and management system;
- Communication and motivation system; and
- Information provision system.

These relevant systems are subsystems to support a higher system which is to maintain and improve the reputation of the profession by ensuring high standards of entry into the profession (see Figure 5.1).

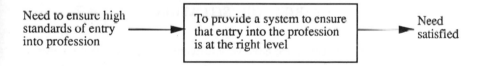

Fig. 5.1. The examination system for the Professional Association

Our working root definition was:

'A system owned and operated by the Professional Association to administer the examinations by registering, supervising, recording and notifying students accordingly.'

When we came to write the root definition, we had particular difficulty about the client. At first the obvious client was the secretary, but on further analysis, the client changed to the education secretary. Yet as a computer solution became very likely, the person exercising power proved to be the treasurer, a member of the Financial Committee who would only give his consent to purchase a computer system if it was a particular brand - that which he was experienced at using (and one which, the analysts felt later, was inappropriate to the examinations system). There was nothing that the analysts could do about this political in-fighting, but at least we were aware of the problem. It is sometimes difficult to produce a rigorous root definition because of these political or other problems. Sometimes it is impossible to resolve differences. However, unless they are resolved, they may be a source of difficulties later, as shown by the choice of hardware in the case study.

The CATWOE criteria was used to check and revise the above root definition as follows:

Customers	Members of the Association, the secretary, education secretary and treasurer.
Actors	The Professional Association, its members, students attempting to join, and its full time staff
Transformation	To provide examinations which will ensure entry at the right level to the profession
Weltanschauung	Computer systems are efficient
Owners	General Committee of the Association (representing members of the Association)
Environment	The particular profession

Thus the first use for the root definition is to:

CLARIFY THE SITUATION

People involved in an enterprise have very different views about that enterprise. These views are frequently at cross-purposes. This holds true even when the same words are used to describe things. This is because the differences are usually in the unstated assumptions or different perceptions of the environment. More significantly, there are sharp differences of opinion about whose problem the analysts are trying to solve, that is, who is the owner and who is the client. The next section looks at ways of attempting to resolve these differences, though it may not be possible and one root definition - a preferred root definition - might be chosen from the alternatives and used to further develop the information system.

5.4   RESOLVING DIFFERENCES IN VIEWS

Root definitions are particularly useful in exposing different views. We will look at an information system for a hospital to illustrate this. The different people involved in a hospital will look at the system from contrasting positions. Furthermore, these viewpoints in this problem situation are very emotive as they have moral and political overtones. In some situations this can lead to deliberate fudging of issues so as to avoid controversy. This is likely to cause problems in the future. Even if the differences cannot be resolved, it is useful to expose them.

Here are three different root definitions of a hospital system. They all represent extreme positions. In practice, anyone trying to start such a definition would make some attempt to encompass one or more of the other viewpoints, but any one of these could be used as the starting point for the analysis of the requirements of an information system in a hospital.

THE PATIENT

CUSTOMER	Me
ACTOR	The doctor
TRANSFORMATION	Treatment
WELTANSCHAUUNG	I've paid my taxes so I'm entitled to it
OWNER	'The system' or maybe 'the taxpayer'
ENVIRONMENT	The hospital

This could be expressed as 'A hospital is a place that I go to in order to get treated by a doctor. I'm entitled to this because I am a taxpayer, and the system is there to make sure that taxpayers get the treatment they need'.

THE DOCTOR

CUSTOMER	Patients
ACTOR	Me
TRANSFORMATION	Treatment (probably by specialised equipment, services or nursing care)
WELTANSCHAUUNG	I'll treat as many people as possible within a working week.
OWNER	Hospital administrators
ENVIRONMENT	National Health Service (NHS) versus private practice. My work versus my private life.

'A hospital is a system designed to enable me to treat as many patients as possible with the aid of specialised equipment, nursing care, etc. Organisational decisions are made by the hospital administrators (who ought to try treating patients without the proper facilities) against a background of NHS politics and my visions of a lucrative private practice and regular weekends off with my family'.

THE HOSPITAL ADMINISTRATOR

CUSTOMER	Doctors
ACTOR	Me
TRANSFORMATION	To enable doctors to optimise waiting lists
WELTANSCHAUUNG	Create a bigger hospital within cash limits
OWNER	Department of Health and Social Security (DHSS)
ENVIRONMENT	Politics

'A hospital is an institution in which doctors (and other less expensive staff) are enabled by administrators to provide a service which balances the need to avoid long waiting lists with that to avoid excessive government spending. Ultimate responsibility rests with the DHSS and the environment is very political'.

We could therefore develop three very different information systems depending on the view taken. The patient would have the system centred around patients' health records; the doctor would have the system designed around clinic sessions and the administrator around the accounts.

These definitions have been deliberately controversial, but they attempt to show the 'private' views of the participants as well as their publicly stated positions. There is no reason why definitions need to be formal and cold. Wilson (1984) carries out a similar exercise concerning the prison system. Dependent on the view taken, amongst other possibilities, the prison system could be seen as a:

• Punishment system
• Society protection system
• Behavioural experiment system
• A criminal training system
• Mail-bag production system
• People storage system, or
• An exclusive storage system.

These contribute to the eventual primary task definition:
'a system for the receipt, storage and despatch of prisoners'.

The alternative root definitions (briefly expressed above) indicate the difficulty of reconciling different viewpoints, and yet if one is not agreed, it will be even more difficult to agree on a final information system. Information systems are designed to serve the needs of people, and analysts are always brought directly into contact with power struggles between individuals and between viewpoints. Analysts have to make decisions, consciously or unconsciously, about which particular view of the situation or combination of views to work from. One option is to attempt to be 'scientifically detached', but this is only one of the options.

In Scandinavian countries there are laws or public agreements which state that the views of the workers have to be sought and clearly represented at all stages in the analysis, design and implementation of computer-based systems. In the USA, the analysts usually go by the opinion of the people who are paying their fees. Many analysts in the UK argue that they are making 'objective' decisions, innocent of any prejudice, but these may be based on personal and political assumptions that are never made explicit unless attempts are made to establish a root definition.

The manager of a small firm contemplating a microcomputer system may find this process rather long-winded and unnecessary. The system of communications is likely to be easier in smaller firms. Nevertheless, the undercurrent in a small business can be just as much at cross-purposes. The manager of an office in one small firm known to the authors wanted a computerised records-handling system. The present system was both inefficient and inaccurate. In view of the gains in efficiency, it was surprising that the owner of the firm kept fudging the issue. It was only after considerable time that the analyst realised the it was not in the owner's interest to make it apparent to the low paid staff or the Inland Revenue just how profitable the business was. The most suitable system for the owner was indeed a messy poorly-defined paper one.

5.5   SUMMARY

The first stage in the systems design process is the analysis of the human activity system. It is necessary to understand the purposes of the organisation before designing the information system. It is also necessary to consider the people in the organisation, how they react with each other and with the outside world, and to identify sources of conflict. The overall picture serves as a framework to consider the comments of people in the organisation during later stages of analysis.

The analyst must produce a definition of the purpose of the system before attempting system design, even if the definition has to be refined at a later stage. This helps in two ways: it ensures that the analyst is starting in the right direction and it makes available a control mechanism. In other words, does the proposed system achieve the objectives stated at the start?

Root Definitions (along with Conceptual models which are discussed in the next chapter) are the main images or metaphors utilised in the Multiview methodology. Root definitions are the high level abstraction of the salient features of a human activity system. In building these there is a construct remembered by the mnemonic CATWOE which stands for Customers, Actors, Transformation, Weltanschauung, Owner and Environment. As we shall see in Chapter 6, conceptual models are then represented in diagrammatic form from the root definition.

The Human Activity Systems approach is used to explore situations by constructing systems models via root definitions. As Land (1982a) shows, this exploration in information systems is used for different interest groups or stakeholders:

'on the recognition that different participants working within or in association with the system each view the system from a different perspective and as a result have a different understanding of the system and different expectations and objectives.'

The results of this exploration and debate are:

'attempts to get an agreed, or at least clarified analysis of the situation, and the beginnings of a specification of desirable and feasible changes.'

5.6   EXERCISES

1   For a problem situation of your choice, attempt to play different roles and suggest conflicting answers to CATWOE and hence create different root definitions.

Chapter 6
The Human Activity System:
Building the Conceptual Model

6.1   BUILDING THE CONCEPTUAL MODEL

The preceding stages of the analysis give us an overall view of the organisation whose information processing is to be computerised to some extent at least. It also provides some key definitions of the purposes to be furthered by the information system. To complete the analysis of the human activity system, we need to build a model which shows how the various activities are related to each other, or at least how they ought logically to be arranged and connected. This is called a **conceptual model** or an **activity model**.

If the analysis of the human activity system is to be helpful to the organisation, then it will show any discrepancies between what is happening in the real world and what ought to be happening. This may lead to changes in the organisation of human activities. The purpose of introducing a computer-based information system is to improve things, not just to 'automate the *status quo*', though many computer information systems do little more than this. Thus, at the conclusion of this phase we will have a model of the required activities which will serve as the foundation for the information model *and* a set of recommendations for an improved human activity system.

What do we mean by a conceptual model and what is it for? Perhaps these questions are best explained by analogy. If an architect designs a building he must produce two things: first a set of artist's impressions and a scale model to show the client what is proposed and second a set of plans to give the builder. For the purposes of this book these would together constitute the model. They represent all that needs to be created for the parties concerned to decide whether to go ahead with that design, modify it or to choose an alternative. They also enable the builder to say how much it will cost and how long it will take.

The model serves three purposes:
- It is an essential element in the architect's design activities
- It is a medium of communication between architect and client to enable the right design to be selected
- It is a set of instructions to the builder.

In computing we also try to create models which will serve these three purposes, but the process is not so well known, or so well tried and tested, as it is in building. There are probably in use almost as many ways of describing a proposed system as there are design teams. This creates problems for users and designers as they try to understand what is being proposed. Multiview offers standards in information systems design and specification.

We do not have in Multiview a clear-cut distinction between artist's impressions and the engineer's blueprints. There is not one version of the model for the user and another version for the programmer. Some may argue that this would be a valid goal, but furthering our analogy, artist's impressions are notoriously optimistic and vague about difficulties, and engineer's blueprints are very difficult to interpret by all but the trained. It is not satisfactory for the untrained to have to accept the statement: 'trust us, we're the experts'.

This means that the systems user and the systems builder must both understand the conceptual model. Of course the information represented on a model can be complex, but Multiview has been designed so that difficulties in understanding the model are real ones, that is, they result from the complexities of the situation and not from any confusion about what the words and figures are meant to convey.

The rich picture gives a context for the conceptual model. It is redrawn at this time to show the major information flows. Figure 6.1 will be explained later, but readers will already see that it makes an interesting comparison with Figure 4.1. It shows the main activities of the examinations system, and consequently the information to support these activities prior to computerisation.

The conceptual model is formed from the chosen root definition as follows:

- **Form** an impression of the system to carry out a physical or abstract transformation from the root definition.
- **Assemble** a small number of verbs which describe the most fundamental activities in the defined system.
- **Use** the idea of a 'formal systems model' (see Section 6.2) and decide what the system has to do, how it would accomplish the requirement and how it would be monitored and controlled.
- **Structure** similar activities in groups together.
- **Use** arrows to join the activities which are logically connected to each other by information, energy, material or other dependency (Checkland uses the term **logical contingencies** to describe what the arrows indicate).
- **Verify** the model against a formal model of a Human Activity System and then correct it.

The conceptual model shown as Figure 6.1 was derived from the root definition which was, for the Professional Association:

'A system owned and operated by the Professional Association to administer the examinations by registering, supervising, recording and notifying students accordingly.'

We start by taking significant aspects from the root definition and naming subsystems which will enable us to achieve what we require, that is the subsystems to register students, supervise the examinations, record the results and notify the students.

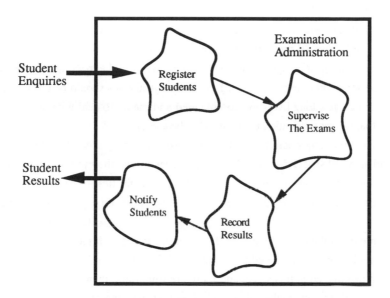

Fig. 6.1. Professional Association - Level 1 Conceptual Model

In order to get agreement between problem solver and problem owner on these systems, it is important to ensure that there is a mutual understanding of the real world meaning of the terms. It is necessary, for example, for the analyst to get to know what is involved in vetting enquirers and selecting potential students for registration in order to understand the pre-exposition preparation system. But the analyst is concerned with 'what is logically necessary' and not 'how the work is managed'. It does not matter, for example, how the enquiries are received or the forms are sent out to be completed or which member of staff deals with them.

So as to ensure that the most useful subsystems have been identified and understood, they are described in more detail in words and diagrammatically. In other words, there is a second layer in the conceptual model set. This is carried out in the second case study which is described in Chapter 7. (All the techniques described in Chapters 4 to 6 are covered in more detail in this case study.)

In order to get agreement between problem solver and problem owner on these systems, it is important to ensure that there is a mutual understanding of the real world meaning of the terms. It is necessary, for example, for the analyst to get to know what is involved in registering students (and vetting enquires and selecting potential students for registration, which would be at the level 2 conceptual model) in order to understand that subsystem. As we have said above, the analyst is only concerned with 'what is logically necessary'.

The conceptual model needs further development. It is a model of the human activity system. Its elements are therefore activities and these can be found by extracting from the root definition all the verbs that are implied by it. The list of active verbs should then be arranged in a logically coherent order. We would expect the number of activities to be somewhere in the range of five to nine. Activities should be grouped to avoid a longer list, as a long list is too complicated and messy to deal with. A shorter list suggests that the root definition is too broad to be useful.

Having listed the major activities, some of these may imply secondary activities. These should also be listed and arranged in logical order around their primary activities. We did not find it necessary to create a second level of activities in the Professional Association case study. But they are seen in the distance learning case study (Chapter 7).

New elements to the conceptual model, not found in the rich picture or the root definition, should not be introduced at this stage. This will cause inconsistencies. If omissions are discovered at this stage, and these are important, then it is necessary to return to the rich picture and include them in it. It will also be necessary to return to the analysis of the human activity system.

Conceptual modelling is an abstract process. The purpose of going into this abstract world of systems thinking is to develop an alternative view of the problem situation. When this alternative view has been developed, we can return to the real world and test the model. It is constructed in terms of **what** must go into the system, and it can therefore be set alongside the real world. We are not concerned at this stage with how the system will be implemented.

6.2   TESTING THE CONCEPTUAL MODEL

At this stage it is necessary to check the conceptual model against a **formal systems model**. This is essentially a compilation of features which have to be present if a set of activities is to comprise a system capable of purposeful activity. This compilation has been founded on a number of years' study of a variety of systems in a number of organisations. The general systems model proves to be useful in a wide range of applications in organisational settings that can be construed as human activities.

These features are:

- *A continuous purpose or mission.* In engineering applications and other 'hard' systems, this could be something like maintaining the correct temperature of a furnace in a steel-making system. In a soft system, it could be something more general that can only be aimed for, like 'high profitability', 'international repute' or 'long term survival'.
- *A measure of performance.* This provides a means of indicating relative success or failure in pursuing purposes or trying to achieve objectives. We want to know whether the system is achieving its objectives.
- *A decision-taking process.* This is viewed in terms of management and the role of the decision-taker. There has to be some mechanism for initiating actions which will get the system back on course if it seems to be failing to meet its objectives.
- *Components which are themselves systems.*
- *A degree of connectivity or interaction between the components.*
- *A boundary,* separating the system from its environment. It defines the area within which the decision-taker has power to cause action to be taken. It also defines the area within which the decision-maker can dispose of physical or abstract resources.
- *Some guarantee of continuity and long-term stability,* and the ability to recover stability after some disturbance.

6.3   CHOOSING THE CONCEPTUAL MODEL

The conceptual model can be defined as a logical model of what ought to be happening to achieve the objectives specified in the root definition. There is normally more than one way of doing something and so choices will have to be made about the structure of the conceptual model. Many systems analysts come from an intellectual background - which relies on 'scientific method' - where they are encouraged to believe that answers are either right or wrong. School science subjects tend to instil this view and not all people have this prejudice shaken out of them. An inexperienced analyst may put a flowchart in front of the user and ask "is this right?" Users who may have had many years of coping with 'messy' reality may well be reluctant to answer so positively. Unfortunately the politics of the situation may be such that they may be forced to say 'yes' if they recognise some resemblance between the flowchart and reality. Alternatively they may be left to 'pick at the details'. One of the problems that the user faces is the inappropriateness of the flowcharts used in conventional systems analysis, and a strength of the conceptual model is its usefulness as a communication tool.

This logical model needs to be compared with reality to see whether improvements should be made to the way in which activities are organised. For example, the conceptual model might highlight bottlenecks, such as too many small decisions waiting for the manager or too many assistants waiting to use the same price catalogue. It may also show up circuitous routes for transferring information.

In small organisations, information handling is very informal, everyone sees what is happening or works alongside the people who know. As work diversifies and more staff are taken on, information flow is based around the experienced staff who become 'walking databases'. Such an arrangement can then ossify and become increasingly irrelevant to new functions and new personalities. Many apparently efficient offices are thrown into disarray by the loss of the one person 'who seems to know everything'.

The first question on comparing the conceptual model with reality is *"Does the information flow smoothly?"*. There are two extreme forms of organisation: where one person sees a job through from beginning to end or where each person handles a specialised part of the work. Of course, most organisations have aspects of each, and both have different implications for information flow.

Many factors must be taken into account when matching functions to staff. These include the capabilities and aspirations of staff, the demands of different aspects of the business, and the need for management to keep control of what is going on. A number of these may change if a computer system were to be introduced. The conceptual model can be used as a tool for thinking about how subsystems *should* be organised in order to achieve the purposes set out in the root definition. Questions can be asked about which subsystems should be linked together and whether they can be handled more efficiently if they are kept separate.

The conceptual model can also be used in the design of new human activity systems, such as the setting up of a new company or department, because it shows what activities should be carried out and how they should be related to each other.

Figure 6.2 shows, amongst other things, how the conceptual model is compared with what is actually happening, in order to uncover discrepancies and to recommend changes.

One of the problems here is that one is not comparing like with like: system models are represented in systems language, and the initial perception of reality is expressed in another language, usually relating to the users' interest groups. To alleviate this problem and to make a meaningful comparison, the language of the users' interest groups ought normally to be used so that users can participate fully in the comparisons. In making these comparisons Checkland (1981) outlines four models:

* General discussion
* Historical construction
* Question definition, and
* Model overlay.

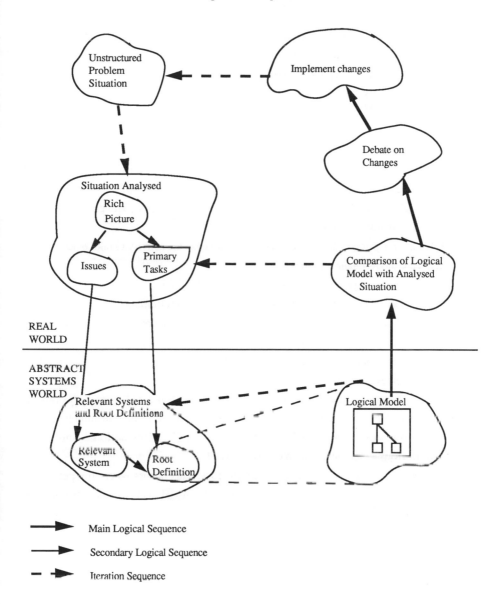

Fig. 6.2. Problem situations and abstract systems thinking

General discussion is normal for issue-based models relating to interest groups, although sometimes it is used for primary task models. The method is to generate discussion resulting from the use of contrasting images.

Historical construction consists of 'operating' a model using a relevant example and comparing the resulting scenario with an account of an historical equivalent in the same situation.

Question definition is the normal method for models conceived with applications in information systems. The method generates questions defined from its model, and audits the real world perception by asking:

- Does the activity exist?
- How is it done?
- How well is it done?

and so on.

In information systems, it is sometimes difficult to ascertain whether the activity exists or not. This can normally be achieved by determining what the output of the activity might be and by looking for the existence of that output. The general case can be described as follows (Wilson, 1984):

- What are the primary activities in the area that cause the activity to take place?
- What are the resultant activities?
- What outputs are generated by performing the activities?
- What activities are initiated internally and what are their outputs?
- What additional (secondary) inputs are initiated by doing the total set of activities?
- What are the constraints under which the activities are done?
- What are the sources of inputs (primary and secondary)?
- Who receives the outputs?

This comparison is useful and can help to produce a 'validated' primary task model for information systems definition. The model is validated in that all interest groups agree that it represents the activities 'taken-to-be' reality. This notional model is a framework from which information can be derived.

The final comparison method is *model overlay*. This occurs where the perception derived from the human activity view is laid over the model to allow a detailed point by point comparison.

6.4   SUMMARY

After completing the study of the human activity system as a whole, the systems designers create a conceptual model. This task includes listing all the activities associated with the root definition, grouping them coherently, and then drawing them together as systems to perform these activities. These systems charts should show the main relationships between the various activities and the environment.

At this stage, therefore, we have primary task and/or issue-based root definitions and conceptual models where we have a description, in words, of what the system *will be* (the root definition) and an inference diagram of the activities which the system *will do* (the conceptual model).

The conceptual model may then be compared with reality to see whether any improvements can be made in the way that activities are actually organised. Differences are noted from the above comparison and the changes are debated and planned for implementation. Some of these changes will include non-information system related changes. These changes are debated, agendas are drawn up and implemented to improve the problem situation. In some cases these improvements may be sufficient for people to feel that the subsequent stages in Multiview are unnecessary. In other cases, however, this is not enough, and a more formal information definition process is needed. The input to these stages should be a well-formulated consensus primary task root definition together with its conceptual model of the agreed notional system. Normally, these would be carried on to Stage 2 of Multiview (analysis of information) as a basis for information definition.

6.5 EXERCISES

1 Draw a series of conceptual models (including second level models and descriptions) for the root definition formed in Exercise 5.6 (1). Read Chapter 7 if you are not sure how this might be done. Validate the conceptual model against the formal systems model.

2 Decide on: the purpose or mission; the measure of performance; the decision-taking process; and the boundary, for that system.

3 Compare the conceptual models formed above with what is actually happening, using Checkland's four models described in Section 6.3.

Chapter 7
Case Study 2: The Distance Learning Unit

The second case study looks at the Distance Learning Unit (DLU) at a Polytechnic in the UK. This case is fully described in Wood-Harper *et al* (1985) and Wood-Harper (1989). Pertinent details here are discussed from the analyst's viewpoint within this project. Parties which were affected by this case included the Polytechnic itself, the Manpower Services Commission (MSC) and the Paintmakers Association, a professional association for paintmakers (*not* the subject of the case study in Chapter 3). The DLU was attempting to provide educational services to train members of the Paintmakers Association who were scattered in small groups throughout a wide area. The MSC was responsible for monitoring the process. The rich picture, shown as Figure 7.1, provides a summary of the situation.

The rich picture places in perspective the elements of the DLU and its environment - the Polytechnic (in particular the administration), the Manpower Services Commission and the Paintmakers' Association, including the departmental boundaries of the Polytechnic.

The problem owner in the case study is shown in the rich picture as the head of the DLU running an academic support unit of the Polytechnic. He wished to set up the unit to provide a service to the paint industry in the UK. The problem owner and the DLU are central to the case and drawn as such in the rich picture. The problem owner was expected to become the system user (though in fact an administrator was appointed by the Paintmakers Association later).

The factory shape at the top of the page represents the Paintmakers Association of Great Britain. Their members are all paintmakers who are based at factories distributed throughout the UK. This was seen as an important element of the structure of the problem situation, hence the outline of England, Scotland and Wales included in the rich picture. Distance learning is viable because the small number of trainee paint technicians at each site make local college courses uneconomic.

This left the problem owner with three problems:
• Getting funds to establish all the necessary training materials and other requirements of a distance learning situation;
• Maintaining the right academic levels; and
• Keeping track of the work of several hundred students across the country.
These problems are simplified into the 'think' bubble relating to him.

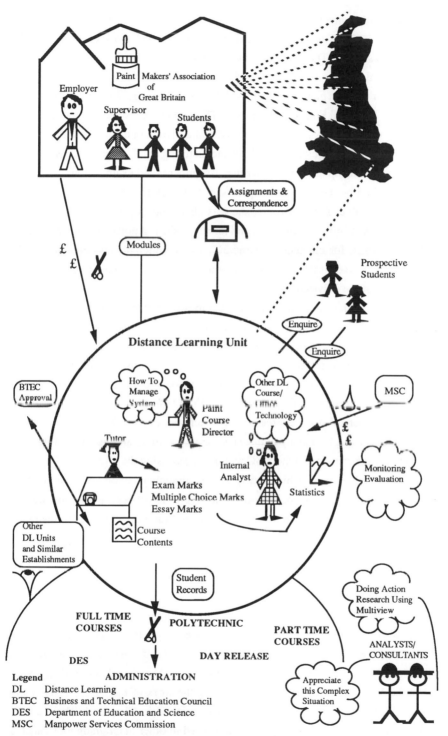

Fig. 7.1. The rich picture of the problem situation

Funds actually came from the Manpower Services Commission which was set up to funnel UK government money into the expansion of technical and vocational education beyond the classroom. The MSC is shown by a 'beady eye' in the right of the picture looking for 'value for money'. The academic content, set up by the lecturing staff (marked 'tutor' in the picture), is ratified by the education authority. This is the Business and Technical Education Council (BTEC) which sets standards for the content and teaching of courses at this level in the UK and is shown in the left of the picture.

We have already discussed one role of the lecturing staff. Another is dealing with enquiries and setting up and marking written assignments and examinations. Some tests would be marked by the industrial supervisor. Although the internal systems analyst was a problem solver for the system, she was also about to set up a second, similar course in the area of office technology, and therefore she is a potential user as well.

Having looked for elements of structure, we consider process elements which include tutoring and assessing students, and transmitting student records to the administration of the Polytechnic.

The climate of the situation, that is the relationship between structure and process, highlighted problems coming from the mismatch of the established structure and new processes formed in response to the new situation. As the new DLU was being set up, the Polytechnic administration was trying to stretch its existing structures to cope with an activity for which it was not designed. The symbol of crossed swords between the DLU and the Administration highlights this possible cause of conflict.

There are other soft facts expressed in the rich picture. The MSC wants to ensure that it is getting value for money in this new training venture and the head of the DLU wants to know the criteria that the MSC will use in assessing the DLU.

An additional problem which emerged was agreement upon 'ownership' of the system. Although the issue was identified through the process, a solution was not agreed. Decisions were being made by the DLU and the Polytechnic administration, and yet the MSC and the Paintmakers Association were financing the project. This political problem made the consensus, which was desired in the first stage, difficult to achieve. (This issue later developed into a 'battle' over copyright - the software was highly marketable.)

We have used various symbols to express all this in the rich picture. As well as the crossed swords showing conflict and the large beady eyes to suggest groups (such as the MSC and the DLU's competitors) looking at the DLU from outside, we have used pound signs suggesting money (in this case financing the project), and little graphs to suggest the MSC are monitoring and evaluating the work of the DLU. We have also used the think bubbles and people symbols mentioned in Chapter 4. These are not standard symbols in the same way as symbols used in other diagraming tools, such as data flow diagrams and entity models which are discussed later in this book and elsewhere. Rich pictures are essentially discussion documents for use by people in the problem situation. Whatever symbols are most appropriate for communicating the ideas, facts, problems, and so on in the problem situation, to the people in that problem situation, should be used. However, the symbols here have been used by the authors over many projects, and they seem to be understandable and helpful to most people.

From the rich picture we could identify primary tasks. We decided that the task central to the problem situation was that 'the DLU has to educate students at a distance', and everything else is carried out to achieve this end. There were many issues that the rich picture has highlighted, the major issue being that of identifying the problem owner related to the complex financial support coming from the MSC, the Polytechnic, and the Paintmakers Association (whose members were to be educated by the DLU).

Once we have thought more about our system for educating students at a distance, it will help us to understand the information handling that is required. This will, in turn, help us to solve the problem in hand, that is, to create an appropriate information system. It will help in other ways as well because we are concerned with more than this. For example, the paintmakers are interested in solving an industry problem of which educating their trainees is a part. The MSC are interested in the way in which training is administered and delivered. However neither of these 'definitions' is relevant for our purpose. Any light they shed is from the 'side'. The relevant system must be relevant to the process of improving the problem situation, and our situation is one of handling the information processing aspects of the distance learning course.

Throughout the process, the following major concerns were:

1 Efficient administration and management within the constraints of the equipment already purchased.
2 Communication with and motivation of physically isolated students.
3 Keeping sufficiently accurate records to satisfy the auditors.
4 Building a good reputation for the DLU.

Within this, we isolated three major components which are relevant systems. We concluded that the issues and primary tasks described above could largely be resolved by the following relevant systems:

• Administration and management system
• Communication and motivation system
• Information provision system.

The information provision system was seen as particularly important by the staff of the DLU. The DLU system was new, but it can be compared with a classroom situation. One thing that was most important in the design of the DLU system, over and above the recording of students' progress, was the need for progress reports for the project manager and the MSC on the success of the course itself, just as if it were a product being sold commercially. In a conventional course, the primary concern is to get 25 or so suitably qualified people together at the right time. It does not matter much if there are 25 who applied or 250, because there is nothing that can be done for the others. Nor is there much that can be done if some of the students prefer some slightly different combination of subjects. With a distance learning course it is possible to be much more flexible in the number of students that can be taught and in the combination of subjects offered. There is therefore a whole new opportunity to do market research relating to who is looking for training and what qualifications they already have. In order to do this, it is necessary to collect a lot more information than is needed to satisfy the strict needs of student registration. This should be reflected in the conceptual model for the DLU.

These three relevant systems are subsystems to support the higher system which is to provide courses to increase technical skills and knowledge in the paintmaking industry by distance learning. When we came to write the root definition, we had particular difficulty, already mentioned, about deciding on the owner. There was nothing that the analysts could do about this, but at least we were aware of the problem. It is sometimes difficult to produce a rigourous root definition because of these political or other problems.

Our working root definition was:

'A system owned by the Manpower Services Commission and operated by the Paintmakers Association in collaboration with the Polytechnic of the South Bank's Distance Learning Unit, to provide courses to increase technical skills and knowledge for suitably qualified and interested parties, that will be of value to the industry, whilst meeting the approval of the Business and Technical Education Council, and in a manner that is both efficient and financially viable.'

The CATWOE criteria which was used to create, and then check and revise the above root definition was as follows:

Customers	Paintmakers and their employees.
Actors	Polytechnic Distance Learning Unit and administration staff. Staff and students in the paintmaking industry.
Transformation	To provide courses to increase technical skills and knowledge for suitably qualified and interested parties.
Weltanschauung	Both efficient and technically viable (implicit in distance learning).
Owners	MSC (and perhaps the Paintmakers Association)

Environment   The paintmaking industry, BTEC approval (for course validation).

The conceptual model was derived from the root definition, and we took significant aspects from the root definition and named subsystems which will enable us to achieve what we require. We identified the following:

ASPECT	SUBSYSTEM
Technical skills and knowledge	Course exposition system
Monitor and Control	Report and information provision system, and Monitoring and evaluation system
Administration and management	Administration system, Report and information provision system, and Pre-exposition preparation system

The top-level conceptual model (Figure 7.2) shows these subsystems and the information flows between them and those coming in and out of the system. So as to ensure that the most useful systems have been identified and understood, they are described in more detail in words and diagrammatically through lower level conceptual models (Figures 7.3 to 7.7).

Pre-exposition Preparation System. This relates to the design and organisation of the courses, including organising the tutors to take courses and prepare material, identifying the target student population and designing the course structure. Student motivation needs to be considered when deciding on the sorts of material to provide as well as the technical skills and knowledge to be transmitted. The production of materials and its transmission to the students has to be managed.

Course Exposition System. This is the system which transmits the technical skills and knowledge to the students. It includes their learning and undertaking of examinations and other work for assessment, as well as the provision of materials from which to learn and contact with tutors. We must consider in this system the communication and motivation problems of the students in a distance learning situation. It is necessary for communication and feedback to be fast in order to maintain the students' motivation.

Administration System. This is the system to administer the sending of work, receiving and marking the work, and keeping records on the students and their progress, and to perform accounts and stock control, as well as answering routine enquiries from students, tutors and employers.

Report and Information Provision System. This system collects information on student marks or particular assessments to produce reports. These will include statistical reports for the various bodies involved.

Monitoring and Evaluation System. This system collects the information from the reports and administration records, and analyses it under various criteria in order to evaluate the viability of the course, its usefulness and so on.

In the first level conceptual model, each of the subsystems is shown in context with the other subsystems (Figure 7.2). The large arrows represent flows of physical things, such as reports, materials, monies, and so on, both within and out of the system. The small arrows represent information flows between the subsystems. Secondly, each subsystem is broken down into its component subsystems with their interactions. This is represented by the level 2 conceptual models (Figures 7.3 to 7.7).

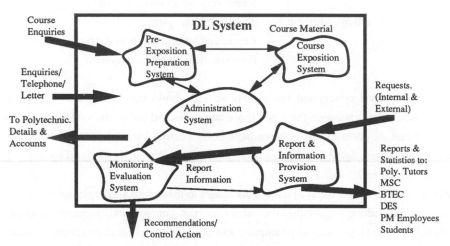

Fig. 7.2. Conceptual model level 1

The next stage, shown in Figure 6.2, is normally to compare the conceptual model with what is actually happening, in order to uncover discrepancies and to recommend changes. In the case of the DLU, this was impossible as there was as yet no real world system in operation. Thus the conceptual model represented our recommendations for the real world organisation.

As we have mentioned, this particular case differs from the first case, and also the other cases described in the book, in that it was dealing with a situation for which no predecessor existed. In addition, the nature of the MSC constrained the flexibility of technical alternatives that might have been chosen. The MSC required that each project be considered separately, so projects which might share equipment (the office automation project for example) could not be considered in terms of their possible total benefits.

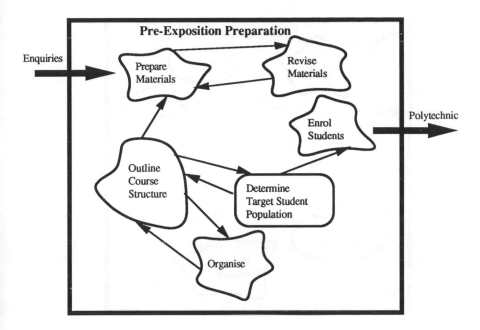

Fig. 7.3. Conceptual model level 2 - pre-exposition preparation

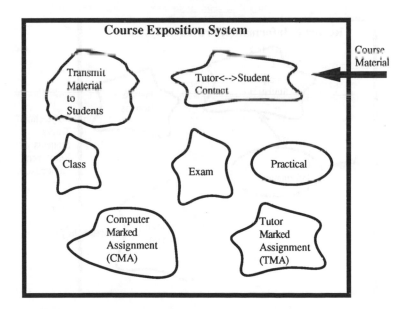

Fig. 7.4. Conceptual model level 2 - course exposition system

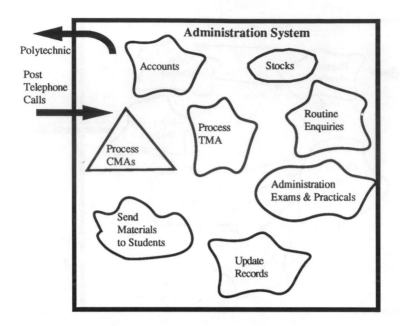

Fig. 7.5. Conceptual model level 2 - administration system

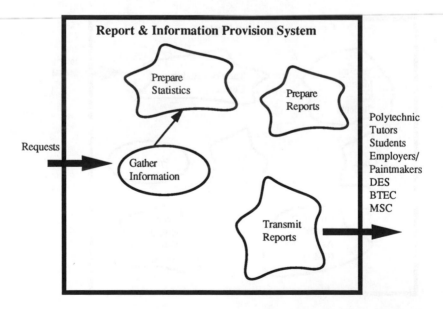

Fig. 7.6. Conceptual model level 2 - report and information provision system

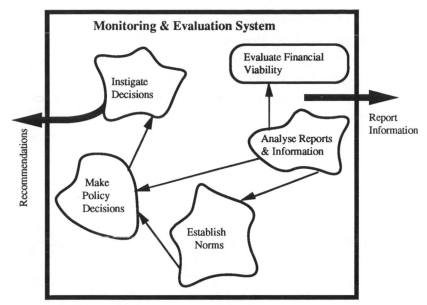

Fig. 7.7. Conceptual model level 2 - monitoring and evaluation system

Because the 'system' did not exist in any form within the Polytechnic, the flexibility of Multiview's model became apparent. No staff existed for the 'system'; they were still to be hired. Nevertheless, a significant amount of participation was available. The internal analyst for the DLU (Lyn Antill, one of the authors of the original book on Multiview (Wood-Harper, Antill & Avison, 1985)) served as a member of the problem solving team, along with an external analyst (one of the authors of this text) and his team.

The problem solving team appeared to have worked very well and to have been one of the successful dimensions of this case. However, the role of the external analyst differed from that assumed in the first case study, because he adopted the role of **facilitator**, rather than that of adviser or solution provider. This was because of the different backgrounds of the staff in the two situations. A facilitator helps the users in their choices. Traditionally, systems analysts have tended to impose their choices on the users.

By the time that this work was carried out, Multiview had evolved through a number of application experiences, and its use had become more polished. In this particular case, the mix of experience of the analysts plus the participation of the users worked together well. It saw the entire range of products from Multiview presented to the problem owner (the rich picture was shown as Figure 7.1, Figures 7.2 to 7.7 showed the conceptual models, and further outputs are described in Part Three of this text). The multiple perspectives identified by the rich picture can be a problem if conflict exists and resolution is not forthcoming. The rich pictures as a representational form, however, worked extremely well. However, uninitiated users did not always see the significance of the conceptual models. Sometimes the movement from one conceptual model to one at a different level was difficult and not clearly directed.

This case also saw the importance of top management support in the process. Further, the problem solving team were knowledgeable in educational environments and this provided a basis for understanding and communication between the team and top management.

PART THREE

MULTIVIEW STAGE 2:
INFORMATION ANALYSIS

Chapter 8
Functions and Events

8.1   THE FUNCTION CHART

Stage 1 of the analysis gives us an overall view, called the rich picture, of the organisation whose information processing is to be investigated. It also gives us some key definitions of the purposes which are furthered by the human activity system. These are the root definitions. The next stage involves the creation of an overall picture of the information flow in the organisation showing the relevant systems, by building a conceptual model. The creation of this model takes us from the analysis of the human activity system to the entity/function analysis, that is, the detailed analysis of information flows. This is the second stage of Multiview. The conceptual model serves rather like an engineer's drawings. It shows what the new system should do.

The purpose of Stage 2 is to analyse the entities and functions derived from the **notional system**, that is, the primary task root definition together with its model and its associated universe of discourse. The analysis proceeds independently of any considerations about how the information system will eventually be implemented.

This stage combines the concepts of data modelling and structured analysis as outlined in Martin & McClure (1984) and Shave (1981) with the practical orientation of Avison (1985), Macdonald & Palmer (1982) and Rock-Evans (1981). The concepts utilised are the entity-function models as outlined for a database environment in Davenport (1978). Three main phases are involved:

1. Development of the functional model.
2. Development of an entity or data model.
3. Interactions of functions and entities, and verification of the model.

The next two chapters look at the information model. In this chapter we look at functions and events, and in Chapter 9 we look at the entity model and the verification of the information model as a whole. Before looking first at entities and events, there is a possibility that the term 'conceptual model' is a source of confusion. Unfortunately, as information systems is a new discipline, there are a number of instances where consistency in the use of terminology is not fully resolved. In some texts and in descriptions of alternative methodologies, the term conceptual model is used for what we have described (and will develop further in the next chapter) as the entity model. In this text we follow Checkland's use of the term conceptual model, as described in Chapter 6, and this shows the relationship between the activities which are logically necessary to support the human activity and the flow of information and money. We will use the term entity model for the result of the process of data analysis and the term information model for the combined function and event models and entity model. The information model shows what information is needed to carry out the various tasks and when it is needed in order to achieve the objectives of the organisation.

The first step in this part of the methodology is to create a **function chart** (or **function model**) which details in a hierarchical manner all the functions that have to be performed within the new information system. At the same time we can show what events trigger the various actions or tasks when needed.

The function chart takes the major information processing functions of the system and breaks them down into their components. This **functional decomposition** is exactly comparable to the process of top down decomposition or a similar technique (known as step-wise refinement) used in structured programming. It is also used in some methodologies of information systems development, see for example Gane & Sarson (1979), deMarco (1979) and Yourdon (1989) which emphasise the structured aspects of systems analysis and design. The function chart is formed by taking the major function of the system and putting its name in a box at the top of the paper. The next stage is to decide which secondary functions are needed to fulfil this primary function. These are placed in boxes on the second line, and so on.

We have implied the use of pen and paper, but there are now a number of computer packages or 'tools' which will help to draw function charts. We used one such package to draw the diagrams in this text. Indeed there are now many tools which will help draw most of the types of diagram shown in this text.

The process of creating the function models has already been started as we build the conceptual model. We are taking the conceptual model one stage further by removing all the physical things such as documents, monies and goods, and concentrating on the functions to be performed. We do not at this stage consider the flow of information through the functions. This will be built up separately as we create the data flow diagrams. These are discussed later in this chapter. We also look at more sophisticated versions of these charts later in the text (Chapter 18).

Functional decomposition is not difficult. It is simply the breaking down of functions into smaller and smaller tasks. However it is important that discussion takes place between the analyst or problem solver and the problem owner (see Section 5.4) to ensure that the functional decomposition that is agreed on is the most useful in the situation. As always with human situations, there can be no one right answer, though many methodologies seem to imply that there is this utopian situation. In fact there will be a number of 'solutions' which help to understand the problem area.

The analyst's role, along with the other people involved, is to choose the best from a number of appropriate models. Of course there are also a large number of inappropriate models.

The function chart (or function model) represents, at any one level, all the functions that the information system needs to operate (not just the functions to be computerised). The lowest level is the most detailed. The functions are not arranged in the sequence in which they occur, as many will occur in parallel.

In the DLU case study discussed in Chapter 7, the highest level of function is 'Operate Distance Learning Course'. This is the top box in Figure 8.1. This is broken down into five sub-functions:

- Pre-exposition preparation
- Exposition
- Administration tasks
- Report and information provision
- Monitoring and evaluation.

These correlate directly to the five subsystems identified in the conceptual model (see Figure 7.2), that is, the model of the activities necessary to realise the objective system.

In Figure 8.1, we see that the 'Pre-exposition preparation' has been broken down into 'Course preparation' and 'Student preparation'. These are logically distinct. The breakdown of 'Exposition' and 'Administration tasks' is not drawn on that page because of lack of room. The letter in small circles show the connections to diagrams in later pages.

'Report and information system' is broken down into 'Services to internal bodies' and 'Services to external bodies'. Again these are logically quite distinct, but may turn out in practice to overlap in some places. For example, we could well use reports generated for one body to satisfy the information needs of another. To avoid confusion it is necessary to differentiate between what is 'logically necessary to do' and 'the method by which it is convenient to do it'. Sending the same report to two different bodies is a decision about **how**, whereas we are presently concerned with **what**.

The functional decomposition continues to a third level as 'Services to internal bodies' is broken down into 'Student enquiries', 'Employer enquiries' and 'Tutor enquiries'.

The complete functional decomposition is shown in Figures 8.1 to 8.9. The fact that there was no existing system to study meant that we did not have complete confidence in the function chart. We were fairly sure that there must be things that we had missed out and would discover when we came to create the system. However, we have made considerable progress and this would be unlikely to have been achieved without this modelling technique.

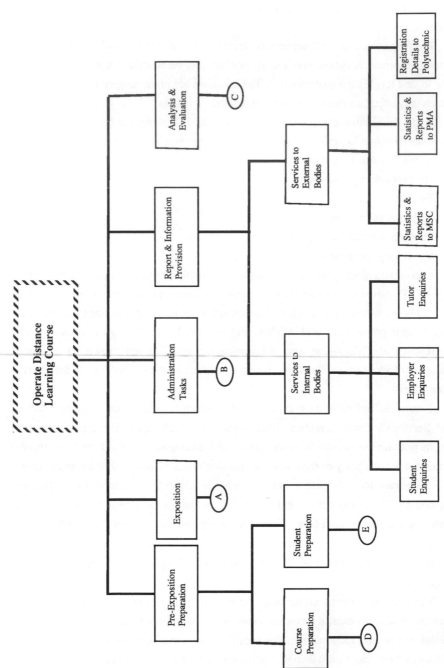

Fig. 8.1. Function model diagram

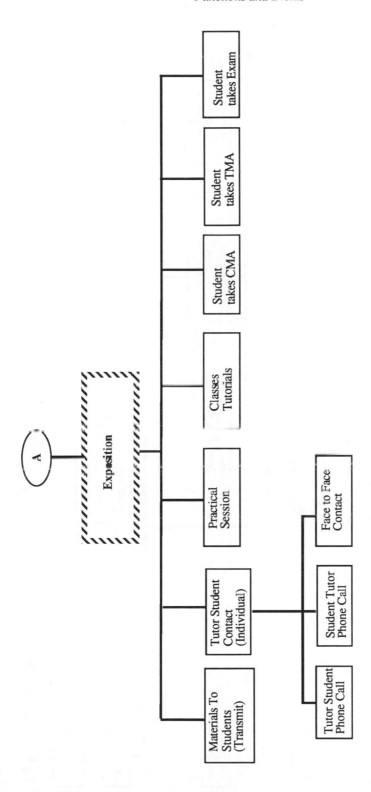

Fig. 8.2. Functional model: exposition

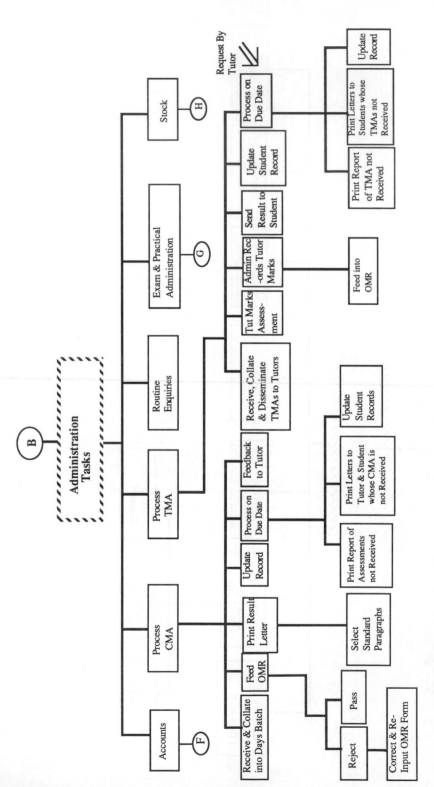

Fig 8.3. Functional model: administration tasks

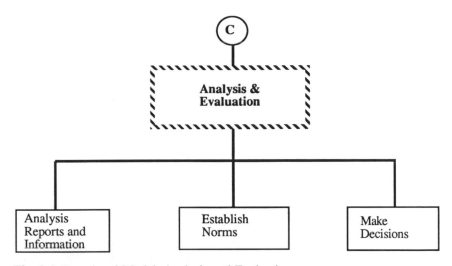

Fig. 8.4. Functional Model: Analysis and Evaluation

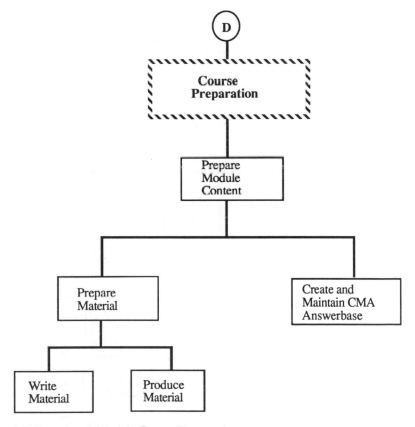

Fig. 8.5. Functional Model: Course Preparation

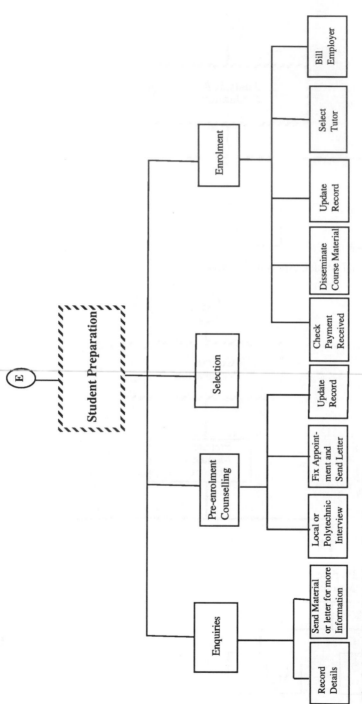

Fig. 8.6. Functional model: student preparation

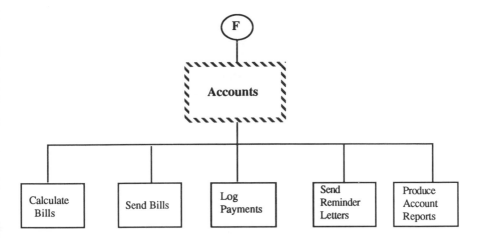

Fig. 8.7. Functional model: accounts

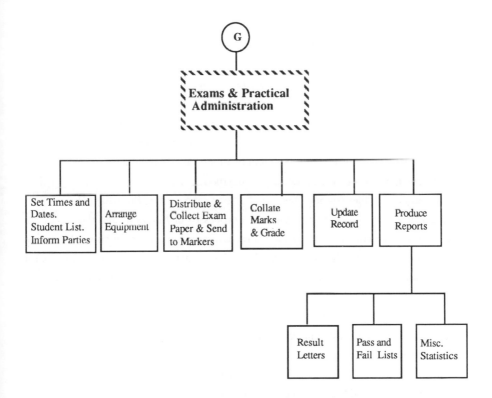

Fig. 8.8. Functional model: exams and practical administration

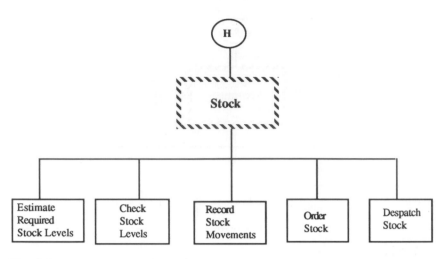

Fig. 8.9. Functional model: stock

8.2   EVENTS AND DATA FLOWS

The next stage is to think about what **events** trigger each of these actions (sometimes referred to as operations), and what information is involved. An event (also called a transaction) is a stimulus that initiates a function. The event 'request by tutor' is arrowed in Figure 8.3). There are two types of events: internal and external. An internal event occurs inside the model and is a function of completing or starting. An external event occurs outside the domain of the model. These events can be depicted on the function hierarchies (through the use of arrows) and on data flow diagrams.

Data flow diagrams give precedence to processes or functions and the use of the data. The analyst constructs these data flow diagrams by examining how information flows in and around the function hierarchies. These diagrams create a good basis for the questions that the analyst must ask the user who is doing the job, and who is the source of the analyst's information. The data flow diagram acts as a check on the previous diagrams. By using this diagram, entries missing from the functional chart can be checked. Formally, this checking can also be done by a Function/Event matrix (described later in this section). This chart can be used to check the accuracy and completeness of the models. Each function should be triggered by at least one event and every event should trigger at least one function.

We will look first at a simplified form of the data flow diagram. Figures 8.10-12 are simplified data flow diagrams showing some of the DLU activities. To complete the model we would draw similar diagrams for all the data flows through all the other functions. This is a methodical process which uses up quite a lot of paper (or iterations

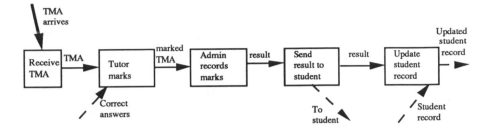

Fig. 8.10. Simplified data flow diagram 'Process TMA'

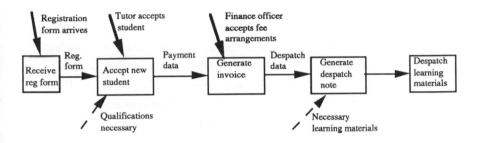

Fig. 8.11. Simplified data flow diagram 'Enrolment'

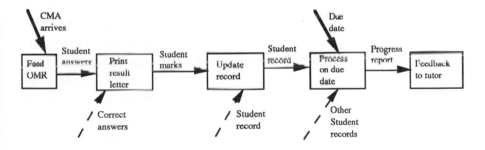

Fig. 8.12. Simplified data flow diagram 'Process CMA'

when using a computer package). The process can be compared with that of completing the engineering drawing when designing a machine or building.

The functions are shown in boxes, and they correspond to the boxes on the bottom row (or near bottom row) of the function hierarchy chart. Figure 8.12, for example, is represented in the functions of the third level of Figure 8.3. They represent the individual actions that need to be performed for the DLU to carry on its business.

Data, which is unprocessed information, flows from left to right across the page undergoing various changes on its way as it is processed. The 'bold' arrows going into the box show the information that is captured during that function. It is collected during some processes, passed on to others and stored. Later on it may be retrieved from the store so that it can be used in another function. Some of this data is input (shown as dotted arrows in the Figure) because the information is necessary for the particular processing. Thus in Figure 8.10, the correct answers are necessary for the tutor to mark a student's TMA. Chapter 9 discusses the whole question of the way that the information model deals with data, information, fields and records.

As we have seen, events are depicted in these simplified data flow diagrams as coming in from above the function boxes. Events correspond to happenings in the real world, and so are easy to understand. In Figure 8.11, for example, a registration form arrives, the tutor accepts the student, and if the finance officer accepts the fee arrangements, this event leads to an invoice being despatched along with the learning materials. Early attempts at information analysis concentrated on 'data' and 'processing', as the events are straightforward in business data processing. However, ignoring events is a mistake as it might, for instance, lead to sales not being recorded and potential customers not being served. In computer controlled systems, such as those at oil refineries and nuclear power stations, the data and processes to be programmed are usually relatively straightforward, but a failure to respond correctly to an event could result, in these examples, in a dangerous explosion or a radioactive leak.

Some functions that are performed at present may have an external justification. For example, external bodies may lay down certain rules about student enrolments. One of the objectives of our system must be to provide the information that is required by statutory bodies. Other functions may be performed because 'it happens to be a convenient way of doing things'. These may be changed on implementing a computer system if a better way is found of doing these things. The analyst has to distinguish between functions that 'serve an organisation's purpose' and others that 'serve the needs of a previous information system'. Analysts must design systems that serve the needs of the *organisation*, not its habits.

Figure 8.10 shows what happens when a tutor marked assignment (TMA) arrives. We have not shown any receipting or batching process at the start, although these may well need to be carried out. On the diagram the TMA is passed to the tutor who marks the assignment. The marked assignment is passed to the administration which sends the result to the student. Data about the marks are also added to the student record. On the date that the assessment is due for completion, all the student records can be scanned to find out who has completed the work and who has not, and students who have not completed the work are sent letters to remind them that they have not submitted by the due date.

Figure 8.12 shows what happens when a computer marked assignment (CMA) arrives. Again, we have not shown any receipting or batching process at the start. On the diagram the CMA is read by the optical mark reader (OMR) and the computer system reads off the answers that the student has marked (they are multiple-choice questions). The computer system now has the data on the student's answers. The computer system can compare these with its list of correct answers along with a list of responses to make to all possible answers. A letter can then be generated on the assessment and give the marks. Data about the marks are added to the student record. On the date that the assessment is due for completion, all the student records can be scanned to find out who has completed the work and who has not, and who has passed the assessment and who has to make a second attempt. Finally, a progress report can be written out for the tutor.

Readers might be surprised when reviewing Figure 8.12 (and Figure 8.3) that there is clear indication as to the possible physical solution (or at least part of it) in the description of what should be a logical view. Writers of text books argue that a data flow should specify *what* flows, not how it flows - it should not differentiate, for example, between data flowing using carrier pigeon or twisted copper wires. However, in Figure 8.12 a computer system using an optical character recognition device for inputting the students' marks (from the CMA) has been suggested and the diagram shows the processing that follows its arrival. Considerations relevant to the implementation have been depicted in the logical description. This shows one of the ways that the contingencies of the 'real world' can differ from the 'text book ideal'. The computer solution was made early on and the equipment ordered. It is not sensible to pretend that the decision had not been made. Analysts need to accept these 'facts of life' and methodologies should still be useful even when working under these constraints.

Since, as we have shown, we can write the contents of these diagrams down in words, what is the advantage of the data flow diagram? The main one perhaps is that it takes an important step from the infinite subtlety of the human being to the simplistic approach of the computer. When one person is explaining a system to another it is possible to move gradually from one phase to another, explaining in more depth where it seems necessary. Computers need every small step to be programmed, the programmer cannot 'assume' steps in a way that one human can when talking to another. The construction of these simplified data flow diagrams represents a phase in the process of breaking complex processes into logical flows of simpler steps. They also identify the information that is passed between these steps and that obtained from files. Finally, they identify the events that call the processes into action. In Figure 8.12, 'feed OMR' and 'print result letter' are two of the steps; 'student answers' and 'student marks' represent information passing between steps; 'correct answers' and 'student record' represent information coming from files; and 'CMA arrives' and 'due date' represent events.

It is true that researchers working in the field of artificial intelligence and knowledge-based systems are attempting to create computer systems that function more like human beings. Some of the effort is directed at making them easy to operate and understand, and we discuss this later, but much of the research is directed towards making the computerised representation of the information more subtle and flexible. However, the business systems available at the moment distinguish between programs, data and events, which call the programs into action. These distinctions must be shown in the model if it is to serve as a representation of the way the system is to work.

Readers should study Figure 8.11, which is the data flow diagram for enrolment, and answer the following:

- For each of the events shown at the top of the box, what is actually happening in the office?
- For each of the functions, what sort of information would have to be retrieved from the system before it could be done?
- What new information would have to be recorded after each function?

These are precisely the questions that the analyst must ask when creating the diagrams in the first place. He starts with the functions that have been spelled out on the hierarchical function chart and then goes on to see how the information must flow in and out of them. The creation of this diagram provides a good basis for the questions that he must ask the users who are doing the job, and who act as the source of the analyst's information.

The diagram also acts as a check on the previous diagrams. When 'thinking through' a set of actions it is possible to identify something that has been missed off the function chart or some information which is needed but has not been represented on the information flow picture. This is another very important function of the model - making sure that all the pieces are there and that they fit together.

We have so far described the construction of a simplified form of data flow diagram and these were used in the DLU case study. However, data flow diagrams are very useful in the analysis of functions and events and the diagramming technique has been extended in Multiview, as in other methodologies. Figures 8.13 and 8.14, taken from Avison and Fitzgerald 1988, give two examples. These data flow diagrams (DFD) have four basic constructs: data flow, process, data store and external entity.

The data flow: Data flow is represented by an arrow (as it is in the simplified model) and depicts the fact that some data is flowing or moving from one process to another. A number of analogies are commonly used to illustrate this. Gane and Sarson suggest that we think of the arrow as a pipeline down which 'parcels' of data are sent, and Page-Jones (1980) states that data flow is like a conveyor belt in a factory which takes

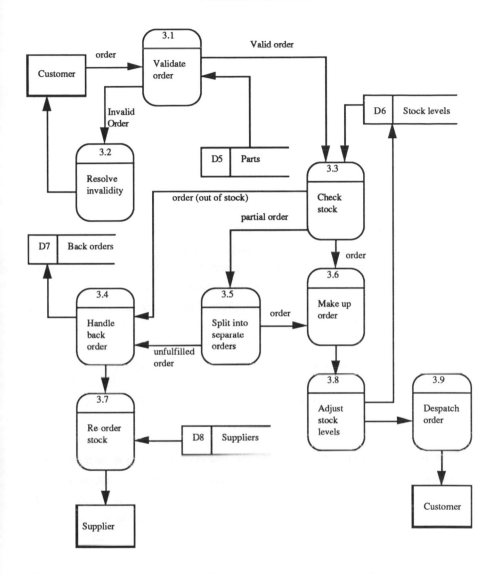

Fig. 8.13. Sophisticated data flow diagram for sales order processing

data from one 'worker' to another. Each 'worker' then performs some process on that data which may result in another data flow on the conveyor belt. These processes are the second element of the DFD.

The processes: The processes or tasks performed on the data flows are represented in Figure 8.13 by a soft box (a box with rounded edges) as against the 'hard box' of the simplified model. The process transforms the data flow by either changing the structure of the data or by generating new information from the data. In Figure 8.13, 'validate order' is a process, and this has transformed the order data flow by adding new information to the order - whether it is valid or not. Invalid orders flow out from the validation process in a different direction to valid orders. In this example the conventions used for the process symbol are as follows. The top compartment contains a reference number (3.1) for the process and the lower compartment contains the description of the process. A process must have at least one data flow coming into it and at least one leaving it. There is no concept of a process without data flows, a process cannot exist independently.

The data store: If a process cannot terminate a data flow because it must output something, then where do the data flows stop? There are two places. The first is the data store, which can be envisaged as a file, although it is not necessarily a computer file or even a manual record in a filing cabinet. It can be a very temporary repository of data, for example, a shopping list or a transaction record. A data store symbol is a pair of parallel lines with one end closed and a compartment for a reference code and a compartment for the name of the data store. For example, in Figure 8.13 the process of validating the order (3.1) may need to make reference to the parts data store (D5) to see if the parts specified on the order are valid parts with the correct current price associated with it. The data flow in this example has the arrow pointing towards the process which indicates that the data store is only referenced by the process and not updated or changed in any way. If the arrow points to the data store, this indicates new information is being added to the store (for example, the arrow from process 3.8 to the stock levels data store (D6)).

The source or sink (External Entity): The second way of terminating a data flow in a system is by directing the flow to a sink. The sink may, for example, be a supplier to whom we send an order for stock. The supplier is a sink in the sense that the data flow does not necessarily continue. Sinks are usually entities that are external to the organization in question, although they need not be, another department may be a sink. It depends on where the boundaries of the system under consideration are drawn. The original source of a data flow is the opposite to a sink, although it may be the same entity. For example, a customer is the source of an order and a sink for a despatch note. Sinks and sources are represented by the same symbol which is a square (thickly lined on two sides) in our convention. Sources and sinks are often termed 'external entities'.

One of the most important features of the data flow diagram is the ability to construct a variety of levels of data flow diagram according to the level of abstraction required. This means that an overview diagram can be consulted in order to obtain a high level (overview) understanding of the system. When a particular area of interest has been identified, then this area can be examined at a more detailed level. The different levels of diagram must be consistent with each other in that the data flows present on the higher levels should exist on the lower levels as well. In essence it is the

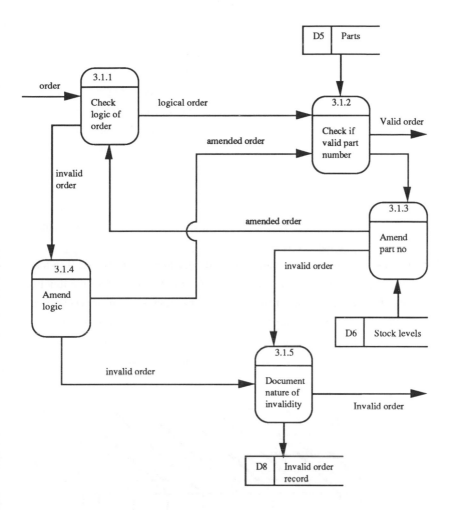

Fig. 8.14. Lower level data flow diagram for validate order process

processes which are expanded at a greater level of detail as we move down the levels of diagram. This 'levelling' process gives the technique its top-down characteristic.

If Figure 8.13 is examined we may require more detail of any of the processes on the diagram. Figure 8.14 is the next level down (or an *explosion*) of the Validate Order task. The overall process is expanded into five tasks with various data flows between them. However all the data flows in and out of Validate Order (reference 3.1) in Figure 8.13 can be found on Figure 8.14. The new data flows are either flows that only exist within the Validate Order process, that is, they are internal to it and are now shown because we have split this down into separate components (for example, Amended Order), or because they are concerned with errors and exceptions.

The details of errors and exceptions are not shown on high level diagrams as it would confuse the picture with detail that is not required at an overview level. What is required at an overview level is 'normal' processing and data flows. To include errors and exceptions might double the size of the diagram and remove its overview characteristics. For example, Figure 8.14 shows new processing concerned with amending an order and even a new data store which did not appear on the higher level diagram. The problem is that it is sometimes difficult to decide what constitutes an error or an exception, and what is normal. Some common guide-lines suggest that if an occurrence of a process or data flow is relatively rare, then it should be regarded as an exception. However, if it is financially significant, it should be taken as part of normal processing. Overall, it depends on the audience or use to be made of the data flow diagram as to exactly what is included. At the lowest level, all the detail, including errors and exceptions, should be shown.

Another way of checking the accuracy and completeness of the model is to take a piece of squared paper and write all the events down on the side and all the functions across the top. The next step is to put an X at the intersection between an event row and a function column if that event triggers that function. Every event should trigger at least one function and every function should have a triggering event. If there are any gaps, then the analyst must find out what has been forgotten. Note that Figure 8.15 has only been partially completed.

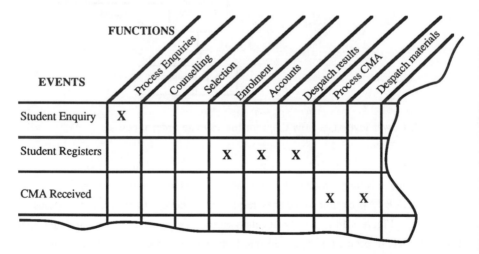

Fig. 8.15. Function/event matrix for DLU case (part)

If there are things that have been overlooked, or a better way of breaking down the functions into their component activities has been identified, then it is necessary to alter the relevant parts of the diagram. This seems a nuisance but it will be much worse later if a system is implemented which is incomplete. Further, as mentioned previously, there are a number of computer tools available which facilitate the drawing and, more importantly, the easy updating of the various diagrams including these more sophisticated data flow diagrams (such a package was used in constructing Figures 8.13 and 8.14).

Unless there are peculiar difficulties, analysts working on a small system should get the information model about right after a second or third attempt. If you are still struggling ask yourself the following:

- *Am I trying to represent every conceivable circumstance in too great detail?* Small systems cannot cope with infinite variety. Keep the formal system to the essentials and let the people operating it use their discretion in applying it to particular circumstances. Alternatively, build in a reference to the supervisor/manager where things do not fit the normal pattern.
- *Does the business really require that almost every transaction is unique?* Unless most of the work can be processed according to a set of broad rules which you can trust the operators to interpret, then a computer system is unlikely to help.
- *Am I still searching for the 'perfect' model?* Remember that there are no right answers, only ones which are more or less useful and more or less complete. The question to ask is whether a system based on this model would serve better than the one that is available now, and whether it is worth the effort to change over. If you really are in two minds about the best way to represent the model, then try out two alternatives in detail to see which works out better. You could even go to the suppliers with both models to see which one can be supplied more easily.

8.3   SUMMARY

There are three main elements to an information model - functions, events and information. Information modelling starts with the overall picture of the information flow in the conceptual model and develops the activities in this into the function hierarchy chart. The actions identified at the bottom of the hierarchy chart are then used to create a simplified data flow diagram. These attempt to link inter-related information activities within the hierarchy. This takes a natural grouping of functions and shows the information flowing into them and the new information flowing out. Above each function is shown the event that triggers it. A distinction should be made between functions which are essential to the business and those done to serve the needs of particular information systems, because the latter can be changed if there is a better way of handling information. A more sophisticated data flow diagram can then be drawn which distinguishes between internal stores and external sources and sinks.

It is important to cross-check between the charts to make sure that no events, functions or information flows have been left out. The charts should be checked by all the people involved. An additional check can be made by creating a function/event matrix. This shows which functions are triggered by which events and vice versa. Even if the only interest is in buying a software package rather than designing and implementing a tailor-made system in-house, it is still necessary to go through the design phase. This is because it is only when the list of functions to be performed is drawn up that it is possible to check whether a particular software package caters for them.

8.4   EXERCISES

1   Draw a set of function charts for an organisation.
2   Complete the set of simplified data flow diagrams and function-event matrix for the DLU case study.
3   Draw the sophisticated data flow diagrams for the DLU case study.

Chapter 9
Analysis of Entities

9.1 KEEPING RECORDS

Stage one of Multiview looks at the activities of the organisation to see what are its major objectives. Stage two is the analysis and creation of a model of the information processing that is needed to achieve these objectives. This information model shows the relationship between events, functions and data. As well as being a design tool in its own right, the model serves to help the users see whether the proposed system will meet their needs and it is also a specification against which, later in the project's life, to test the offerings of hardware and software suppliers or systems developed in-house.

We have looked at the overall information flow in the conceptual model (Chapter 6), the breakdown of the major functions of the organisation into its essential components and the events that trigger each of these functions and the flow of information through the functions (Chapter 8). By doing so, we have tried to work out answers to the questions: "What needs to be done?", "when should it be done?" and "what information is needed to do it?".

We will now look in more detail at the information needed to support these functions. There are a number of things that companies may keep records about - customers, orders, employees, stock items, credit lines, and so on. Some of these are about people, for example, employees. Some are things or collections of things, such as stock items. Others are activities. Sales orders, for example, represent transactions performed by customers. Some of the things are more abstract, for example, a credit line. This is actually a rule. It is a record of a decision about how much credit to allow a customer.

There are standard ways of recording information relevant to the organisation and useful to people working in it. These recording systems (double-entry book-keeping, ledgers, invoices, record cards, orders in triplicate, and so on) are all suited to paper as the recording medium. Paper has many advantages, in particular it can be read by people, and changes in content and format can be made conveniently. However, it is tedious to produce reports from a file of paper records and analytical statistics are particularly difficult to produce. Furthermore, the transfer of paper from one location to another is slow - although 'fax' or facsimile, a system that reproduces documents at a distance, is beginning to overcome this problem.

Computerised systems have different strengths and weaknesses so it is important not just to transfer a system designed for paper across to a computer, because it is unlikely to fully exploit the particular strengths of the computer system. For this reason, analysts should start by looking at the nature of the information prior to the implementation of an information system. They need to separate the logical model of information from its implementation considerations.

The nature of information can be ascertained initially by the process of identifying entities, relationships and attributes. The process occurs in parallel with the formulation of the functional model. For this reason we recommend that analysts should start again by looking at the information needs of the organisation and deciding on what records it needs to keep.

9.2 ENTITIES AND RELATIONSHIPS

An **entity** is something about which records are kept and is any object of interest to the organisation under analysis, any part of the system or any object about which data can be stored and collected (Veryard, 1984). Identification of entities is the first step of data modelling.

An entity can be real or conceptual, an activity, a passing state or a grouping. An **entity type** is given to a class or a set of objects, for example, a car, university or hospital. Each of these is represented by an **entity occurrence**. This is sometimes referred to as a record. Each occurrence of the entity customer will have a set of data items associated with it. These data items could include 'name', 'address' and 'telephone number'. Each record or entity occurrence would be composed of the same set of data items, although the actual value will differ from one record to another. For example, all customer records will have the data item 'name', but the actual contents could be 'Smith', 'Jones', and so on.

Some entities are obvious physical things, like customers or stock. Others are transactions, like orders, sales and hospital admissions. Some entities are more or less artificial. These are rather like catalogue entries in the library: the only reason to have them is to help people find books which would otherwise be difficult to locate.

Data modelling, which is a diagrammatic technique, represents entities as 'soft boxes' in most conventions. A soft box is a rectangle with rounded corners. The name of the entity type is written in the box. The second step in data modelling is to identify the connections between entities. These connections give structure to the data model. If such a connection between two entity occurrences can be generalised and named so that it can be applied to several situations, that is then called a **relationship**. Any two entity types (may) have a relationship between them. For each course we could have one or more occurrences of the entity student, as one course can be given to (or taken by) a number of students. It is necessary to relate a particular course record to the equivalent student records. The relationship is expressed in the diagram by a line between them and a 'crow's foot' at the 'many' end (in this case at the end of the entity 'student'). The **degree** of a relationship is based on the number of occurrences of the entity types that can be related to one another. The possible degrees are:

- *One-to-one* - represented by a line without a crow's foot
- *One-to-many* (or many-to-one) - represented by a line with a crow's foot at the 'many' end
- *Many-to-many* - represented by a line with a crow's foot at both ends.

The entity model is static and not time-dependent. Because of this:

- A model must contain *all* entity types possible throughout the life of the information system; but at different time points, some of these may not exist.
- A model assumes that all entities of a given type participate in the associations of that entity type. Again, at different times this may not be true.

Figure 9.1 shows the basic structure. It contains the additional information that a course consists of many modules.

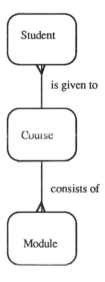

Fig. 9.1. Entity modelling - the basic symbols

The final step is to define all the properties of these objects. These are called **attributes** (we called them data items in the description above). Each entity type has a number of attributes associated with it. Some of these attributes are designated to uniquely identify each entity occurrence. This attribute or set of attributes is usually called the **key** or **identifier**. The aim of the initial analysis of the data is to define the

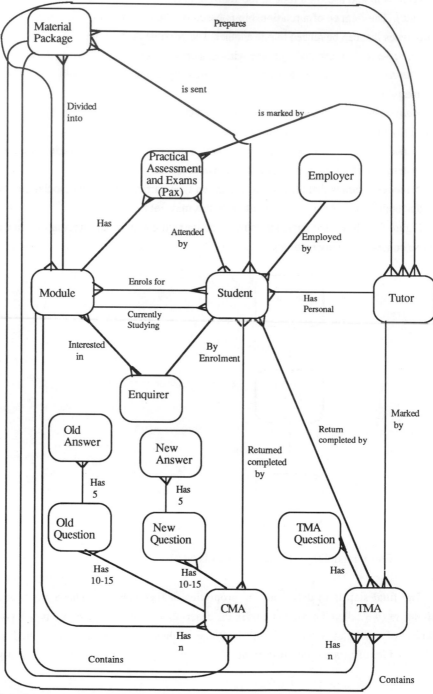

Fig. 9.2. Entity model for Distance Learning Unit (part)

attributes and an identifier associated with each entity. For example, the student reference number may uniquely identify each entity occurrence of the entity 'student' (the student name is unlikely to be unique for all students).

The **entity model** for the DLU is shown as Figure 9.2. As can be seen, the entities are shown in soft boxes, whilst the lines between them show the most important relationships. It is usual to include only those relationships that can be described as 'fundamental to the business', otherwise the diagram becomes too complex to be readily understood, and in any case, later when the model is transferred to a computer system, it would be too complex.

In Figure 9.2, we see that the relationship has been named to describe how the entities inter-relate. Thus, a student 'enrols for' a module. 'Many' means any number from zero onwards. It could be that at a given time no students are assigned to a particular tutor, but the possibility remains that a number of students might be assigned to that tutor. However, one student cannot have more than one employer or personal tutor. In some instances, the number of occurrences have been specified. Thus, the computer-marked assignment (CMA) 'has 10-15' new questions.

Although it is a more formal representation than the rich picture, it is not too difficult to see what is going on by looking at the entity model - at least those aspects of the problem situation that it is supposed to represent.

There are no one-to-one relationships in the DLU case, where for every occurrence of one entity there is one and only one occurrence of another, but if 'husband' and 'wife' in another model were separate entities, the relationship (in most countries) would be one to one.

Other relationships are many-to-many, that is, they have a crow's foot at each end of the line. Such is the relationship between students and computer-marked assessments. This means that each student can take a number of CMAs and each CMA may be taken by a number of students. The large number of these relationships in the diagram illustrates the complexity of the model.

9.3 VERIFYING THE MODEL

Engineers build models to test their designs and this is a major reason for building an information model. It is difficult to test something that only exists on paper, but mistakes *can* be identified, and it is obviously better to show these up at this stage before too many decisions have been made about implementation. In general, the later errors are detected, the more expensive they will be to correct. Testing the information model is part of the process of design specification and the more thorough it is, the better the chance of success.

A good model is one which is a fair representation of the problem situation, and although entity modelling is sometimes described as an 'objective' process, it is subjective and does depend on the skill of the analysts and the views of the users and managers about what is important to the organisation. Different analysts are likely to come up with different activity models and like most of the techniques used in Multiview, should be looked at as 'something for discussion'.

A good way to start the testing is to go to all the people who will use the system and ask them to list the sorts of information that they want to collect and the questions that they will want to be able to answer. Such questions might include "Have you marked the CMA I sent in last Friday?" or "What proportion of students are dropping out before they take the exams?" or "Has Ann Jones completed module 1 yet?". Armed with a list of questions, the analyst looks at the function chart, the data flow diagrams and the entity model to see if the necessary information was collected. Further, this process will detect information on the model that is not used.

As we shall see later in this chapter, there are other ways to verify the entity model, for example, through the study of events. A particular check on the entity model uses the technique of **normalisation**. This technique helps to ameliorate the anomalies when inserting, deleting and updating entity occurrences (see Date 1986 for the rationale and details of the process). It is used in a number of methodologies. The process has three steps:

1   *First normal form*: Ensure that all the attributes are atomic (that is, in the smallest possible components). This means that each has only one possible value and not a set of values. For example, if an entity is presented as:

COURSE, COURSE-NAME, MODULE-DETAILS

module-details has to be defined as a set of atomic attributes, not as a group item, and has to be broken down into its constituents. This has been done in the entity course details in Figure 9.3. Another aspect of first normal form is the filling in of the details, also seen in Figure 9.3. Whereas the order of the **tuples** (each row of the table) is insignificant in the second table, the order is important in the unnormalised version because some of the information would be lost if the tuples were ordered differently. The key (or identifier), which uniquely identifies each tuple occurrence, of the entity course details consists of course and module (a composite key).

COURSE DETAILS (UNNORMALISED)

COURSE	COURSE-NAME	MODULE	M-NAME	STATUS	M-PTS
C14	PAINT FOUNDATION	M17	DESIGN-1	BASIC	4
		M19	CHEMISTRY-1		
		M22	TECHNOLOGY-1		
		M34	COLOUR	INT	6
C15	PAINT QUALIFIER	M41	DESIGN-2	INT	6
		M46	TECHNOLOGY-2		
		M55	COMPUTING	ADV	8

COURSE DETAILS (FIRST NORMAL FORM)

COURSE	COURSE-NAME	MODULE	M-NAME	STATUS	M-PTS
C14	PAINT FOUNDATION	M17	DESIGN-1	BASIC	4
C14	PAINT FOUNDATION	M19	CHEMISTRY-1	BASIC	4
C14	PAINT FOUNDATION	M22	TECHNOLOGY-1	BASIC	4
C14	PAINT FOUNDATION	M34	COLOUR	INT	6
C15	PAINT QUALIFIER	M41	DESIGN-2	INT	6
C15	PAINT QUALIFIER	M46	TECHNOLOGY-2	INT	6
C15	PAINT QUALIFIER	M55	COMPUTING	ADV	8

Fig.9.3. First normal form

2 *Second normal form*: Check that all non-key attributes belong fully to one entity type, that is, they are fully dependent on - give facts about - all of the key. This is called functional dependency. If this check fails, entity types (new or existing) are created which are fully dependent on their whole identifiers. The products from this process are called 'second normal form'. For example, course details, in first normal form, is not in second normal form because m-name, status and m-pts are functionally dependent on - they are facts about - module, which is only part of the key (course and module). They do not represent facts about course. Thus two tables are formed from the first normal form table of Figure 9.3. The entity module in Figure 9.4 will have the attribute 'module' as the key and we are left with a second table consisting of course and module (the composite key) and the non-key attribute course-name.

MODULE

MODULE	M-NAME	STATUS	M-PTS
M17	DESIGN-1	BASIC	4
M19	CHEMISTRY-1	BASIC	4
M22	TECHNOLOGY-1	BASIC	4
M34	COLOUR	INT	6
M41	DESIGN-2	INT	6
M46	TECHNOLOGY-1	INT	6
M55	COMPUTING	ADV	8

COURSE DETAILS

COURSE	COURSE-NAME	MODULE
C14	PAINT FOUNDATION	M17
C14	PAINT FOUNDATION	M19
C14	PAINT FOUNDATION	M22
C14	PAINT FOUNDATION	M34
C15	PAINT QUALIFIER	M41
C15	PAINT QUALIFIER	M46
C15	PAINT QUALIFIER	M55

Fig.9.4. Towards second normal form

If we look at the second table in Figure 9.4, we see that it is also not in second normal form because course-name is functionally dependent on course, which is only part of the key. We therefore have to separate out this table leading to Figure 9.5.

COURSE

COURSE	COURSE-NAME
C14	PAINT FOUNDATION
C15	PAINT QUALIFIER

COURSE-MODULE

COURSE	MODULE
C14	M17
C14	M19
C14	M22
C14	M34
C15	M41
C15	M46
C15	M55

Fig.9.5. Second normal form

We finish with three tables in second normal form, module (Figure 9.4) and course and course-module (Figure 9.5). The course table now only has two entries, as we do not want entries which are exactly the same. The table course-module is 'all key', that is all the attributes are key attributes. Some readers may be surprised that it is not left out because the module and course details are seen in the other tables. However, information would be lost if we did this, that is, modules M17, M19, M22, M34 are included in the course C14, and M41, M46 and M55 are included in the course C15.

3 *Third normal form*: Check to see if the value of a non-identifier attribute can be deduced from the values stored within other non-identifier attributes in the same entity occurrence or occurrences in the same entity type (this is known as transitive dependency). This check is to ensure that redundancy is not present due to dependency upon non-identifier attributes. If this redundancy occurs then the dependent attribute can be removed to new entity types. The resulting products from this process are called the 'third normal form'. In Figure 9.4, the attribute m-pts is transitively dependent on status (not a key) in the table module and the third normal form version has two tables, status and module, for the table module in second normal form.

MODULE

MODULE	M-NAME	STATUS
M17	DESIGN-1	BASIC
M19	CHEMISTRY-1	BASIC
M22	TECHNOLOGY-1	BASIC
M34	COLOUR	INT
M41	DESIGN-2	INT
M46	TECHNOLOGY-2	INT
M55	COMPUTING	ADV

STATUS

STATUS	M-PTS
BASIC	4
INT	6
ADV	8

Fig.9.6. Third normal form

The status table had repeating entries, so these were not included. The final set of tables in third normal form includes module and status (from Figure 9.6), course-module and course (from Figure 9.5). We have used the term tables for the entity lists, whereas most of the technical texts will use the term **relations**.

9.4 DESCRIPTION OF DLU ENTITIES

In identifying the entities for the DLU system, we kept in mind the following definition; 'An entity is any thing or object which has characteristics that are important to the system under study'. Most of the entities shown in Figure 9.2 are listed below, along with a short description.

ENQUIRER	A person who displays interest in a paintmaking course
STUDENT	A person enroled in a paintmaking course
EMPLOYER	A company financing students on the paintmaking course
TUTOR	A member of the DLU academic staff
MODULE	The basic unit of a course of study. The system will need to store a wide range of information about a module for administration and statistical purposes
MATERIAL-PACKAGE	This represents a collection of study material that is presented or posted to students studying the relevant module. The systems will store data about this entity for stock recording purposes.
CMA	The Computer-Marked Assessment is a set of questions sent to students who return them completed for marking.
TMA	Tutor-Marked Assessment is a marked version of the CMA
PAX	This entity details practical assessment and examinations, including times, locations and grades.

These descriptions are not detailed, but allow the client to comment on whether we are 'on the right lines'. It is important to distinguish this dialogue with the user from the technical aspects which come later. The entity model is an input to the technical design stage where more detailed questions are asked. The entity definitions are also written in the jargon of the user. The academics who received this report were aware, for example, of the significance of computer-marked assessments. The jargon associated with the DLU may not be familiar to all readers, however, and to help them, we give further descriptions of the entities.

A module is a logical unit of the course. The purpose of breaking a course down into modules is to offer students more choice. Some modules are at a basic level and these permit students to reach the academic standards required for a course for which they would not otherwise have been eligible. Conversely they may be exempted from some modules of the course in which they can demonstrate that they already have the required competence. In a conventional classroom situation timetabling these modules is very difficult, but distance learning presents no such problems.

The material package is the set of module documents that help the student study the topic. Tutors have to design, write, illustrate, edit, print and check this material.

The CMAs are used to test students' grasp of the written material. In practice they are difficult and time-consuming to write. The questions are sent as part of the material package. The records system has to hold the correct answers and responses to incorrect ones. These will be printed out when the CMAs are marked. A response might be:

'This is incorrect, but a common mistake. If you look at page 12 you can see that.........'

This sort of feedback would normally be provided by the teacher in a classroom situation, although the CMA is likely to give the individual student a much more detailed response. Statistics about CMAs have to be produced to ensure that they are not too difficult or easy or to show that the material package needs to be improved because students are consistently getting wrong answers relating to one section of the notes.

9.5 DESCRIPTION OF DLU RELATIONSHIPS

A description of the more important relationships shown in Figure 9.2 is as follows:

STUDENT enrolls for MODULE:	A student will enrol on a course and in doing so enrol on the one or more modules that make up the course. Conversely, several students are enrolled for a particular module at any one time.
STUDENT is currently studying MODULE:	At any one time, a student will only be studying material from one module.
MODULE is divided into MATERIAL PACKAGES:	Material to be sent to students is collected into study packages. A 'whole module study package' might overwhelm a student starting on a module, therefore a material package contains only a portion of that study content.
STUDENT has studied MODULE:	A student may have studied a number of modules already. This information forms an integral part of the student record. Some modules are prerequisites for others. Students must pass a certain number of modules before qualifying for their certificate. Viewed from the other direction, the relationship provides statistical information on past student performance for a given module.

The language used and the concerns of this stage of the analysis are both oriented towards the user. The analyst is trying to understand what is significant to the user about the data that could be recorded.

9.6   ATTRIBUTES

An attribute is an item belonging to an entity. Filling in the attributes of an entity provides a further level of detail. We list below the attributes of two entities in the DLU as examples.

ENQUIRER   Name, Address, Sex, Source, New/Old Student, Course
                          Interested In, Comments
EMPLOYER   Company Name, Address, Employer Number, Phone Number,
                          Registered Counsellor, Registered Practical Centre, Association
                          Member, Number of Employees, Contact Name, Industry

The idea of attributes will be familiar to people who have kept records or who have used data handling software (database or file management systems). Analysis is carried out by discussing with users the sorts of information that they want to keep and ensuring that the list of attributes is complete, consistent and unambiguous.

9.7   ENTITY LIFE CYCLE

The entity life cycle shows the changes of state that an entity goes through over time. It is a technique which represents a dynamic view of the system. For example, we will trace the life cycle of an occurrence of the entity 'enquirer' in the DLU system. There will always be an entity type 'enquirer', even if there are no enquirers presently in the system. If we look at a particular enquirer (an entity occurrence of the entity enquirer) then it will change state if any of the the following happens:

• The enquirer enrols as a student;
• The enquirer withdraws by saying that he is not interested; or
• The tutor declares that the enquirer is not suitable for the course.

If none of these happens, the enquirer could remain in the system for ever. It would be sensible therefore to declare a time limit for enquiry data after which it will be deleted from the system. There could be good reasons for maintaining this data, however, as an enquirer may be encouraged to re-apply in the following year or may want to hear of new modules and courses as they develop.

The entity life cycle chart, such as that shown in Figure 9.7, shows the progress of any particular type of entity. The things that cause the state of the entity to change are functions and events. Entity life cycle analysis identifies the various possible states that an entity can legitimately be in. There is always a starting point, usually an event, which sets the entity into its initial state and a terminating point to finish the cycle. In the example, the initial state of the entity is as 'applicant'. This is triggered by an event, which in the example is the receipt of an application. The entity changes state as a result of the admissions function which either causes the applicant to be rejected or accepted. The resultant entity states are rejected or accepted. The accepted applicants start their courses and become registered. They may or may not become qualified, so that their final state is either qualified professional or unqualified. It should be noted that a function can be depicted that does not change the state of the entity. In this case the arrow points back to the same entity state. 'Progress to next year' is an example of this; it is a function that does not change the state of the entity, the student is still registered.

In this example there are a number of terminated states, but some conventions suggest that there should only be one. In this case we would simply add an extra state, called, for example, archived, and draw arrows from all our terminated states to this archived state.

It can be seen that the technique is useful in identifying the states of an entity, the functions that cause the states of an entity to change, and any sequences that are implied. It is also important to identify the terminating states of the entity. Some systems have not always done this and have found that at a later date they have no way of getting rid of entity occurrences.

The diagram is a good communication tool that enables users to validate the accuracy of the analysis. It can form an outline design for transaction processing systems. A by-product of the analysis process is that functions in which the entity type is involved are identified. The process is therefore useful as a validation of the other function analysis techniques. These charts should be drawn for all the entities.

The entity/function matrix and the event/entity matrix, both drawn in a similar manner to the function/event matrix shown as Figure 8.15, are useful as a further check for completeness.

9.8   TESTING THE SYSTEM

A good model is one that is a good representation of the organisation or department or whatever is being depicted. The process of entity modelling is an iterative process and slowly the model will improve, particularly as other techniques are used, as a representation of the **perceived reality**. The modelling process can be looked on as

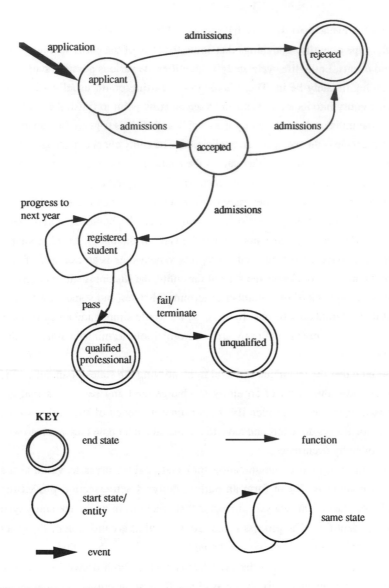

Fig. 9.7. Entity life cycle for enquirer entity type

the creation of discussion documents and its coincidence with the real world is verified in discussions with the various users. It is particularly helpful to ensure that questions from users are addressed by the various models.

We list below some of the questions that users were likely to ask of the system. They are taken from a list of questions that each user wished the system to answer in relation to the DLU course and its students. It is important that the model has the information available to provide the answers. We also comment on our reactions, which include amendments to the model and pointers towards possible reports and information retrieval requirements of the final system.

Tutor Enquiries:

1 *Who has completed a particular assignment?* An entity 'CMA taken' was added to the model with the attributes: Student Number, CMA Number, Date, Received/Not Received, Reason, Result, Mark, Letter Sent Y/N. A list of students whose assignment has been received needs to be printed at the request of the tutor.

2 *What are the top/bottom/average marks for the assignment?* This can be obtained by analysing the CMA Taken and TMA records. A statistics report needs to be printed at the tutor's request.

3 *What is the progress of a particular student?* All necessary information is provided in the student record, for example, the attribute Date of Last Assignment Received will be useful in this context. A student profile report needs to be printed from the student history and student record files.

4 *What are the names of the postponed or withdrawn students?* This can be extracted from the records for individual students.

Student Enquiries:

1 *Has a particular assignment been received?* Assignments must be logged as they arrive.

2 *When will the next block of work be received?* Each student must receive a course calendar telling them this information at the beginning of the module. The calendar should be generated by the system from the student's date of starting. If they lose it, the system should be able to generate a new one.

9.9 IMPLICATIONS OF INFORMATION ANALYSIS FOR A COMPUTER INFORMATION SYSTEM

A study of Figure 2.2 shows that there are outputs of this second stage in Multiview which are passed on to Stage 4 (design of the human-computer interface) and Stage 5 (design of the technical aspects) - which are stages concerned with the design of the computer system - as well as the next stage (analysis and design of the socio-technical aspects). In this section we present aspects of the information modelling stage which provide pointers to the computer information system.

In fact the conceptual modelling phase gives some help to later computerisation, because it shows what, in outline, the new system should do. It can therefore be used as a first basis on which to evaluate the information system. Does it perform all these functions? But we need more detailed guidance to help the designers in Stages 4 and 5.

The function chart provides more details on what is involved in each of the functions identified in the conceptual model. The events identified at this stage are also important inputs to later stages: how will the information system deal with the processing triggered by these events? As we mentioned in Chapter 8, ignoring events could lead to mistakes such as students on the DLU scheme not being awarded their certificates if they pass the course. When we create the data flow diagrams, we show how the flow of information passes through the functions. We have many pointers to the design of the application subsystems which is part of Stage 5.

Of course, the logical subsystems described in Chapter 8 may not exactly match the computer applications and computer programs. Their design may be based on other factors, such as the efficiency requirements related to computer systems (indeed some of these subsystems may not be computerised at all), but the logical subsystems will need to be handled in some way by the information system.

The process of entity modelling described earlier in this chapter is suitable to computerised handling of data, whether using the integrated database approach or separate computer files. In either case, each entity *can* become a file, each entity occurrence a record (and its attributes will be data items), and each record occurrence will be identified on the computer system. We have italicised 'can' because, again, the final organisation of the data will depend on the facilities of the computer system, but we have very strong pointers to the design.

The relationships will be used in the information retrieval system, because there will be situations when information from more than one entity (or file) will be required to service a request for information. A student might request information on the telephone regarding his results. Access to the student file might locate his or her student number and this might be used to access the TMA and CMA files for the marks.

The degree of complexity highlighted by the entity model (the one shown as Figure 9.2 is only moderately complex) might be too high for many computer packages to handle, particularly using microcomputer systems. Of course the user is not interested in how the computer achieves the task of relating records. The same logical relationships may be handled in different ways by different systems. Provided the system can answer all the questions like "Which students have completed CMA 47?" and "Which students are being tutored by Peter Barnes?", then that is all that matters. The details of design can be left to the final stage of Multiview which is the design of the technical aspects of which the database is a major part. Even though packaged software is available in a wide variety and is becoming more versatile and computer hardware is ever improving in terms of speed and memory, it cannot encompass the infinite variety of human activities. Further, aspects not discussed at all so far, such as maintaining reasonable speeds of access to individual records and ensuring that arrangements are made to protect data from unauthorised access, become major problems when we come to design the technical system.

In Sections 9.3 and 9.8 of this chapter we have started providing input to Stage 4 of Multiview, because we have begun to ask questions of the human-computer interface. However, in the information modelling stage we have only shown the *what*, that is, what questions need to be asked. We have not given pointers to the *how*. It is at Stage 4 that such things as dialogue styles are decided. This will depend on, for example, the experience that the users have had with computer systems.

In conclusion, in the stages of Multiview so far discussed, we have been describing the logical models. This describes what happens conceptually, whatever form the physical implementation takes. This information forms the inputs to the design stages, but these analysis stages are separate from the implementation aspects.

The next stage of Multiview begins the process of moving away from the analysis discussed so far in this text towards the design issues we have been discussing in this section. This concerns the balancing of the social and technical needs of the organisation.

9.10 SUMMARY

The second stage of Multiview consists of Information Analysis. This is the analysis of entities, functions and events. This stage is summarised as Figure 9.8.

In this chapter we have been concerned with entities. An entity is something that we ought to keep records about, because it has characteristics, known as attributes, which are important to the information system under study.

Care must be taken to ensure that the entities that are identified are the ones that are important to the organisation, and not just copies of records that have been kept on paper or cards in any previous manual system.

Computer systems are not very flexible in the number of entities and relationships that can be held efficiently. This means that it is important to note those entities and relationships that are most vital to the system. The relationships can be one-to-one, one-to-many or many-to-many.

The information should be tested by getting all users concerned with the system to list details of the information that they will need to retrieve from the system, and then studying the model to ensure that it is capable of providing that information.

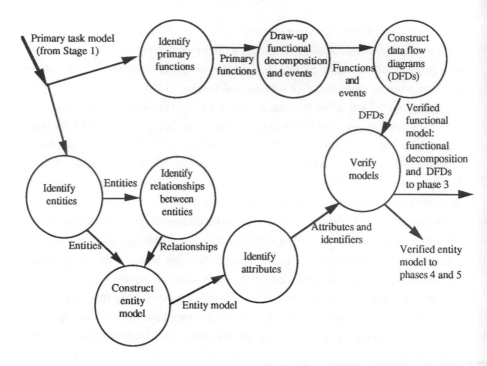

Fig.9.8. Summary of stage 2: information analysis

9.11   EXERCISES

1   For a particular application area, such as a library, draw up a list of entities.
    Construct an entity model by filling in the important relationships. Write the names
    of the entities and the relationships. List the attributes of the various entities.
    Complete the entity life cycle for each of the entities.

2   Following completion of exercise 1, describe those aspects of your analysis which
    give pointers to the systems analyst designing a computer information system for
    the application area.

3   Complete the exercise introduced in the first paragraph of Chapter 10.

Chapter 10
Case Study 3: The Freight Import Agency

The import agency was a small freight agent situated at a local airport. The purpose of the study was to identify the systems requirements and postulate solutions. Because the information modelling phase of the DLU case study was discussed in great detail in Chapters 8 and 9, we have only outlined these stages in case study 3. However, we hope that the outline of the problem situation using the background provided in the narrative and the diagrams is clear. It would be a useful larger exercise for you to develop this case by developing the models provided and thereby constructing the missing aspects, such as the function/event matrix, a description of the entities and relationships, the lists of attributes, the entity-life cycle, through to the process of testing the system. Obviously you will have to make assumptions. Some of these may have to be made because of flaws in the models provided!

The two main actors within the company were an ex-freight manager of a large local freight company and his secretary, both of whom had broken away from their previous company to set up a rival company. The operational function of the company was well-defined and both people were familiar and skilful with the necessary tasks required to fulfil this function, including such activities as receiving goods and filling in complex customs forms. Other auxiliary functions, however, were not well-defined; for example, the marketing and planning functions were run on a 'gut feeling' ad hoc basis. At the time of the study, the import agency was doing well and was confident in its affairs. With the unstructured and uncertain future strategy, the real state of the company was unknown.

Neither person involved had had previous experience with systems analysis and design. A major task in the study was to develop a degree of mutual understanding between the analysts and the users.

Problems identified included uncertainty about the rate of expansion. For example, should they keep a low profile in the midst of powerful competitors who had not yet taken action to combat the new competition? The company, however, was expanding, with a backlog of accounts and plans to provide other services that would further expand not only their customer base, but also the paperwork.

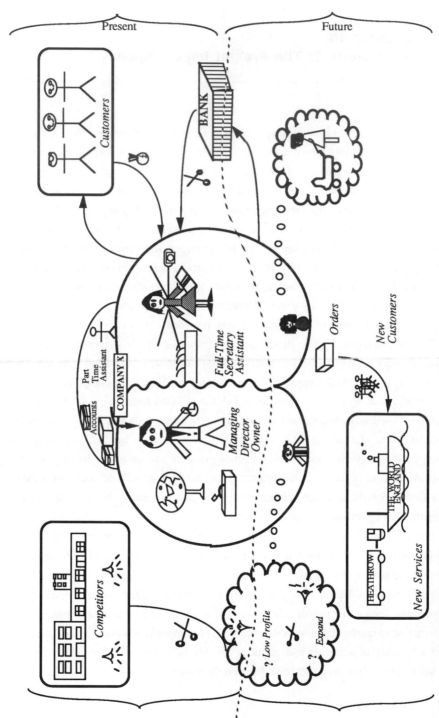

Fig. 10.1 Rich picture of the freight import agency

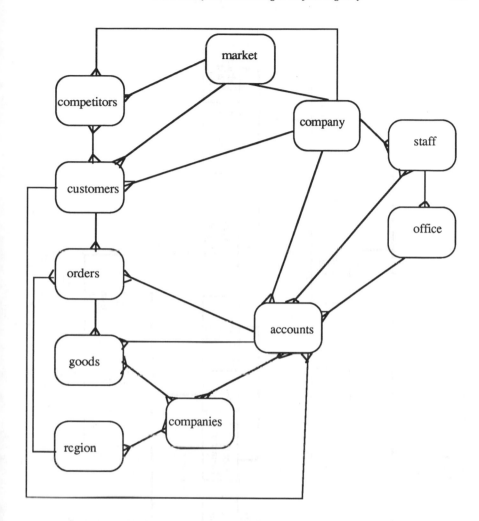

Fig. 10.2. Entity model of the import agency (part completed)

Staffing was expected to be a problem, since the full-time secretary wished to leave and start a family in the near future. Because of her skill and knowledge of the company this could mean a major restructuring of the business in terms of staff and technology. With an increasing work load, this problem would get worse. A part of the rich picture of the situation can be seen in Figure 10.1.

The company chairman participated at least partially in the design process. Although not particularly pleased with the entity model (Figure 10.2 shows the part completed version with the main entities and some of the relationships), the functional model (Figure 10.3) was appealing to the Chairman, and he got involved in altering and redefining the model himself. This improved his understanding of the data flow diagrams at a later step (Figure 10.4).

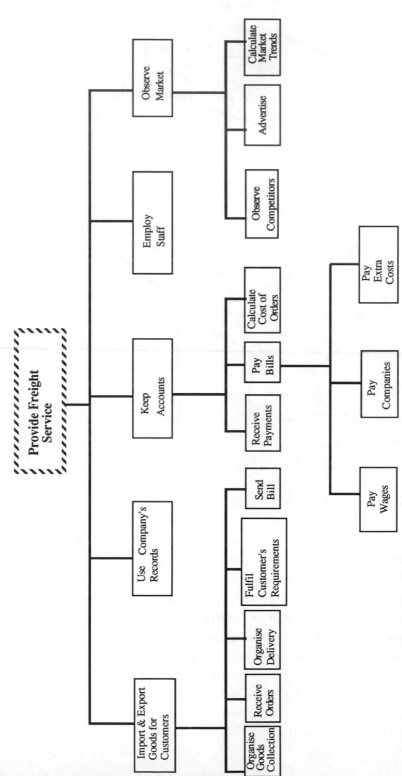

Fig 10.3. Functional Model of the Freight Import Agency

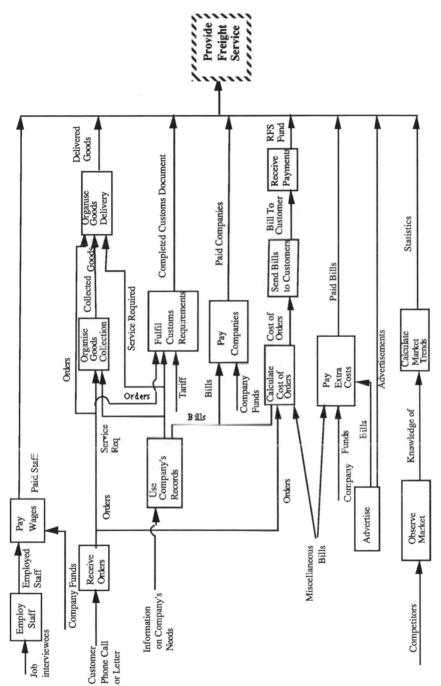

Fig 10.4. Simplified data flow diagram of freight import agency

PART FOUR

MULTIVIEW STAGE 3:

ANALYSIS AND DESIGN OF
SOCIO-TECHNICAL ASPECTS

Chapter 11
The People Using the Information System

11.1 SOCIO-TECHNICAL DESIGN

As we enter the third stage of systems design, we have already developed an understanding of the problem situation, and we have created a model of its information needs. The information system must obviously serve the needs of the organisation, but it must also be compatible with the needs of the staff who will use it. If a system is to be successful, it must be fitted comfortably into their working lives. This is why the third stage of Multiview is concerned with the analysis and design of the socio-technical system.

In many organisations all the major decisions are made before consulting the users. 'Consultation' then means 'doing a public relations job to placate the staff'. This is not what *we* mean by consultation.

Job satisfaction is one of the central ideas of the socio-technical theory which can be defined as calling for a good fit or match between the expectations that employees bring to the job and the requirements of the job as defined by the organisation. In the following framework, this can be assessed under five dimensions (Mumford and Weir, 1979):

- **The Knowledge Fit.** This is the degree to which the employee's job allows him to use and develop his skills and knowledge and the degree to which these skills are being developed.
- **The Psychological Fit.** The degree to which the employee's job allows him to further his private wishes for achievement, recognition, advancement, status or whatever. Herzberg (1966) described them as being **motivators** and they vary according to age, background, education and class.
- **The Task-Structure Fit.** The degree to which the job meets the employee's requirements for variety, interest, feedback, task identity and autonomy in the job. It is a measure of the job in terms of it being demanding and fulfilling. Technology can affect the task-structure fit substantially, and sometimes has reduced the fit by simplification and repetitiveness.
- **The Efficiency Fit.** The degree to which the job offers financial rewards, work controls and supervisory controls which are acceptable to the employee.
- **The Ethical Fit.** The degree to which the values or philosophy of the employer are compatible with those of the employee. Organisations differ in their goals: profit

maximising, providing the best service, and so on.

The ideas of this work utilise the principles of socio-technical design today as seen in Figure 11.1, which is taken from Fok, Kumar and Wood-Harper (1987).

---

1 *Assumptions about the organisation:*
- Organisation as an open system interacting with the environment.
- Organisation as work system with two independent but interrelated subsystems, social and technical.

2 *Assumptions about people:*
- 'Theory Y' orientation towards people, hence it is morally right to let them participate in decision making.

3 *Socio-Technical Design goals:*
- Jointly satisfy the organisational technical requirements (efficiency goal) and the quality of work life (social goal).

4 *Assumptions about the Socio-Technical Design process:*
- Workers should participate.

5 *Socio-Technical Design concepts:*
- Work system, not single job, as design unit.
- Work group, not individual job holder, becomes central in design.
- Internal regulation of group.
- Redundancy of function, not redundancy of part.
- Members have discretion, not highly prescribed work.
- Develop flexible learning system.
- Autonomous work group is a superior form of organisation.
- Role changes:
    designer: facilitator, not 'expert'.
    worker: 'designer' of the system.
    manager: boundary manager, not supervisor of workers.

6 *The Procedural Steps of Socio-Technical Design:*
- Select target system.
- Identify unit operations.
- Identify key variances and their interrelations.
- Draw up variance control table.
- Ascertain social system members' perception.
- Understand neighbouring systems.
- Understand boundary-crossing systems.
- Consider the context of general management system.
- Consider design proposals for target or neighbouring system.

Fig. 11.1. Principles of the Socio-Technical Approach

The activities of the workforce *are* the activities of the organisation. If the information system is to serve the needs of the organisation, then operating that system must not conflict with other essential activities such as making things, selling things and providing services. For example, if sales information is to be recorded, then this should not keep the sales assistant from serving other customers. This could easily happen if the system is too slow, the entry terminal is not conveniently situated on the counter, there is frequently a queue of people to use it, or if it is difficult to use or unreliable. Any of these could lead to lost sales, a deterioration in service provided, and also lead to lower staff morale and even trigger industrial action by disgruntled employees.

People actually doing the job usually know more about it than the people who direct it. Thus, whilst managers are the best people to make strategic decisions, the people doing the job may be the best informed about day-to-day working. However, not all companies are willing to consult their employees about issues like the purchase of a computer, and those that do often do not have any clear idea of how to get the best out of such discussions. This chapter looks at ways of handling the whole question of integrating a computer system into people's work.

One approach, which has the force of law in Sweden, and is regarded as normal working practice in Norway and Denmark, is to consult with worker representatives at each stage of design and implementation. This has certain merits in that everybody knows what is going on and possible difficulties can be identified early. But it is a policing system, setting up minimum standards for employee protection, rather than a way of showing everyone how to get the best out of the situation.

Scandinavian countries also require that information about proposed computer systems is written in plain language so that all involved can understand what is happening. However, being able to read the language and being able to see the practical implications of the proposal are not always the same thing. A better approach is to decide on the way in which the working day should be organised, and then see to what extent the computer system can help to achieve that.

Some systems designers, for example Professor Enid Mumford of Manchester Business School, have used user participation as the cornerstone of their systems design philosophy. The approach can be successful even in large bureaucratic organisations where change is not normally regarded positively and where the flow of information between offices can be very complicated. Normally in these circumstances it is very difficult for analysts to work out what is happening. It may well be that employees in these organisations, at the first hint of computerisation, do not cooperate as they fear the loss of their jobs or simply think that "change has got to be for worse".

The socio-technical systems approach also recognises different interest groups or stakeholders:

> 'the method seeks to discover their social, technical and organisational objectives
> which are perceived by the interest groups' (Land, 1982a).

This method utilises the idea of user participation which helps to eliminate or reduce
communication problems, and perhaps conflict, between the analysts and users. There
are three categories of participation (Land, 1982b):

consultative	where users provide ideas and suggestions to the system design process, but analysts make a majority of the decisions. It is the lowest level of the three forms of participation.
democratic	where all user interest groups have an equal say in the development of the information system. Here the users make the decisions, but management makes sure that decisions are implemented.
responsible	where all the participants make the decisions and are responsible for implementing them.

One way to achieve a better rapport is to organise staff into advisory committees
and assign a systems analyst to each committee. Initially users may be unsure of what
to do or take a 'militant' stance, but over time the analyst may be able to discuss
problems in the present way of doing things. Later, users may 'take over', suggesting
ways of improving *their* system. At that point the analyst begins to take the role of
technical consultant, rather than leader.

Users obviously play a role in developing the information model, as we have
shown, as they describe the data that has to be processed, but we are concerned here
with the decisions about fitting the system into their working life. Questions such as the
following are typical of those that have to be asked at this stage:

- "Are we going to wait until the end of the day before printing out all the reports?"
- "Is everyone going to have a terminal on their desk?"
- "Are we going to re-train existing workers and re-classify their jobs?"
- "Are there going to be any redundancies?"

There are a large number of computer-based systems on the market and a very large
number of suppliers. Yet there are actually not all that many options. In most
fundamental respects, the systems that they offer fall into only a few categories. The
differences tend either to be about the business ability of the supplier or else technical
matters that are of more concern to the computer specialist.

What sort of options are we discussing in this stage of Multiview? To help us answer this, here is a further list of questions that ought to be asked:

- How much of the work is to be done by the computer and how much by the staff?
- Is the system to be used by trained experts, users with some training, or anybody who needs access to the information?
- How urgently will different pieces of information be needed from the system?
- What, if any, alterations will be necessary to the physical workplace? For example, will there be special computer workstations, acoustic panelling around the printers or improved lighting?
- What changes will there be in the number of jobs, staff gradings, or the working day of individual staff?
- Who will have what responsibilities for which aspects of the computer operation?

The whole business of fitting machines into people's working lives has been given the title 'socio-technical design'. In any large technologically dependent organisation it is obviously a matter of great importance. It can also be a minefield of industrial relations' problems and there is great scope for getting it wrong and setting up mechanisms which are very inefficient to operate. The problems for users in small organisations may be easier to solve, but they are still there.

Within the socio-technical stage of the Multiview approach, participation is used for these reasons:

- Ethical, because people have the moral right to a major input into the design process of their working situation. This allows users to protect their interests.
- Pragmatic, because detailed knowledge of the working system is possessed by the people who work within the system. Therefore, participation is the best way of acquiring this knowledge.
- Psychological, because people do not mind change if they know the reason.

Participation will occur when the users are concerned with decisions about fitting the information system into their working lives. This method is outlined in the next section.

11.2   SOCIO-TECHNICAL ALTERNATIVES

The best way for the people involved in a system to decide what they want is for them to be presented with a realistic set of alternatives. They can examine each of these, preferably 'acting them out' in some way, to see which alternative seems the most comfortable. The alternatives are often easier to set out for a microcomputer system because they will consist of some arrangement of microcomputers with packaged software used in a particular way. Provided that a demonstration of the packages that could fit the need can be arranged, then it is possible to visualise what it would be like to implement the application with them.

It is important, however, that the set of alternatives provided is not too limiting and narrow but illustrates the wide range of opportunities that exist. Otherwise, users will have no real choice and the user is offered only lip-service to the decision-making process.

Suppose that you were considering a book-keeping system. Two alternatives might be to put the actual debit, credit and balance figures on a very simple computerised system, and deal with any additional calculations yourself, or to buy a sophisticated system that would permit any foreseeable work (for example, budgeting and reporting) to be handled on the computer as well. The first of these alternatives would be easy to set up but is likely to leave you with a residue of potential problems, and occasional sessions writing up reports from the data. This could be a good choice, however, where ease of setting up is particularly important and where there are few unusual transactions or sophisticated reports required. A more sophisticated system would be more expensive and is likely to be more difficult to set up, but is likely to be much more powerful. Before making such a choice it is important to make a list of all the factors affecting that choice. A good method is to follow the exercise outlined in Figure 11.2.

In order to be successful in defining and ranking alternatives, the analysts and the users must predict the future environment. A tool applicable to this situation is called **future analysis** (Land, 1982a and 1987). The tool is based on the idea of forecasting the expected life-span of the information system. The analyst and the users together predict the planning horizon as the period of time during which the designed system will meet the organisation's needs and expectations. The idea here is a trade-off between flexibility and design costs. This technique can be described as consisting of four steps:

1   Predict kinds of changes which are possible. Are they technological, legal, or economic changes for the organisation?
2   Predict the likely outcome of the information system in the future.
3   Evaluate which features (decomposing the information system into parts) of the proposed system are more susceptible to these changes.
4   Determine the planned horizon of the information system and consequently ascertain the flexibility of the system to be catered for.

Once the future environment has been predicted, the rest of the socio-technical design can be carried out.

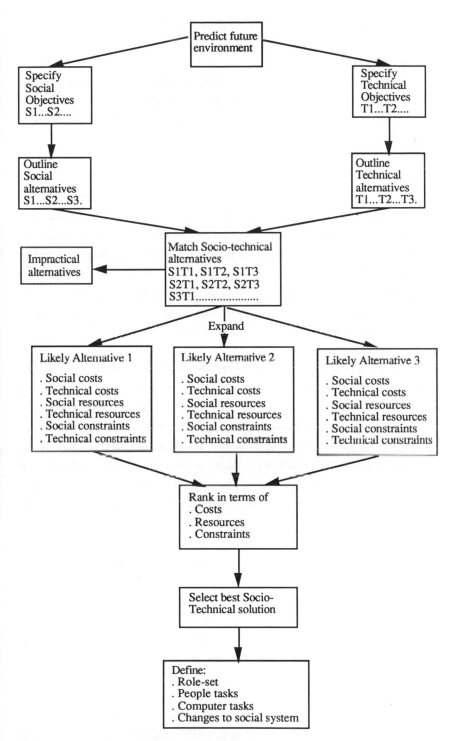

Fig.11.2. Principles of socio-technical design

11.3   SOCIAL OBJECTIVES AND ALTERNATIVES

What are the most important social issues related to the system? It may be to take the pressure off staff harassed by paperwork. It may be to facilitate better communication between staff. It may be linked to issues like career progression or reducing the number of boring repetitive jobs. It may be about getting better and quicker information to key decision makers.

Although there may be existing social problems lowering staff morale, there may also be the fear that a new system would disrupt an otherwise happy office. Keeping what is good about a working situation is very important and easily overlooked. We often concentrate on problems only to find that the cure is worse than the disease. It is important therefore to identify elements that should be retained in any new system.

It is therefore possible to set out the various objectives of the system and then to formulate ways of achieving the objectives. For example, if we want to reduce paperwork, do we streamline the paper flow or have the computer carry out the processing; if we want to support salesmen more, do we give them their own computer with access to the accounts files or do we make accounts staff more readily available to provide the information required?

These social issues are based on the ideas of improved job satisfaction and quality of working life (Mumford, 1983a and 1983b). Achieving job satisfaction can be defined as achieving a good match between the expectations that the employees have, the requirements of the job as defined by the organisation, and the employer's need. The employees' job expectations are formed partly as a result of personality characteristics and partly as a result of conditions in the work situation and society at large (Mumford & Weir, 1979). Depending on the social situation of the work, this job satisfaction can be assessed formally by a questionnaire or it can be done informally in smaller information systems.

The social issues may manifest themselves in the present working situation and they need to be taken into account in any new information system. These will be defined in the form of job satisfaction reducers and contributors as defined by Mumford (1985).

'Job satisfaction reducers are those frustrations which cause staff dissatisfaction as well as reducing efficiency [whereas] job satisfaction contributors are positive factors which enable staff to get interest, stimulus and a sense of achievement from their work'.

In doing this analysis, the beneficial features need to be kept and the bad features need to be improved. It is important for the analyst to listen to what managers and users are saying about their work. Social objectives need to be set and social alternatives formulated. For example, if the social objective is to reduce boring repetitive work, then task rotation could be a viable solution.

Here are the major social objectives of the freight import agency:

- To be acceptable to the people who perform all the main roles in the company.
- To maintain and perhaps increase the job satisfaction of staff.
- To enable the managing director to stay in control.

Here are some of the general questions that could be asked about a prospective computerised system:

- Are the existing staff going to use the system?
- Will some staff be lost or redeployed?
- Are all staff who need the information going to have access to the computer or will some get their information prepared for them (for example by printed reports)?
- What good features of the existing system are to be kept? Such features could include an acceptable level of job variety, easy interaction between people, and a friendly atmosphere.
- To what extent will the system affect the work of different users?
- Are there specific objectives, for example to improve performance of key personnel or to enable faster throughput of work?
- What emphasis is to be given to general objectives such as improving job satisfaction or acceptability to all employees?

There are other questions that could be asked. It is important for the analyst to listen to what managers and users are saying about their work. It is all too easy for computer professionals to get so enthusiastic about the technical objectives that they are not sufficiently sensitive to the users' social objectives. Further, it is unlikely that users will come forward with social objectives unless they are prompted. This may be because they do not think of the possible improvements or disruptions. They may feel that they will just have to put up with changes and that they have no power to influence decisions. User attitudes may depend significantly on the experiences that they have had with change in the past. Another reason may be that they are not sure how they will react to the new situation. If key staff are uncomfortable about the information system, it could cause its failure. User attitudes may depend on their experience of change in the past.

Of course, not all social objectives will be met. Therefore another useful task is to decide on priorities. This could be negotiated between analysts, managers, users and other interested parties, such as the trade unions. There may be an agreement that there are no compulsory redundancies and this has top priority. This might allow some freedom to negotiate redeployment and an understanding that staff levels will be allowed to drop through natural wastage.

As can be seen from Figure 11.3, in the freight agency case study, the social alternatives were first that the information system had to be acceptable to the staff of the company, job satisfaction was regarded as important, and finally that the managing director wished to stay in control of the system. A particular alternative distinguishes between a slow response (implemented using a batch system) and a faster response (through using an on-line system). In a batch system, the various transactions are assembled together and then processed as a batch. The results may not be given to the user for a few hours or even longer. In an on-line system, it is possible to deal with each transaction as soon as it has been submitted and the results may be given to the user in a second or two. A batch system might be chosen because of better control, and easier recovery from failure or because it is cheaper to run. The main gain of an on-line system is its potential speed of processing.

Social alternatives relate to different ways in which social objectives might be achieved. Getting rid of boring repetitive work could be achieved by:

- Grouping tasks so that each individual has two or three tasks to do instead of one
- Putting people into teams and giving each team a certain amount of work to see through from start to finish, leaving the team to decide who should do which parts of it
- Rotating jobs so that people only spend a few weeks on any particular task, even though each task is still repetitive.

11.4   TECHNICAL OBJECTIVES AND ALTERNATIVES

By 'technical' we are not referring directly to aspects of information technology but rather to things that are now technically possible for the organisational situation. This might be quicker throughput, bigger volumes, more accurate accounting, or information more readily available to the people who need it. Sometimes the term 'efficiency objectives' is used instead.

These objectives should be visible in the analysis of the human activity system. They can be inferred from the agreed primary task root definition. The objectives are the reasons why the information system is being installed. They are the overall objectives rather than specific detailed ones. At this stage we are concerned with the information situation as a whole and it will not be possible to satisfy all the technical objectives. We may want to increase throughput and cut costs, but either we have to choose between these objectives or accept a trade-off between them. Technical objectives have to be ranked in terms of priority, and the users should carry out this ranking. It is the analyst's job to lay out the alternatives and to spell out the implications of them for the creation of the information system.

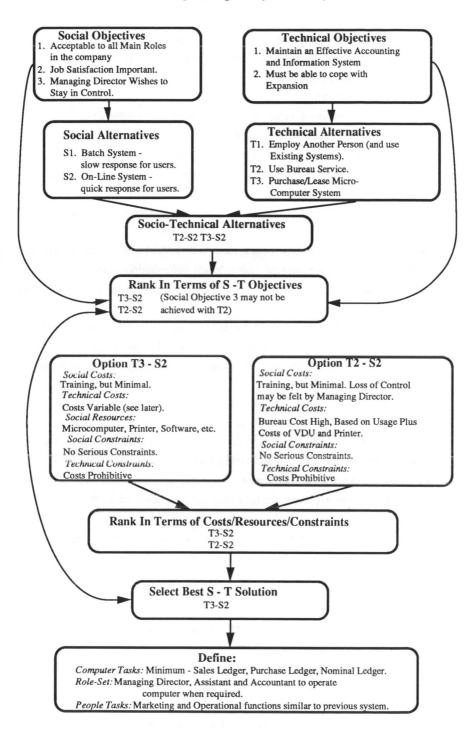

Fig. 11.3. Socio-technical outline for freight agency

Technical alternatives are the different ways of organising the work on the computer and of splitting the work between computer and manual operations. Some of the standard alternatives for a large system are:

- A large central computer
- A distributed system with several smaller computers each handling part of the work and able to communicate with each other
- Intelligent terminals hooked up to either of the above alternatives which will permit users to process their own data locally as well as having access to shared files
- A central computer and a number of independent microcomputers.

In the freight import agency case study described in Chapter 10, the following analysis was carried out:

- What technical tasks would the new system have to deal with? Answer - maintain an effective accounting system and general information system (within the constraint that it must be able to cope with the expected future expansion of the company).
- Would it be possible to maintain the present manual system? Answer - yes, though it would be necessary to employ one extra staff member immediately, this would increase, and within three years it would be necessary to computerise the information systems.
- Would each type of computer system, microcomputer in particular, be able to cope with the likely expansion of the company? Answer - after making some 'ball-park' calculations, it was obvious that there are microcomputers available which are big enough in terms of memory and processing speed.

This gave two further technical alternatives:

- Would it be possible to process the data externally using a bureau service? Answer - yes.
- Would it be possible to purchase or lease a microcomputer so that the data could be processed in-house? Answer - yes, though this would be more expensive than a bureau service in the short term.

11.5   RANKING THE SOCIO-TECHNICAL ALTERNATIVES

By listing the social alternatives and the technical alternatives, it is possible to throw out those which are not feasible and concentrate on the few options that might be feasible.

Two alternatives that were open to us included:

- A batch system where users got all their information in reports
- An on-line system which could respond to queries immediately.

Since user satisfaction would be lost because of a loss of control using a batch system, an on-line system was recommended.

Recommendation   A menu-driven system which could take input for processing as required, generate standard reports, and accept one-off enquiries. This system would have to retain some flexibility because many of the requirements would only emerge as the system developed (as the agency grew). However, the standard procedures should be very similar in use to that of the manual system, otherwise there would be loss of job satisfaction.

Of the three technical alternatives, it was decided to abandon the possibility of employing another person for keeping the manual system, as this would only be a short term solution. The two socio-technical alternatives which were viable were an on-line system using a bureau service or an on-line system using an in-house microcomputer system.

Recommendation   It was decided to choose an on-line system using an in-house microcomputer system because this would maintain the managing director's control over the system, which was one of the social objectives.

In most other circumstances, evaluating the socio-technical alternatives would require much more work. Here are some of the things that ought to be taken into account:
- What are the costs of the alternatives, in money, time and in terms of work disruption?
- What are the benefits of the alternatives, in the short, medium and long term?
- In terms of the cost/benefit equation, which alternative represents the best value in meeting the social and technical priorities?

In Figure 11.3, a more detailed consideration is given to the two options in terms of social costs, technical costs, social resources, social constraints and technical constraints.

11.6 THE SOCIO-TECHNICAL DECISION

The task of working out potential costs and benefits may be quite considerable. Even so, there are no guarantees that there will be enough information to ensure success. The decision will still be a difficult one. There will be some people or groups who will not be happy about the system. Indeed, there will be some situations where the new system is a direct assault on vested interests and involves a power struggle.

At this stage the problem owner will have made a decision about what type of computer system to go for, assisted by the alternatives which have been set out by the problem solver. This is not a commitment to a particular computer or supplier. The hardware and software selection belongs in the technical design stage. We are still creating the specification against which particular offerings will be judged: computer tasks (the 'computerised' part of the function/data flow model), people tasks (the 'manual' part of the function/data flow model), changes to the social aspects of the work situation and the role-set.

In the freight import agency case study, the computer tasks to be performed were sales ledger, purchase ledger and nominal ledger, as well as related information provision; the role-set included the managing director, his assistant and the accountant who could operate the computer when required; and the people tasks were such that the marketing and operational function were similar to the previous clerical system.

11.7   SUMMARY

The third stage of Multiview deals with the way in which the information system is to be fitted into the working lives of the staff of the organisation. This is known as Socio-Technical Analysis and Design. It is a stage both of analysis and design where the problem solving team (consisting of analysts *and* users) lays out the alternatives and the problem owner decides which alternative to adopt.

Firstly the future environment is forecast. Then the social objectives have to be spelled out. These may include statements about the categories of staff that will have to use the new information system, whether there will be redundancies and staff regradings, and how urgently different members of staff need particular information from the system. These objectives have to be put in order of priority. Some of the objectives can be stated negatively as constraints.

Once the social objectives are ranked, the analysts together with users in the team, can put forward various alternatives for achieving the objectives. These may include different methods of work organisation and different degrees of computerisation.

Technical objectives have then to be spelled out. These may include faster throughput of work, greater accuracy, better reporting, and easier access to information for certain key staff. These technical objectives have also to be ranked.

Technical alternatives for achieving these objectives are laid out. These do not refer to specific pieces of hardware and software, but to general types of information system. The alternatives could be 'distributed versus centralised systems', 'dumb terminals versus on-line microcomputers', 'batch verses on-line systems' and 'software packages versus tailor-made programs'.

Each technical alternative is put alongside each social alternative. Some will be excluded at once, but a few are likely to be left for further investigation. The costs in time, money, and difficulty for each alternative need to be estimated as well as their benefits in terms of meeting the stated social and technical priorities. A decision needs to be taken about which type of system to acquire. This is not a technical decision about particular hardware and software, but a general statement about the type of system. This statement forms part of the input to the technical design (Stage 5) and the design of the human-computer interface (Stage 4).

11.8 EXERCISES

1 For a problem situation with which you are familiar, follow the method for social and technical ranking as described in the chapter.

Chapter 12
Case Study 4: The Computer Consulting Company

The fourth case to be discussed concerns a small newly established computer company. The Multiview methodology was used to identify possible problem areas and solutions. The work is further described in Episkopou and Wood-Harper (1984) and Wood-Harper (1989). We will look at the background of the company and go through the early stages only briefly, using draft and outline models to avoid too much repetition with work discussed in previous cases. At the end of the overview of the case study, we will consider the reactions of students who used this case for practical work. This formed part of their course on systems analysis.

The three main actors within the company were two recently graduated students (one computing graduate and one accountancy graduate) who were both directors, along with the chairman, who is a university lecturer. Unlike the freight import agency case, all three people had previous experience of systems analysis and design theory and practice. The relationship between analyst and user was one of mutual understanding and cooperation even before the study began.

Another major difference was that the roles and functions in the computer company were not well-defined. This was partly due to the inexperience of the participants in the task involved and partly due to a conflict of views on the basic purpose of the company. At the time of the study, the future of the company was uncertain, although its potential was high. Morale and confidence were changeable.

One problem which was identified was the confusion of management structure (a vague organisational chart) and job definitions, due to a lack of formal assessment of staff utilisation. In addition, the chairman, being an academic, was unable to devote himself completely to the company. Relationships between the chairman and directors did not seem to be a problem.

A full range of products were provided for this case, and we show below early and incomplete drafts of the rich picture, the function model, the entity model and socio-technical alternatives (see Figures 12.1 to 12.4). You are invited to develop them further and suggest conceptual models, entity life histories, and so on.

We will look at the socio-technical aspects (Stage 3 of Multiview) of the consulting company in more detail, as it was the subject of Part 4 of the text. As we see from Figure 12.4, we saw two social objectives. The first was that the information system should be acceptable to all staff. This was important because, being a small company

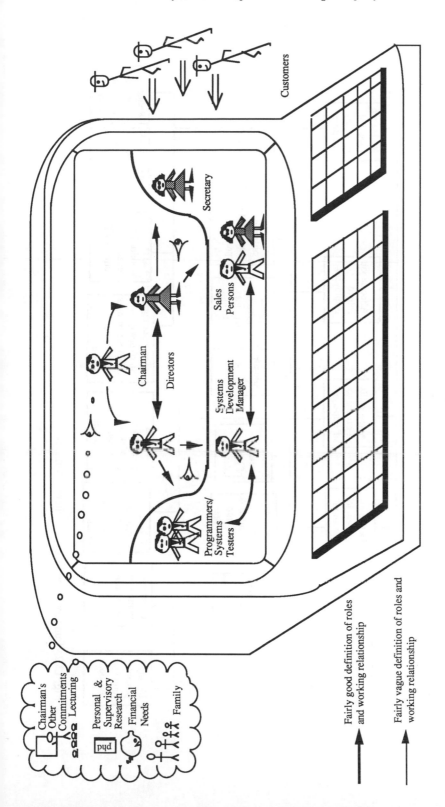

Fig 12.1. Some elements of the rich picture of a computer consultancy company

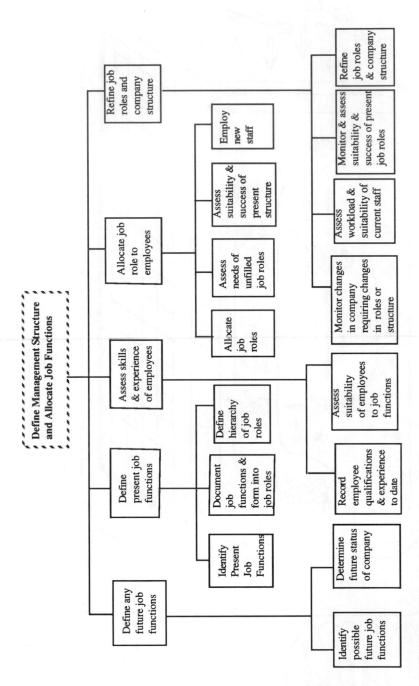

Fig. 12.2. Functional model of consultancy company

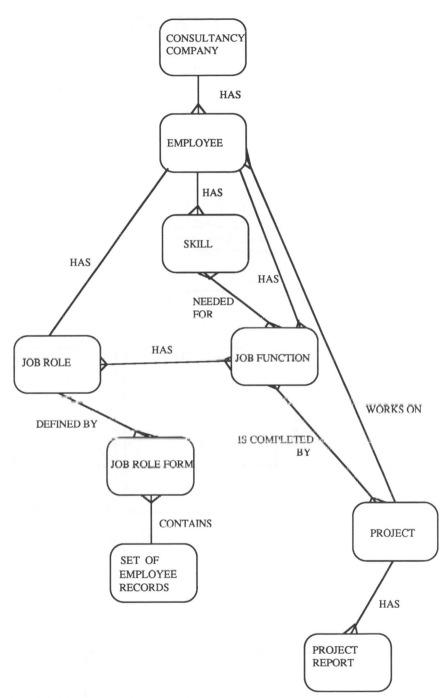

Fig. 12.3. Entity model of consultancy company

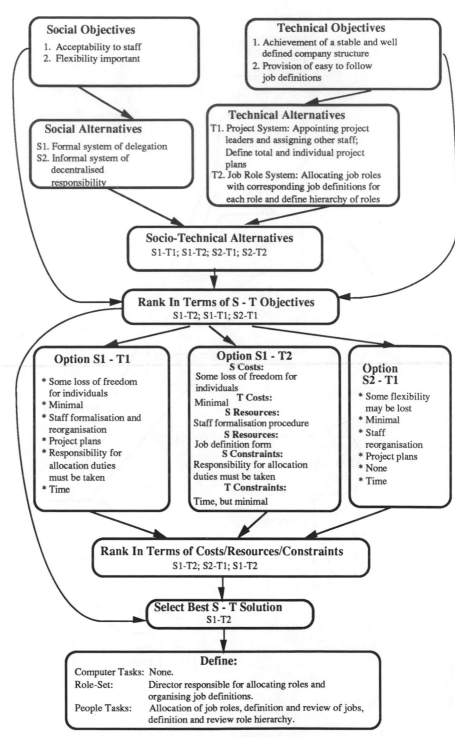

Fig. 12.4. Socio-technical outline of consultancy company

with the staff all playing key roles, it was essential that no staff member became disaffected. The second was the importance of flexibility. The three directors were not sure in what direction the company might develop. Two social alternatives were proposed. The first was a clerical system which was formal in type. In other words, there would be a hierarchy developed and a system of delegation through that hierarchy. The second was a clerical system of decentralised responsibility. In other words, there would be consensus of all the staff.

There were also two technical objectives. In a new company, likely to grow fast, there was a need for stability and a well-defined structure. The second was the provision of easy-to-follow job definitions. The two alternatives were:

Project System   The appointment of a project leader and assigning other staff and defining both total and individual project plans.

Job Role System   Allocating job roles with corresponding job definitions for each role and defining a hierarchy of roles.

As can be seen from the socio-technical outline, only one of the possible four combinations was dismissed. The informal system, with decentralised responsibility, along with the job role system, with its hierarchy, would be mutually exclusive. The other three possibilities were ranked. The option combining the formal system of delegation along with the job role system scored best. This was partly because the time technical constraint was least strong (and the directors felt that it was necessary to put some sort of system in place as soon as possible) and also because it was a more flexible option.

The choice, therefore, was a non-computerised solution. This may be seen as ironic because of the particular type of company and the background of its staff. But it does show that computerisation is not always felt to be the sensible way to progress. Nevertheless, although this solution proved capable of dealing with requirements for a year or so, as the company grew it proved unsatisfactory. In fact it was only fifteen months following its implementation that the need came to develop a computer solution. Aspects of this are described in the following two chapters.

This case and that of the freight import agency looked at in Chapter 10, showed that the methodology allowed the user to take on different perspectives, sometimes at different stages of the process. These two cases also showed that the methodology worked well in the small business environment. We found that in each case, the nature of the organisation affected the emphasis placed on various stages.

The people in the import company did not find the conceptual process of the identification of human activity systems to be as valuable, whereas those in the computer company, trained to think in this fashion, benefited more. The differences in the clarity of their functions and roles led to more emphasis being placed on functional modelling where the functions were well-defined. Interestingly, the computer company felt that Stage 2 was of less value, since it did not identify any new perspectives for them to consider.

We also used these two companies as a training ground for student groups who were effectively 'naive analysts'. The student groups (who specialise in either computing or accountancy) were enrolled in a second course in systems analysis and design. Their contribution has also provided some added understanding of the process. The most significant lesson was in the elicitation of multiple perspectives, as more than one group would work with the company. They had received formal training earlier in the use of the methodology and its philosophy. Each group perceived the 'same' problem content differently. This has brought home to us that the methodology itself is not a sufficient guarantor of truth. Each group seemed to perceive a different reality. Further, we feel that there was a noticeable difference in the way that computer science and accounting students viewed the 'same' situation.

The group involvement in the process has also been enlightening. Many students expressed displeasure with working in groups, mentioning the additional time required for group meetings and for negotiations and resolution of disputes. Yet, at the end of the study, the vast majority of students felt that the group work was very useful.

We observed that the group results were usually more constrained and conservative, where the individual work was often more creative and flexible. A trend worth noting was that many of the students found that, as they used the methodology more, they began to use it more as a series of techniques rather than as a framework for creative thought. As a result, their products began to show less creativity. The groups also had their own observations about the methodology. Some of the groups felt that Stage One was useful; other groups felt that the first stage was too complex for small organisations. Many of the students felt that the complexity of the methodology might exceed the complexity of the organisation! The methodology does not indicate, nor did the groups derive, measures of performance. The only measure of performance - at least to Stage Three of Multiview - was that a system specification emerged from the process.

PART FIVE

MULTIVIEW STAGE 4:

DESIGN OF THE
HUMAN-COMPUTER INTERFACE

Chapter 13
Human-Computer Interaction

13.1 HUMAN-COMPUTER DIALOGUES

The fourth stage of Multiview is concerned with the way in which individual users communicate with the computer. They may be inputting data, instructing the computer to run programs, or interpreting output. This all has to be done in a way that users find easy to understand. The particular way appropriate will vary according to the background and experience of the users, and the particular process required. Many users are 'happy' with the jargon of computing. Some users, particularly those who need to use the computer only occasionally, may not be familiar with this jargon. They may not want to be trained in computers and very often it is not appropriate for them to learn these skills.

Some computer systems have been designed for 'occasional' or **casual** users. One obvious way of making computers easier to use is to display the various options from which they may choose on a screen as a **menu** rather than expect users to remember the names of particular **commands**. These command-driven systems are a remnant of computing in the early days when the 'user', most often a computer programmer or computer operator, had to remember a string of complex commands or refer frequently to the relevant manual. It is much easier to choose from a list of options on the screen, though it can be irritating for the more experienced user. If users are still unsure of the effect of the various options, the system should be capable of providing further help so that their meaning is made more clear.

This whole area of computing is frequently called the man-machine interface, human interface or user interface. We also use the term human-computer interaction to represent the dialogues between the computer and the user. The use of the word 'human' rather than 'man' avoids the implication that users are necessarily men. The word 'machine' suggests 'engineering' which is also inappropriate. We use the term **dialogue** to represent the form of this interaction, as this term carries the right tone of formality whilst indicating that information is going two ways. Sometimes this is referred to as a 'conversation', but the degree of friendliness and lack of formality implied by a conversation is not representative of most of these dialogues.

There are various things that humans can be 'saying' to computers, for instance:

- They may be issuing an instruction, for example to run a program, print a report or compute a value;
- They may be putting data into the computer; or
- They may be requesting some information from the computer.

Even though the computer will only react in the way that it was programmed, it is important for users that it react in a way that they can relate to. If humans have certain expectations about the way that statements should be interpreted, they will have to spend emotional and intellectual effort getting used to the computer if it reacts differently.

Psychological and linguistic factors must be taken into account when designing the computer part of human-computer dialogues (that is the computer message to the user). For example, if the user makes an error when storing data, the response by the system should not normally be an error number without further explanation. It is not the response that people would expect when dealing with other people. Whilst we know that it is only a machine and it is not trying to be rude, it is very difficult not to become irritated by this type of message. Yet it is still a common form of error message.

A natural language dialogue may seem to be an obvious goal for systems designers, but natural languages such as English are not well structured and they have very large vocabularies. They are also prone to ambiguity, usually a delight to read in a novel, but not acceptable for communication with a computer system. It is therefore difficult to represent true English dialogue on a computer system. Some **speech recognition systems** are effective in that they are capable of 'memorising' a few hundred words which the user can use as commands to the computer. This list of commands might include 'read file', 'write file' and 'delete file' in a database system. Such a system might be useful, but such interactions do not constitute a dialogue.

Another interesting development is the use of icons, that is, the pictorial representation of the tasks that the computer can perform at each stage. This interface has gained most users through its use on the Apple Macintosh computer, but is available on a wide range of computers. There may be a picture of a filing cabinet to represent the option to store data; a wastepaper basket to delete data; or a printed sheet to print it out. The analogy of this type of interface is that of the **desk-top** as all the features of the desk-top are provided on the computer screen. This approach is often associated with a 'mouse', a device, shaped like a small box, which can be moved around on the desk-top and this movement is tracked on the screen. The mouse can be used to point to the icon representing the option required. A button on the mouse will then be pressed to effect that option. This reduces the use of the keyboard, which is said to discourage some users.

Some methods of data capture reduce the need for keyboard skills for the input of data. These include optical character recognition, optical mark reading, magnetic ink character recognition, bar code reading, and magnetic strip reading.

An **optical character recognition** (OCR) device can read text directly from a book or a report. Until recently, OCR devices required a standard typeface such as Elite and Courier or the OCR standard fonts OCR-A and OCR-B. They were restricted in other ways such as requiring double-spaced typing, wide margins and special quality paper. As the technology has improved, such restrictions have proved to be temporary, as it is possible for some OCR readers to be 'trained' so that they could read non-standard fonts. Some systems have already been developed that can read a newspaper page with headline, captions and the body of the text even though they are in different fonts. Even poor quality photocopies can be read with good results. Other OCR readers can read neat and regular handwriting.

Optical mark reading (OMR) is frequently used as a way of reading data into files. The documents may be in the form of cards or paper forms. OMR documents include survey response sheets, catering arrangements, order forms, time allocation records and wage time sheets. The document is designed so that the person completing the form marks the options required, usually using an HB pencil. The OMR reader recognises these marks and reads the data into the application package.

Magnetic ink character recognition (MICR) is less usual in standard business applications, although it is used commonly in the banking sector (for example in processing cheques). A cheque has the account number and bank branch number pre-printed in the form of magnetic ink characters. The money amount is later keyed on the cheque using magnetic ink and the cheque is then read into the computer.

Bar coding is commonly used on products in a shop or warehouse. When the strip is read at the point of sale, the product number is read into the system. As the price and other details can be obtained from computer files, it is not necessary for any keying in. A **magnetic strip** is commonly used in the banking sector and on membership cards. A credit card, for example, can have the user's number encoded in the magnetic strip. These methods of inputting data are used because of improvements in processing speed, accuracy or security which might be required in particular applications.

These facilities were not required in the computing consulting company case, but in the DLU system (described in Chapter 7), the use of an optical mark reading system for recording students' answers to questions was used. The questions were of the multiple choice type which required either 'A', 'B', 'C' or 'D' to be marked in each case, rather than a narrative response, and therefore appropriate to this form of input. Once input into the computer system, it was easy to count up the scores, give the scores to the students and tutors, and use the information to compare students, and so on. It proved to be a very efficient way of assessing students on the course, though the type of questions are rather limited in style.

13.2   COMMON DIALOGUE STYLES

The traditional dialogue in computer systems is command-driven. The system waits until the user types in a command which is recognised by that system. As we have seen, this is not appropriate for users who are not familiar with computing systems. The use of special keys on the computer keyboard, known as function keys, to represent particular commands can help, but these systems are still not easy to use without considerable experience and are not usually regarded as 'natural' by most users.

The first advance to 'user-friendliness' is the menu. This is a display of the choice of options available. Menus are normally hierarchical. Having chosen a first option, the user is presented with another menu which displays a series of further alternatives in that option. Going through the hierarchy of menus could be tedious to the experienced user, as it might be necessary to pass through a number of menus until the desired place is reached and there should therefore be ways to by-pass menus.

In the second part of the computer consultancy company project, a computer information system was developed. In this system, the first level menu gave access to the major functions. These were, as shown in Figure 13.1, accounting, stock control and customer records.

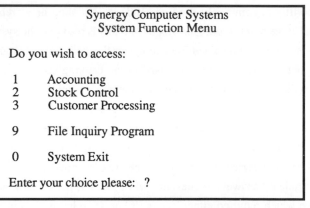

Fig. 13.1. Main Menu

Form-driven systems present another advance on command driven systems. The programmer sets up a replica of a paper form on the screen. This is usually referred to as a 'soft copy' form. This could be identical to the input form that is used in the real world system (the 'hard copy' form). A very simple form is shown as Figure 13.2. For products added to the stock, the user keys in the product number and the quantity added to stock. The system displays the description of the item from the product file so that it is easy for the user to verify that the correct product number has been input. The question 'OK? Y or N?' is displayed at the bottom of the form. If the user is happy with the input, he will key in 'Y' and the data will be used to update the master files. Otherwise he will type 'N' (in fact, anything other than a 'Y') and the user then has the opportunity to correct the data or quit (leave that part of the system).

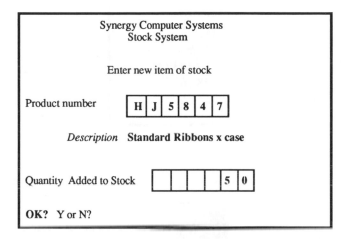

Fig. 13.2. A soft copy form for the computer consulting company

Displaying a form is also a convenient way of making a lot of information about an individual person or transaction available to the computer. During input, the cursor jumps from box to box as each box is completed. By using the cursor control keys (the 'arrow' keys) on the keyboard, the user has control to over-ride this. It is then possible to go back to a box and correct it. If the computer system detects an error, this might be indicated by flashing the offending item and displaying an appropriate message which informs the user of the nature of the error.

The touch-sensitive screen available on some microcomputer systems has made the form mode easier to use, and it is useful for other types of interaction. This permits the computer to record information about items on the screen that the user is pointing at. A light pen can be used with similar effect. These methods usually locate records quicker than cursor control keys.

Most computer systems include software for creating graphs, and a graphical representation of data is usually assimilated quicker than tables. Figures 13.3 and 13.4 give a comparison of methods to represent sales figures for the computer consultancy.

For some human-computer dialogues, the use of graphical methods may also be appropriate. As we have mentioned, using icons proves an effective way to display options. Again, the use of a visual symbol can be more effective than words, particularly jargon words.

SYNERGY COMPUTER SYSTEMS SALES YEAR TO DATE	
PRODUCT	SALES
4	£6.086
7	£8,522
9	£10,958
10	£12,173
15	£18,261
TOTAL £56,000	

Fig.13.3. Sales for year to date

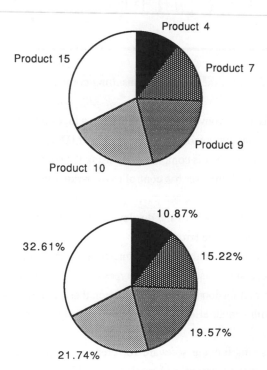

Fig.13.4. Two pie chart representations of sales for year to date (Figure 13.3)

13.3   DIALOGUE ANALYSIS

The field of human-computer interaction has two aspects: **what** information does the user wish to interchange with the computer and **how** should this interaction be implemented. The question **why** will have been tackled when analysing the human activity system. Systems analysts have to find out the 'what' and communicate these requirements to the system builder, in particular the programmer, who will decide on the most effective 'how'. This is true of the whole range of systems analysis and design activities. The rest of this chapter looks at the analysis of what interactions need to take place in the proposed system, and the information that is needed to create the most appropriate human-computer interface.

Different sorts of dialogue can be created for different categories of user. Therefore, for each computer function to be carried out, we need to identify the categories of staff who will be using it. We can divide users for this purpose into three types:

- Trained operators
- People who routinely use the computer for some part of the job
- Casual users.

For the trained operators, the dialogue is best made as terse as possible so that they will be able to get any particular task done in the minimum time. The difficulty here is in creating a dialogue that is terse but clear and unambiguous. There is a limit to the ability of even the best trained operator to deal with long strings of command codes.

For the casual users, the problem is one of letting them know what is available and how to get it. One possibility is to provide users with a printed directory which lists the various information that is available and a number associated with each set of information. This number is typed by the user. Once in the right 'area', progress is made by selecting the required items from a menu. This is a rather tedious way of moving around a database, but it is straightforward to use.

The middle category of people who use computers as some part of their job is becoming increasingly important. They want to communicate in terms that are familiar to them and their work and not in those of the computer system. They want the dialogue to be efficient, but they are quite likely to forget details about the way in which the system is operated. Menus and help routines can be appropriate to this category of user. It is also possible for different levels of help to be given to the user. At the first level, a list of the basic commands could be listed on the screen permanently. More experienced users, who are familiar with these basic commands, can request that the more 'advanced' commands are displayed instead. Finally those users very familiar with the system can opt for the screen to be clear of this list of commands (they will know these off by heart), leaving the maximum screen size for the text (if a word processing system), spreadsheet or whatever.

We have discussed the level of computer literacy of the user. The analyst must also consider the concepts and vocabulary that the user will be comfortable with. These may also vary, according to the education, background and experience of the particular user. Thus even in situations where two systems are both going to be used by casual users, the sorts of dialogues for the two systems may be very different.

For each function to be performed, it is necessary to design the dialogue needed. Figure 13.1 showed the top level menu for the computer consulting company and Figure 13.5 shows the next level menu assuming that the user has keyed in '1' (for accounting).

```
┌─────────────────────────────────────────────────┐
│              Synergy Computer Systems            │
│                   Accounting                     │
│                                                  │
│    Do you wish to access:                        │
│                                                  │
│    1     Sales ledger                            │
│    2     Purchase ledger                         │
│    3     Nominal ledger                          │
│    4     Sales order processing                  │
│                                                  │
│    9     Return to previous menu                 │
│                                                  │
│    0     System Exit                             │
│                                                  │
│    Enter your choice please:   ?                 │
└─────────────────────────────────────────────────┘
```

Fig. 13.5. Second level menu

There are a set of menus and assuming that the user keyed in '2' for purchase ledger, there would be a further set of options including the ability to make an enquiry for a particular supplier. The system then asks:

STATE SUPPLIER NUMBER

and assuming that '8734' was keyed in, the user is presented with the screen displayed as Figure 13.6.

For every function that requires an interface between user and computer, it is necessary to specify the category of user and the flow of information between the user and computer. Where there is more than one type of user, the design of the dialogue is not straightforward. Two possible options for the designer are: design one dialogue, with shortcuts for the sophisticated, or tailor the dialogue to each category, producing several distinct but equivalent dialogues. The results of these decisions become the input to the technical design phase. It is also an output from Multiview, because it

```
┌─────────────────────────────────────────────────────────────────────┐
│ Synergy Computer Systems                      8 November 1989         │
│                   Purchase Ledger Inquiry                             │
│                                                                       │
│  Account Number 8734                                                  │
│  John Burns Paper,  Federal Street, Birmingham                        │
│                                                                       │
│  Balance     Current    30days     60days     90days                  │
│  £259.25     £-300      £58.00     £0.00      £501.25                  │
│                                                                       │
│  Date        Our Ref    Their Ref  Credit     Debit    Balance        │
│  04/05/89    B567       7987       £184.75             £184.75         │
│  19/08/89    B668       8045       £201.25             £386.00         │
│  17/10/89    B901       8098       £358.00             £559.25         │
│  01/11/89                                     £300.00                  │
└─────────────────────────────────────────────────────────────────────┘
```

Fig. 13.6. Purchase ledger inquiry for computer consultancy company

becomes the specification of some of the clerical procedures surrounding the computer system.

13.4   ERROR PREVENTION

One of the major concerns, after the dialogue has been specified, is that every possible precaution should be taken to prevent errors occurring. Error trapping has long been thought as part of program design, and many of the techniques for preventing errors and detecting them relate to program design. Nevertheless, error prevention should be regarded as the responsibility of the systems analyst and systems designer.

It is important to make sure that dialogues are clear and unambiguous. If the user knows exactly what is happening and what input is required at each point in the dialogue, then mistakes are less likely to happen. Using meaningful prompts is one way of achieving this. A prompt of '?' only, which is the standard on many systems, does not give any help to the user at all, except that the system is waiting for something. In the example in Section 13.2, the user was asked to state the supplier number. A prompt should name the item that is expected and in some situations give information about the format that is expected, for example:

ENTER TODAY'S DATE (DD/MM/YY).

Another way of preventing confusion, and therefore error, is to ensure that the design follows the natural logic of the situation. An obvious example of this would be to use soft copy forms for data entry where the data was originally on a paper form.

Unless there are good reasons for an alternative, the VDU form and the paper form should have the same design. The operator is simply copying the data from the paper to the screen and is much less likely to put data in the wrong place. The user will also feel more 'at home' with the new system.

The system must also allow for all possible error correction. There are many well known techniques for ensuring the accuracy of data input, such as range checks, hash totals, check digits, cross checks and checks with information held in files. These checks, described in Chapter 16, are a feature of most data processing systems. Some artificial intelligence techniques are also being incorporated into commercial systems. One question relevant to the computer consulting company could be:

HOW MUCH CREDIT SHOULD WE ALLOW JOHN BURNS PAPER COMPANY?

The system could answer that question by looking at the previous payment record of the company and making a 'judgement' based on this information and also the credit limits of companies with similar records. Alternatively, this may be done 'behind the scenes', and should the user key in a significantly greater amount, the system may warn the user that this is higher than expected.

Once errors have been detected, they have to be corrected. The sooner the error has been detected, the easier it is to correct. Some 'intelligent' systems are being developed which can correct input by putting it into context. This presupposes that there is enough extra information in the input for that correction to be made. This parallels the sort of corrections that we make automatically when, for example, we hear someone use the wrong word and we correct the sentence in our own mind. This is potentially very useful for typographical errors in text. Spelling checkers are also useful. None of these systems are likely to be fool-proof, though they may reduce the amount of human checking necessary.

The normal method of error correction is to bring the error to the attention of the user. The error message should be clear and polite and should make clear how any correction can be carried out. The system should also make clear whether any action has been taken on other data based on this erroneous information. The operator needs plenty of help in correcting an error because there is a chance that the user will make another mistake when trying to make a correction. This is because correcting, unlike inputting, can never become 'automatic' and routine.

It is also necessary to ensure that the system has recovered from the error. A mistake during data entry is easy to recover from. The operator sees on the screen that the data is now correct. In some circumstances, the option of abandoning the present job should be offered, for example, if the operator is updating the wrong record. Here any changes made on that record ought not to be made permanently. But clear information about the consequences of 'quitting', that is going back to the previous state, should be provided, for example:

QUIT - RECORD IS UNCHANGED? (YES/NO)

This informs the operator of the consequences and permits recovery from the quit instruction should this be an error.

The most difficult error from which to recover is that which has been in the system for some time. It may be possible - though it is likely to be tedious - to 'go back in time' to the point where the error was made and reprocess all the subsequent data. A log of all the transactions affected needs to be kept. There also needs to be manual methods of alerting people to the possibility that they have been using erroneous data and asking them to check their work using the system.

Clearly the systems analyst and the systems designer have to work closely in decisions about errors that must be guarded against and the method by which this can be achieved.

One other aspect about control in general, is that some systems need to conform to established practice. In the accounting application for the computer consulting company, the system needs to conform to legal requirements, and those of the external auditor. Procedures in this application need to be particularly rigorous and comprehensive, otherwise there may be a loss of opportunity to detect fraud and promote efficiency.

13.5 RESPONSE TIME

One other aspect of the dialogue that needs comment is the time that the user may have to wait for the next response, in other words, the time taken between submitting the job and the return of the results. In some situations the dialogue can be handled satisfactorarily by a request for information which is given by return of post (in this case we use the term turn-round time rather than response time). In other situations the information has to be returned in seconds. These are usually not absolute demands. The analyst can ask the user to put a price on increased speed: "How much is it worth to get a response within seconds, minutes, hours?" or " What would happen if you had to wait until the end of the day, week, month?".

With this information, the systems builder can lay out the alternatives and their feasibility. At each end of the spectrum will be the basic choice of on-line or batch processing, although combinations are possible, such as on-line validation of data but regular processing of validated transactions in batch. On-line systems enable fast processing, they have a potential for a turn-round time of a second or two. If this potential is realised, then the system is said to be a **real-time system**, because the state of the computer system is kept in step with the 'real world'.

13.6   SUMMARY

The fourth stage of Multiview is concerned with the design of the human-computer interaction. A number of improvements to this interaction have recently been implemented or researched. These include technical developments such as voice recognition and other data capture methods. Improvements should also come from the study of human factors such as the psychology of the interaction and an understanding of natural language.

The dialogue should be related to the type of people who will be using the system. The major factors relate to the amount of training that can reasonably be expected and to the vocabulary and interests of the user.

For each function to be performed, the contents of the dialogue, that is the information and instructions between the user and the computer, needs to be defined.

The specification of the dialogue and the statements of the types of user for that dialogue are the outputs from the socio-technical design. They are input to the design stage. They also form the basis of the clerical procedures surrounding the system.

13.7   EXERCISES

1   Compare and contrast different ways of data entry, such as soft copy forms, the use of commands and menus.
2   Differentiate between real-time, on-line and batch processing.

Chapter 14
Strategies for Design

14.1 PROCEEDING TO DESIGN

Up to now we have been concerned with WHAT the system is to do. This includes activities, functions, tasks and dialogues. We are now in a position to consider HOW we might achieve an implementation that matches these requirements. Having completed the logical specification, that is, the statement of the user's requirements, we now proceed to the technical specification.

The HOW questions cover things like computers, programs, databases and procedures. The designer is not being asked to create any of these things, as that is the job of the hardware and software engineer. The designer has to specify the particular hardware and software facilities required to meet the users' needs. In some instances however, particularly in a microcomputer environment or where special facilities known as fourth generation languages are used, the designer may also be the system builder.

A computer specification has to be complete. The designer must be rigorous so that, for example, the computer expert does not make decisions which affect the way in which information is presented to the users. The design can be created in many ways, and these are discussed in broad terms in this chapter. In subsequent chapters we follow through the particular strategy adopted in Multiview.

At this stage a more or less rigorous definition of the information system is provided. Ideally this will be very precise because it will be easier to proceed to design. However, this is not always possible, and there are situations when the statement can only be based on people's 'guesstimates' of what might be useful to them.

The analysis is likely to be more rigorous where:
- The situations and activities are well-defined
- Changes in requirements will be minimal because of a static situation
- A meticulous analyst has been given scope to collect and check all the necessary data.

The analysis is likely to be less rigorous where:
- The situation is 'messy', for example, no one knows what ought to be done to solve the problems that they are experiencing
- The situation is unknown, for example, where a system is being set up for a new job

- The situation is changing
- Adequate systems analysis is not available because, for example, there is not enough time, a suitable analyst is not available or a professional job would be too expensive.

The analyst going into a situation does have some scope in making clear how the job ought to be tackled, but the scope is obviously bounded by the constraints of the situation. The best thing for the analyst to do, given a limited scope, is to make clear what can or cannot be achieved within those terms of reference. An analyst might, for instance, say: "I can't give you an exact statement about your requirements, but I can help you to think about what might be useful to you, and produce some alternative suggestions". Unlike some alternative methodologies, Multiview is designed to be effective in non-idealised situations. No assumption is made that it will be used in the most advantageous setting for information systems development.

It is important that both analyst and client are aware of the degree of rigour that there has been in the analysis up to now, because this will influence the way that they ought to go forward. At one end of the scale is the totally rigorous. This could be stated as: "Let us write down every detail of the requirements, then we'll computerise it". Most computer books of the 'sixties and 'seventies were based on this approach, and many analysts take it for granted that this is the best approach. The job of computerising the system started with a feasibility study then went through the stages of definition, preliminary design, detailed design, implementation, then conversion to the new system, and its maintenance (see, for example, Daniels and Yeats, 1972). But it is unwise to prohibit further investigation into the user's needs. An opportunity could well be lost in providing better information in a better way.

At the other end of the scale is the statement: "We've got an information problem, but we've no idea what we want so let's see what's available as that might give us a few ideas". This is the heuristic approach. Analysts should perhaps be clearer about what is available even if any one approach is not forced on the user. They should give more guidance than just to suggest to designers to 'look around'.

Neither of these extreme positions seems sensible to the authors, and Multiview, in attempting to match the heuristic temptations of users to the analytic temptations of computer people, adopts a middle ground. The user is rather like the browser in a dress shop waiting to see something that is 'just right', whilst the computer person is like the dress-maker wanting to work from a pattern without having to make any alterations. Designers taking the middle view go out with some ideas and try to refine them in the light of what is feasible in the particular problem situation.

The next sections look at some alternatives open to the designer. They are packages, prototypes, detailed analysis and design, and end user development.

14.2 PACKAGE SELECTION

This approach is nearest to the heuristic search extreme. An overview analysis may have concluded that the application is of a certain general type, such as stock control or sales ledger, and that the volumes of data and transactions were within the range likely to be catered for by an off-the-shelf package. Such a solution seems to be a straightforward matter, but there are a number of pitfalls.

In order to select suitable software, the requirements need to be specified in more than outline fashion, and some of these requirements may relate to technical matters, for example the way in which data should be transferred from one program to another. There is no standard way of describing software so that the buyer of a package knows exactly what he is getting. The manual provided with the system may help, and it may be possible to buy a copy of the manual before finalising any decision about purchase. But even the manual may be vague and ambiguous about certain points or else optimistic about the capabilities of the system. Some 'capabilities' may refer to aspects that have not been implemented as yet.

Difficulties in evaluating an application package may be caused by not knowing what questions to ask of it. A very common reaction of users to packaged software is to go through the following stages:

- Fantasy about what problems a computer system would banish for them
- Anxiety at the thought of coping with a new system, because they feel as though they are on alien territory
- Delight as they start to get the basics working and discover that they understand quite a lot about it
- Horror when they discover that the package cannot do some of the things that they need for the system to be effective.

The advantage of having been through the Multiview analysis stage is that there is a series of models of how the system needs to work in practice. The salesman and the manual can be probed to ensure that the package will be able to cope with the situations that have been written into the model. Thus, the package must be able to deal with the information processing associated with all the events in the information model. The package should also be looked at in the light of the following questions: "what sort of organisation was this package intended to work in?" and "what sort of people are supposed to be able to operate it?". It may be possible to have the package free on loan for a trial period, so that it can be evaluated fully.

If there is doubt about what is wanted from a computer system, then it is obviously useful to look at what is available. A package that is potentially useful may be seen and even if such a package is not found, then more information about what might meet the needs of the organisation has been gained. It is a common observation that people are better at seeing what is wrong than what is right. If this is true then a reasonable specification may be "what I want is the features of the XYZ package, plus ...., but excluding ....".

It is always worth looking at what packages are available as it is possible to learn about particular applications and the ways in which they are usually handled. Useful features, that were not originally thought of, may be used in your solutions. These features could include good ways of presenting menus, layouts, or error handling routines. Analysts with a strong computer background often over-estimate the user's knowledge of what computers are and what they can do. Demonstrations of packages might be very helpful to the users so that they can see what is available and for the analyst to gauge the capabilities of the users.

When choosing a package, there are a number of questions that should be asked. The first of the following is the most obvious (but even this is sometimes ill-considered), and there are other important criteria that ought to be followed (Avison, 1990b):

- Does it meet the functional requirements?

  This is of course the issue of fundamental importance. If the package does meet the functional requirements then:

  (a)   is all the input required by the package readily available?

  (b)   is its capacity large enough for present use or too restricting for the future?

  (c)   Does it process the data fast enough?

  If only some of the requirements are fulfilled then some other questions should be asked:

  (a)   what percentage of the requirements are fulfilled without amending the application package?

  (b)   are the limitations of the package acceptable?

  (c)   how easily can the extra requirements be fulfilled?

- What resources are required to buy and run the package?

  (a)   what is the basic cost, maintenance cost and the cost of extra hardware and support required?

  (b)   what labour is required to set up and run the system?

  (c)   can the package be run on other computers (which may be important later)?

- How many people are presently using the package?

  (a)   is it possible to get their reactions to it?

  (b)   were there many setting-up and teething problems?

  (c)   has it proved reliable?

  (d)   are they presently happy with the system?

  (e)   are they happy with the help provided by the supplier when requested?

(f)   what would they have done differently now?

- What is the quality of the documentation? Is it geared to computer experts, or are the users of the system likely to understand it? Is it well written? The documentation should be judged on its appropriateness for the people who are going to use the package. Is it good for:

(a)   reading (e.g. to give a general overview of the system?)

(b)   learning (e.g. so that the user can use the package without too much trouble)

(c)   teaching (e.g. so that the trained user can teach others how to use the system)

(d)   referring to (e.g. so that the format of a particular command can be checked)

(e)   reminding (e.g. to allow the user to look at an overview of the system quickly)

(f)   diagnosing problems (e.g. so that the user can soon correct any mistake).

- Are the 'help' facilities provided by the package when using the system on the computer good? If the user does make an illegal command or response, are the messages sensible and does the system provide help to make the correction? This is a facility which is often overlooked when buying a package but a good help facility is vitally important when learning about the system.
- Is there a disk tutorial system? Such a system should lead the user through the use of the package, with carefully chosen examples, in a structured way.
- Can the package be implemented without the need to employ computer professionals? This should avoid expensive setting up costs.
- Are other training facilities provided? These may be in-house or provided at the supplier's base.
- Is it a well-established product? Products that have been on the market for some time are likely to have fewer problems.

One possible way of evaluating packages is to develop a weighted matrix (see Figure 14.1) which shows how packages measure up to requirements (weighted to ensure that the most important requirements are given more importance). In the example, package C is the best option.

The most successful packages perform fairly simple tasks or allow maximum flexibility in the tasks which are required by most companies. Word processing and spreadsheet packages allow the maximum flexibility for the user to generate variety. Systems analysts will not be brought in to specify these tasks, although they might advise on the appropriateness of such a solution. Once the package has been designed and programmed, it can be mass-produced and sold fairly cheaply. Such systems have promoted the success of microcomputers.

The next most available types of package are for book-keeping. This is not because accounting is totally straightforward. In fact even similar companies keep their books

CRITERION/ (WEIGHT)	PACKAGE A	B	C	
1 (2)	6 (12)	9 (18)	8 (16)	
2 (10)	6 (60)	0 (0)	9 (90)	
3 (10)	7 (70)	0 (0)	9 (90)	
4 (1)	7 (7)	10 (10)	0 (0)	
5 (2)	0 (0)	10 (20)	0 (0)	
TOTAL WEIGHTED MARK	149	48	(196)	

Fig. 14.1. Comparing application packages

differently. The reason why book-keeping packages on microcomputers are important, is that every firm is obliged by law to keep certain figures available. Most firms regard this as peripheral to their activities and are prepared to let a software company tell them how it should be done. This gives them a feeling of security because they believe that the people who wrote the software must have got it right, and that the computer printout will placate the tax authorities. There is not a great deal of systems analysis involved in book-keeping except at a detailed level.

There are a lot of microcomputer packages calling themselves 'databases'. It is only in recent times that they have begun to deserve that name. In the early days of microcomputing, most of them were little more than computerised card indexes. It may well be that this is all that the user needs, or at least that some very useful work could be done on them. But the analysis of data and data relationships which was described in Chapter 9, for example, shows us that data is actually more complex than this, and almost any system calls for a variety of inter-connected records. To do work with this kind of application does require a database management system. This covers all aspects of the integration, security and integrity of the data, and the inter-relationships between the data and the programs that access it. Other standard application packages include those for word processing (and desk-top publishing), business graphics and statistics.

Packages for some other applications are much less common and usually more expensive. This is because the market for particular packages can be very small and hard to predict in advance. Often the difficulty of producing one piece of software which will suit enough different buyers is greater than the cost of producing several different versions, each going to a different company. However, there is a move in some user communities to agree amongst themselves what their requirements are and then get funding for a communal software development project. This may be done through a professional body so that packages are developed that are suitable for dentists, doctors, and solicitors, amongst many others.

Ironically, as more packages become available and they become more sophisticated, so it will become more difficult to choose the right one. Eventually it may be possible to specify software from the users' point of view so as to produce a 'standard' for software description that will tell the potential users everything that they want to know. The Multiview approach attempts to cover each of the dimensions in the description that have been found to be important. We use this framework for evaluating software for our clients.

14.3 PROTOTYPING

In all branches of engineering, the creation of a prototype is an essential stage in design. It helps to work out the details of the design and to test them in a way that could never be done on paper. Several different versions of the prototype can be constructed for several different purposes. In order to take advantage of prototyping it has to be possible to build something that enables those aspects of the design that is of interest to be tried out, and this has to be built cheaply and quickly. By spending time on the development and testing of prototypes first, rather than going straight ahead to build the real thing, the finished version should be produced earlier than otherwise.

All these principles can be applied to systems design, and prototyping is now frequently used as part of the systems design process. There are two reasons for this. There is a **demand push** because too many users have been disappointed with a system after waiting a long time for it to be implemented. Many faults in the completed design may have been prevented by comments from users early in its development. But the design needs to be displayed in a way that is meaningful to users. There is also a **technology pull**, because fourth generation programming languages are simpler to use and there are now a number of application generators available which facilitate prototyping.

By implementing a prototype first, the analyst can show the users inputs, intermediary stages, and outputs from this system. These are not diagrammatic approximations, which tend to be looked at as abstract things, but the actual figures on computer paper or on terminal or workstation screens. The formats can be changed quickly, as the users suggest changes, until the users are given a reasonable approximation of their requirements. It may only be by using this technique that the users discover exactly what they want from the system, as well as what is feasible. It is also possible to try out a run using real data.

With the aid of an application generator it is relatively quick to set up something which behaves on the surface like a cut down version of a proposed information system. It may be possible to create part of the system at a time. This prototype does not have to cope with technical problems (like what to do when a disk is full) or with many of the errors and exceptions that the final version will have to cater for. Nor does it have to cope with the volumes of transactions and the speed of response necessary for the final version. It can also be simplified to single-user operation. Its purpose is to give the user an idea of how the system will operate so that it is possible to comment on it. Amendments can be agreed before too much time is spent on coding.

Prototyping helps the design of the system. It allows users and operators to see how the system may look and feel and it may be the only way that they can decide on the features of the proposed system. It therefore enables the analyst and user to make sure that they are on the right lines before too much time and effort have been committed.

Prototyping can therefore be seen as a much improved form of systems investigation and analysis, as well as an aid to design. It is particularly useful where:

- The application area is not well defined,
- The cost of rejection by users would be very high and it is essential to ensure that the final version has got users' needs right, and
- There is a requirement to assess the impact of prospective information systems.

It is also a way of encouraging user participation.

It also helps with the detailed design because it enables users to *act out* the future system. This makes it possible to see what detailed decisions have to be taken, because it forces the analyst to think through all the stages and see how each step will work out in practice. Many situations will emerge in the trial of the prototype that no one had thought about in the verbal specification. Sometimes, even when it is known that there is a situation which causes design difficulties, a solution cannot be found in advance. Computer systems are not very adaptable, and therefore it is necessary to make these decisions so that they are built into the system. Until the day when computer systems are sufficiently flexible that they will respond to unusual situations on the basis of accumulated experience, in the way that human operators would, acting out a situation is the best way of making a decision.

14.4 DETAILED ANALYSIS

This has been the standard way forward until recently. Many analysts prefer working on the basis that systems will be tailor-made, in the same way that most architects usually prefer to design specifically for a customer. A tailor-made solution would also seem to be more likely to result in a system that suited the users. However, if we pursue the architect analogy further, most of us are quite prepared to live in a conventional house but require 'architect designed' adaptations and extensions. In the same way, a package with adaptations, which require tailor-made analysis and design, may prove a good solution. It is likely to be cheaper and quicker to implement when compared to a totally tailor-made solution. Only where an application is quite different from anything generally available is it necessary to revert to 'design from scratch'.

Even if a computer system were being designed from scratch, there is usually no reason to avoid a prototyping phase although sometimes, after trying out various parts of the system, it is realised that the system is so complicated that it is not possible to move from the prototype to the finished version. In these situations detailed analysis of parts of the system are necessary.

The functional analysis undertaken in the information modelling stage (Chapter 8) needs to be used as a basis for program specifications or clerical procedures, depending on whether that part of the system is to be computerised or not. Some of the functions may be carried out by software provided with the system, for example, setting up reports using a report generator.

The entity model (Chapter 9) has to be developed to provide a specification of the database. This has to cover:

- The entities (or files) with their associated fields (attributes) and the keys for each record.
- The relationship between record types.
- The normal access method to individual records. These may be accessed directly, for example, looking up the details of a customer record as the customer comes into the office, or they may be retrieved according to their relationship with something else, for example, retrieving sales order records for a particular customer, following the retrieval of the relevant customer record.

These functional requirements would have to be considered along with those relating to the technicalities of the particular database management system chosen. This includes the procedures for ensuring privacy, integrity and security of the data. We shall look in more detail at the design of the technical subsystem in Chapter 16.

14.5   END-USER DEVELOPMENT

We have assumed so far when describing Multiview that the tasks of creating the computer solution will be carried out by a technically-oriented designer or programmer (albeit with user involvement). However, this is not the only possibility. Even though end users are unlikely to be computer experts and unwilling to spend the many hours necessary in designing, writing and testing programs in a computer programming language, this does not preclude end user development. For example, they sometimes choose a package without help from systems analysts or any computer people. An application package may perform something like 80% or 90% of the requirements in a particular application, leaving 10% or 20% of the work undone. It may be that these tasks can be done manually or that a consultant can be hired to design and write the software necessary to execute these tasks. Some computer packages provide another alternative: the ability to enable the users to write their own procedures. It is frequently not beyond an interested user to write the procedures necessary to fulfil the rest of the required tasks.

Packages adopt one of two approaches. In the first, the user writes procedures in the programming language used by the writers of the application package. But this is likely to be difficult for end users. The second approach is to provide a 'very high level language' which is easy to use and which the package can execute. A specially designed set of procedures is usually much easier to learn and to use than a conventional programming language. These commands should give the user the flexibility necessary to allow the production of routines necessary to 'customise' the package so that it can meet all the user's requirements. Even so, it is probably necessary for the user to have attended a training course in the use of the package, usually lasting a few days, to gain a fair command of the system's capabilities.

As we have described, some applications are unique to a company or at least are so different that it is impossible to find a suitable application package available. If there is no in-house software specialist, there is still an alternative: that of using an **applications generator** or **user workbench**. This is a package designed to help the user build a system without using a conventional programming language. An applications generator may consist of a number of tools, frequently called **fourth generation tools**. The facilities that they provide are likely to include:

* Prototyping
* Screen formatting
* Database handling
* Test data generation
* Report generation
* Data dictionary handling, and

- Documentation generation.

Many of the systems advertised under these banners are designed for applications programmers - aids to speeding up their work - particularly the more mundane work such as screen and report design. However there is a way that even specialist tools can be helpful, for users and programming people can sit together at a workstation and try out a prototype. This is the compromise discussed earlier in Section 14.3. The prototype can be modified a number of times, until a system is developed which is satisfactory to the user. This process of developing application systems has two main advantages: firstly, it is quick, and secondly, because the user is involved, it is likely to produce a system that meets the user's requirements.

This section will concentrate on the attributes of those systems designed especially for the user. There are packages with facilities similar to those described above but usable by the untrained person. These systems will therefore be:

- Easily learned,
- Require few statements to do a particular task,
- Adopt default settings should the user not specify certain details, and
- Provide productivity and cost gains over programs written by programmers in conventional programming languages.

These facilities form a **user workbench** (as against the programmer workbench and analyst workbench, which are subsets of the fourth generation environment designed for the more technical people). Many systems have only a few of the facilities discussed below, but it is likely that newer systems will contain most of these, designed for the user in a complete 'fourth generation environment'.

A **screen painter** (or formatter) enables the user to set up a screen layout for such requirements as menus and screen reports. The system itself generates the programming language statements necessary to produce the particular screen layout required. A series of similar screens can be set up easily. This will be useful for the entry of data which is similar but not the same. The system should also enable screens to be changed easily. This means that the tool is far more flexible than conventional application systems.

One feature that most of these fourth generation systems will have is **database handling**. The user may not have to collect the data for the application, it may be already in the database. However, it is necessary to specify what data is required. The system may do this by asking the user a set of questions - a series of prompts - and, according to the user's answers, generate the code necessary to derive the information required. Alternatively, the user's requirements might be specified by 'filling in a form' displayed by the system on a VDU. It may even be possible to use an 'English-like' code and, should the system not understand this fully, it clears up ambiguity by asking the user a further set of questions. A further facility provided by the database will be the raw material to generate **test data** from the database, so that the users can satisfy themselves that the applications that have been developed do work.

From the user requests, the system will generate code. This code may well be in a high level language but there is no guarantee that the code generated is efficient. Indeed, it is not likely to be very efficient and such systems often require a microcomputer with a large memory as a minimum. The code generated by experienced programmers is normally more efficient, but their time more expensive.

The simplest request is usually one of report generation. This may also be specified by completing a form giving details of:

- Data required
- Headings
- Titles
- Totals
- Page breaks, and
- Sort and print criteria.

As well as having a database, these systems normally have a **data dictionary** which gives details of the data stored. This enables the user to specify the correct name of the data required and to see how the data has been validated, when it was set up, and so on.

Forms may also be created by the user for data entry into the database, and the user should also be able to specify data validation procedures, so that data entering the database is valid. Another important tool is the ability to create menus for future users as well as reports and forms. The menu may consist of a series of options expressed in English phrases or icons. The person creating the application may also wish to set up help screens for users of the system being developed. In designing screens and forms, such requirements as:

- Top and bottom headings
- Colours
- Column placements, and
- When to produce a new page

should be specified very simply using such a tool. All these facilities give the user a powerful soft copy and printed document generating tool.

Another principle of many of these systems is that of development by example. The user 'ticks' those items on the screen that are required. A report screen could also be presented to the user who specifies areas where more detail is required (a 'zoom in') and other areas where a summarised format would be more appropriate.

Although such systems may be used to develop applications, they may also document the systems produced, or at least ease its production. For example, initial 'skeletons' of document types can be provided. These will not only help and speed up the production of documentation, but also ensure that standard layouts are followed and that the documentation is complete. Indexes can also be built up to cross reference elements of the documentation and the system itself. This also means that documents can be retrieved conveniently and altered if necessary.

14.6 CREATION OF THE COMPUTER CONSULTANCY PROTOTYPE

We developed the application system for the computer consultancy company using a series of prototypes. There were already manual versions of some applications. The paper systems proved to be fairly flexible and adaptable though it was difficult to generate reports and statistics from them. Further, they were becoming incapable of carrying out the necessary processing as the company expanded. It was almost as if as soon as we were familiar with operating the paper system it was necessary to change to a computer system and start learning all over again. Fortunately it was possible to transfer many of the records conveniently to the computer.

It was decided to design the prototype on a microcomputer. There were a number of applications. We decided to purchase an application package for the accounts system, and once this was adapted for the particular needs of the organisation, following several prototyping phases, this was successful. In other words the prototype 'became' the live system.

The customer system was developed in house and we had a number of problems, in particular, getting the two applications to 'talk' to each other so that data on the accounts package, such as that included in the sales ledger, could be used in the customer system. The latter was a system very specific to the needs of the organisation, largely to aid management decision-making. A second problem was designing the menu application, seen as Figure 13.1, so that it could call these two different applications, one a proprietary package and the second a tailor-made system.

Readers may find it surprising that 'computer experts' had difficulties in this area, but there are always teething problems when setting up systems, very often ones relating to installation. It *should* have been straightforward, but there were difficulties getting information from the application package suppliers. This is frequently a problem with microcomputers. The weaknesses of the documentation come to light only on trying something out. Suppliers are not always helpful, particularly when it might draw attention to weaknesses in the application package supplied.

14.7 SUMMARY

We have so far answered four of the five questions that are asked of the analyst:
- In the analysis of the human activity system we have identified the organisational purposes that the system is to serve.
- In the entity/function analysis (information modelling) we have identified the information handling requirements of the system.
- In the socio-technical phase we have decided what sort of computer system, in general terms, would best suit the needs, and how it would be fitted into the working lives of the staff.
- In the human-computer interaction study we have looked at the sorts of staff who will be using each aspect of the system and the dialogues that they will need to have with the system.

This statement of requirements will be more or less rigourous depending on both how clear-cut the situation is, and how much expertise has been available for the analysis.

There are four ways of proceeding from this stage towards the design and implementation of the system:
- Package selection
- Prototyping
- Creation of the detailed design for tailor-made applications, and
- End user development.

The difference is largely one of emphasis, as the package solution must be looked at as a possible way forward for at least part of the design, and prototypes are very helpful in creating a detailed design. The advantages of prototypes are that they permit users to visualise and act out those parts of the system that concern them and therefore to make better decisions about what they want. Prototyping is particularly useful in situations where the requirements are not clear-cut.

14.8 EXERCISES

1   For a standard application such as payroll, investigate two or three application packages available. How do they appear to meet the requirements of an organisation that you know? Why are they different? (If possible, try out the packages. You will soon realise that it is not always sensible to believe the 'glossies' of suppliers).
2   Research some application generators and fourth generation systems. How easy are they to use?

Chapter 15
Case Study 5: The District Health Authority

The fifth case to be discussed concerns the analysis, design and prototyping of an information system which fulfils some of the local needs of fourteen nursing and para-medical professions working in the community in a district health authority, whilst satisfying the statutory requirements of the UK National Health Service (NHS) Körner steering group for those professions. Further details of the case can be found in Avison and Catchpole (1987). The work leading to the implementation of a prototype computer information system was achieved through the participation of those professionals who would eventually use the system. This prototype system covers the chiropody and school nursing staff groups.

The case study illustrates the contingency aspect of Multiview, that is, the choice of tools and techniques within the framework and the adaptation of the structure of the framework itself to suit the needs of a particular problem situation. We take the opportunity to discuss ideas, such as action research, implied in the book but not discussed explicitly previously.

In an average health district in the UK (there are 220 in total), the normal health care activity of the community (non-hospital) health services creates tens of thousands of health care interactions annually. These relate to a whole range of activities from the domiciliary midwifery service to the domiciliary care of the terminally ill elderly patient. Current information about these interactions is stored in several discrete and often very separate manual record systems. There is surprisingly little comprehensively organised information available about them and it is difficult to evaluate how effective the services are. The need for the systematic collection, collation and analysis of information of a 'service' nature (type, duration and frequency of interactions) and of a 'clinical' nature (patients' details and reasons for requiring care) has been recognised by NHS management as a valuable information base for planning and organising health care activities. Such a system would provide feedback to the professionals working in these areas. The UK government steering group on health service information chaired by Mrs. Edith Körner has also recommended a minimum amount of data which must be recorded to provide the statistics required by the Department of Health and Social Security.

In current discrete information systems which have operated for many years, data has been collected on forms relating to the provision of services in the community.

Individual practitioners submit data on their activities to managers, usually on a monthly basis. A characteristic of this data is that it is of high volume, which means that it isvery difficult if not impossible to process manually into meaningful information. Data collection is often duplicated by different staff groups. Returns made by staff are frequently stored away for many years without use being made of them. The recording of this data is often carried out merely to fulfil statutory requirements or for no good reason at all.

An increasing emphasis is being placed on caring for clients in the community situation and the potential of community information systems is large. At this particular health authority the number of beds in the district general hospital is 750. One community service, school nursing, has 20,000 registered clients. This data could provide valuable epidemiological and demographic information. The opportunity is presently being lost.

Our remit was to analyse, design and implement a prototype of an appropriate information system for the community health services of the health district, whilst fulfilling the related statutory requirements of the NHS Körner steering group.

In order to achieve this major objective, we wished to test and refine the principles, tools and techniques developed by the authors in a real-world problem situation. It is a characteristic of this **action research**, described fully in Checkland (1981), that though the researchers may come with a framework, this may have to be adapted, and particular ideas, tools and techniques used in that framework may not be appropriate in every situation.

A major strand of action research is that the practitioners should participate in the analysis, design and implementation processes and contribute at least as much as researchers in any decision-making. Thus there is a synergy between the researchers and practitioners: the researchers building up theories and modifying them on the basis of practical experience and the practitioners using and modifying research ideas for solving real-world problems.

The first phase of Multiview is an analysis of human activity systems. Our familiarisation process had two strands. We carried out a survey of computer applications for the community aspects of the NHS, documented in Catchpole (1985), and also talked to the professionals working in community health for the health authority and went on visits with them to clients. It was obvious from our survey that there was no existing information system that could be used 'off the peg', we would have to develop our own.

Having established that it was necessary to develop our own information system, we considered possible frameworks and discussed them with management. There are many information systems methodologies, described in Avison and Fitzgerald (1988), such as Structured Systems Analysis and Design Method (SSADM), widely used in the UK Civil Service. These methodologies prescribe procedures, rules, techniques, tools, documentation and training procedures for developing information systems. Although there are advantages to be gained from standardisation, this type of methodology can be rigid and, as argued in Avison & Wood-Harper (1986) and Benyon & Skidmore (1987), it is unreasonable to rely on a single methodology for all situations. Most importantly, this approach tends to preclude the real (rather than lip-service) participation of the users, the methodology being a strait-jacket preventing them from contributing effectively, and it is our view that people ought to have control over their work environment wherever possible, including the computer systems that they use. For this reason we wished to use a methodology (or more accurately a methodology framework) which would be appropriate for the application area and flexible enough for user groups to have a real influence on decisions made.

Thus the framework to be adopted should lend itself to participation of user groups and at all stages of the development of the informations system, not only the design of the human-computer interface. A second and related requirement was to enable prototyping. This facilitates the demonstration of aspects of a potential system to be made without any irreversible work being done on the real system. There are a number of application generators and fourth generation languages which facilitate prototyping. A quick delivery of a skeletal working system can be made which will test out design principles of a system with users, who can then be involved participatively in the construction of the system. A prototype can be used as a tangible starting point for discussions. It may be possible to use the prototype as a basis for the operational system, it 'becomes' the operational system after many iterations when users regard it as being satisfactory. A final requirement of the methodology was to enable the setting-up of the database in such a way that it could be useful to the various professional groups and managers at the health authority and fulfil the Körner requirements. The approach discussed in Avison (1985) was used as a basis for this aspect of the Multiview framework.

The framework for the methodology to develop the information system therefore was an adaptation of Multiview, and is shown in Figure 15.1. We give an outline of the methodology below (the numbers refer to the boxes in the diagram).

1   *Familiarisation and boundary definition:*
Investigate the organisation, in particular by discussing the application area with members of staff, and draw boundaries around the the area affected by the information system.

2   *Körner analysis:*
This activity is specific to this application area, and involves analysing the various

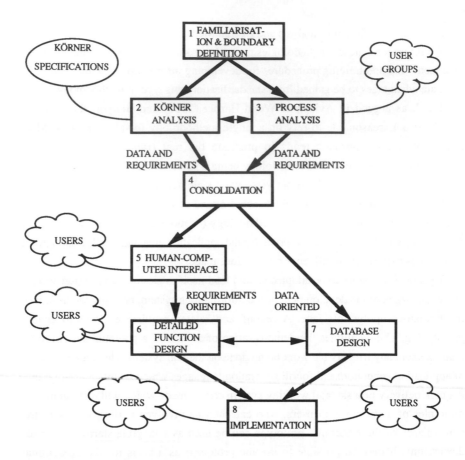

Fig.15.1. The methodology framework

reports (Körner, 1982, 1984a, 1984b) which are relevant to community health and extracting the requirements in terms of data collection and reports and other outputs. Participation is not appropriate here.

3   *Process analysis:*

This involves the construction of a requirements definition, again in terms of data collection and outputs, set out by the system's stakeholders. People with a stake in the project include the staff groups, management and clients. User views are recorded via interviews and group sessions led by the users themselves.

4   *Consolidation:*

The requirements of the various users are merged along with the Körner recommendations to form a consolidated requirements set. The data collected which is needed to support these requirements is also merged to form the basis of a data dictionary.

5   *Human-computer interface:*

The reports and displays identified at Stage 4 are designed in accordance with the users' experience and background. Users are encouraged to experiment with prototypes to determine themselves which approach would be the most appropriate.

6   *Detailed design of functions:*

The functions outlined in Stage 3 are analysed in greater depth and the menus, dialogues and reports designed in detail according to the principles established in Phase 5. Again, the participation of the users is essential to ensure that they get the system that they want.

7   *Detailed design of the database:*

The data requirements identified in the consolidation phase are redefined in a form suitable for the target database management system, which was chosen partly because it could offer the range of user interfaces required in Stage 5. The operational system, unlike the prototype, needs to be designed to fulfil performance, security, privacy and other criteria to a satisfactory standard.

8   *Implementation:*

This phase covers the processes towards changing to the new system and its regular operation and maintenance.

At first glance this structure looks very different from the Multiview framework presented as Figure 2.2. However, closer study reveals that it it not too distinct from that framework, though it has been adapted to suit the needs of this particular problem situation. In this situation, following the familiarisation process (similar to the first stage of Multiview), we wished to make explicit the separation of the Körner analysis (which consisted of analysis of particular information requirements to satisfy legal needs) and process analysis (which consisted of the analysis of data and function needs of users where participation was possible). These had to be consolidated, that is, the outputs of these stages merged. Phases 2 to 4 therefore are similar to Stage 2 of Multiview.

It also proved best in this problem situation to explicitly separate the analysis of functions from the analysis of data. Therefore there are two streams running in parallel, Phases 5 and 6 looking at process aspects and Phase 7 the data aspects. The final phase of implementation included the design of the prototype system, and this required the outputs from both streams.

An important aspect of our approach was to use the newer tools and techniques wherever appropriate. Users were rather unsympathetic regarding computers, and the documentation tools that they had previously used were computer-orientated and very difficult for them to understand and use. In other words, they discouraged participation. The first rich picture (shown as Figure 15.2) proved very useful in our

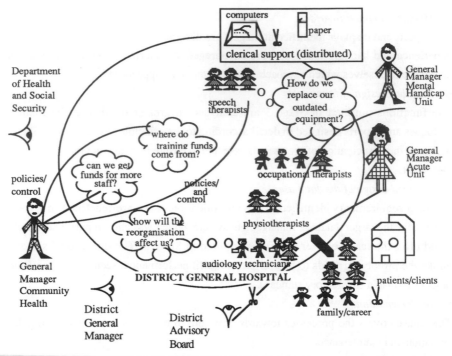

Fig. 15.2. An early draft of a rich picture chart for part of the para-medical services

work at the health district.

Because of the wide area of concern and complexity of this particular case study, a series of rich pictures and other documents were produced (Catchpole 1987). Figure 15.3 shows a sample entity model, Figure 15.4 a sample data flow diagram and Figure 15.5 a function diagram relating to the chiropody service aspects of the community health programme. Special forms were designed for specifying entities, attributes and relationships, and these are also illustrated in this Chapter. Part of the consolidated entity model (Stage 4) is shown as Figure 15.6. This is used as the basis for an entity type specification for the entity 'category-of-programme', shown as Figure 15.7; a relationship type specification for the relationship 'consists-of-2', shown as Figure 15.8, and an attribute type specification for 'category-name' (an attribute of the entity type 'category-of-programme') shown as Figure 15.9. Part of the function/entity matrix is shown as Figure 15.10. Figure 15.11 shows the entity life cycle for one of the entities 'person-in-programme'.

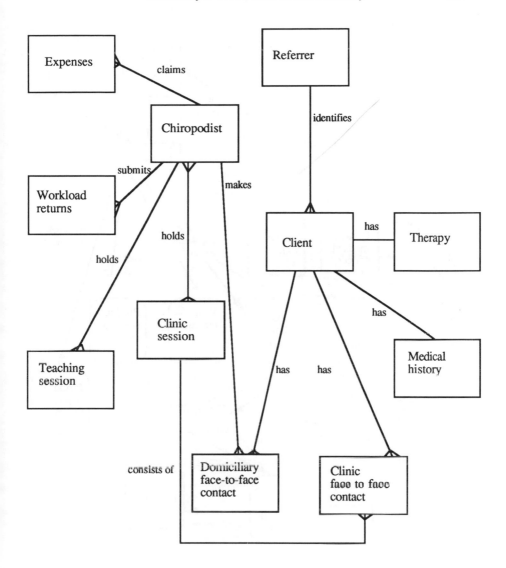

Fig. 15.3. Chiropody service entity model

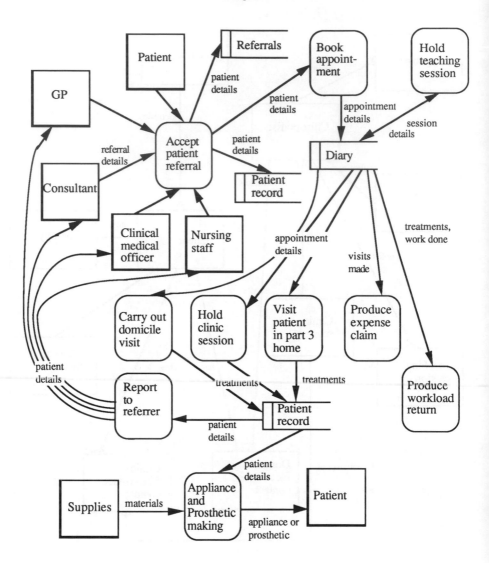

Fig. 15.4. Chiropody service data flow diagram

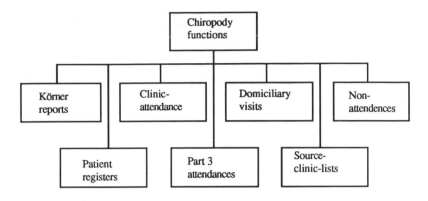

Fig. 15.5. Chiropody service function model

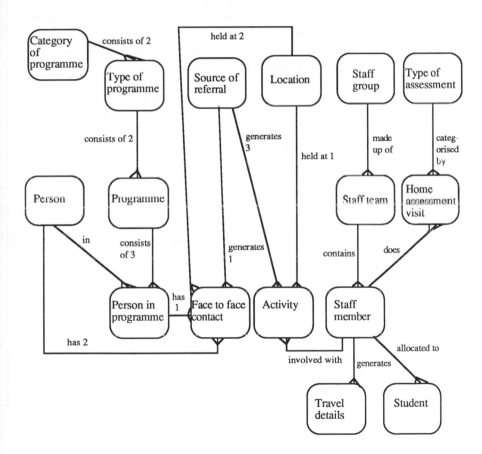

Fig. 15.6. Consolidated entity model (part)

ENTITY TYPE SPECIFICATION FORM			System: CHIS	
Entity name	CATEGORY-OF-PROGRAMME			
Description	A BROAD CATEGORY OF COMMUNITY HEALTH PROGRAMME SUCH AS HEALTH SURVEILLANCE AND THE EARLY DETECTION OF DISEASE			
Synonyms				
Identifier(s)	CATEGORY-NAME			
Date specified	15 MAY 1986	Status (P/V/I)		V
Minimum occurrences	1	Maximum occurrences		10
Average occurrences	3	Growth rate %		
Create authority	HEAD OF DEPARTMENT			
Delete authority	HEAD OF DEPARTMENT			
Access authority	ANY AUTHORISED OPERATIONAL STAFF			

Relationships involved cross reference

      CONSISTS-OF-1

Attributes involved cross reference

      CATEGORY-NAME

Functions involved cross reference

Entity sub types

Comments

Fig. 15.7. Entity type specification form

RELATIONSHIP TYPE SPECIFICATION FORM		System: CHIS	
Relationship name	CONSISTS-OF-2		
Description	A TYPE OF PROGRAMME CONSISTS OF ONE OR MORE INDIVIDUAL PROGRAMMES		
Time state	1 YEAR		
Synonyms			
Date specified	15 MAY 1986	Status (P/V/I)	V
Entities involved (Owner)	TYPE-OF-PROGRAMME		
(Members)	PROGRAMME		
Degree (1:1, 1:m, m:n) 1:m	Optional Contingent Mandatory	MANDATORY	
If contingent, state optional entity			
If exclusive, state paired relationship name			
If inclusive, state paired relationship name and first existence relationship name			
Create authority	HEAD OF DEPARTMENT		
Delete authority	HEAD OF DEPARTMENT		
Access authority	ANY AUTHORISED OPERATIONAL STAFF		
Comments			

Fig. 15.8. Relationship type specification form

ATTRIBUTE TYPE SPECIFICATION FORM		System: CHIS
Attribute name	CATEGORY-NAME	
Description	NAME OF THE CATEGORY THAT PROGRAMME TYPES FALL INTO	
Synonyms		
Date specified	15 MAY 1986	Status (P/V/I) V
Entity cross reference	CATEGORY-OF-PROGRAMME TYPE-OF-PROGRAMME PROGRAMME	
Create authority	HEAD OF DEPARTMENT	
Delete authority	HEAD OF DEPARTMENT	
Access authority	ANY AUTHORISED OPERATIONAL STAFF	
Functions involved cross reference		
Comments		

Fig. 15.9. Attribute type specification form

FUNCTION NAME	STAFF GROUP	STAFF TEAM	STAFF MEMBER	GROUP SESSION	LOCATION	PROGRAMME	CATEGORY PROGRAMME	TYPE OF PROGRAMME	PERSON IN PROGRAMME	PATIENT PERSON
1 GROUP-SESSION-ATTENDANCES	X	X	X	X	X					
2 PROGRAMMES	X	X	X			X	X	X	X	X
3 CONTACTS-TRACED	X	X	X			X			X	X
4 ASSESSMENTS	X	X	X			X			X	X
5 ACTIVITY-SUMMARY	X	X	X	X						
6 ACTIVITY-SUMMARY-OTHER	X	X	X							
7 PROGRAMME-COSTING	X	X	X	X		X	X	X	X	
8 VOLUNTARY-SERVICES	X	X	X							X
9 OTHER-SERVICES	X	X	X							X
10 ACTIVITY-SUMMARY-REFERRAL	X	X	X	X						
11 ACTIVITY-SUMMARY-LOCATION	X	X	X	X	X					
12 CONTACT-ACTIVITY	X	X	X							
13 NON-ATTENDANCES-REFERRAL	X	X	X	X						
14 SOCIAL-SUPPORT	X	X	X							X
15 FUNCTIONAL-IMPAIRMENT	X	X	X							X

Fig. 15.10. Function/entity usage chart

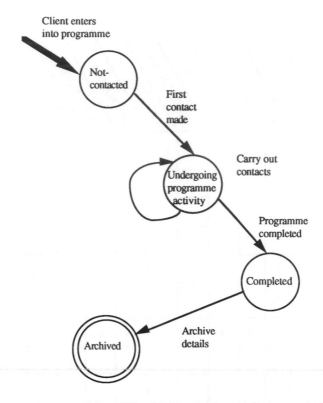

Fig. 15.11. Entity life cycle for 'Person-in-Programme'

It was recognised that there was a need for those people in the organisation who will eventually use the information system to take part in the analysis and, in particular, the design decision-making. Of the three approaches described in Section 11.1, the democratic approach was thought appropriate and selected. This approach was preferable to consultative participation which still leaves the bulk of design decisions to the systems analyst/designer.

The 'responsible' approach would have allowed all members of the community health services to be involved in the systems design process. However, for this particular problem situation, a continual high quality operational service must be maintained and so the approach would have been impractical in view of the lengthy time scales which would have been involved.

A design group was formed consisting of various grades of staff from the community health services representing the professional staff groups. Volunteers were used who had an interest in the development of a system from the non-management grades. The agreement of senior management was obtained to enable the members of the design group to participate.

An important member of the group was the facilitator who led the group in the tasks to be performed. For this problem situation, the facilitator took on an active role, training the design group in the application of the methodology and also carrying out tasks which were not thought appropriate or necessary for the group as a whole to participate in.

The composition of the group is shown as Figure 15.12:

Management Grades

Director of Nursing Services (Community)
Assistant Director of Nursing Services (Health Visiting)
Assistant Director of Nursing Services (School Nursing)
Assistant Director of Nursing Services (Community Midwifery)
Assistant Director of Nursing Services (Psychiatry)
Assistant Director of Nursing Services (Mental Handicap)
Assistant Director of Nursing Services (District Nursing)

Senior Clinical Medical Officer

District Head Occupational Therapist
District Head Physiotherapist
District Chiropodist
Senior Dietician
Senior Audiology Technician
District Speech Therapist

Non-Management Grades

Health Visitor
School Nurse
Community Midwife
Community Mental Handicap Nurse
Community Psychiatric Nurse
District Nurse

Senior Psychologist
Dietician
Audiology Technician
Speech Therapist

The Facilitator

Fig. 15.12. Composition of the design group

The design group met together as a whole and also in smaller teams as appropriate. For the facilitator to gain an initial knowledge of the community health services, and more importantly to become familiar with members of the design group, a period was spent where the facilitator worked with all of the design group members for one day each, to observe the tasks they carried out. For example, for the six nursing staff grades, time was spent travelling around in the community, visiting clients in their own homes. This time proved to be well spent and helped form good relationships between the facilitator and design group members.

There were 110 separate reports defined by the users (see Figure 15.13). The number of reports required to provide all the Körner minimum data set information for the community and para-medical services collectively was 15. By merging all of these reports with those requested by the users, a total of only 38 reports needed to be produced which satisfied all the Körner requirements and 85% of the original user requests. The other 15% of reports were categorised by the users as 'quite nice to have' but not essential for their work.

A second area where the information system requirements of the users and Körner proved less costly than expected concerns data collection. The standardisation in reports

STAFF GROUP	NUMBER OF REPORTS ASKED FOR	NUMBER OF REPORTS INCORPORATED	% INCORPORATED
HEALTH VISITORS	12	12	100
SCHOOL NURSES	12	12	100
DISTRICT NURSES	7	6	85
COMMUNITY MIDWIVES	6	6	100
PSYCHIATRIC NURSES	9	6	66
MENTAL HANDICAP NURSES	8	8	100
CLINICAL MEDICAL OFFICERS	10	6	60
OCCUPATIONAL THERAPISTS	6	6	100
PHYSIOTHERAPISTS	5	5	100
PSYCHOLOGISTS	10	6	60
DIETICIANS	7	5	71
AUDIOLOGY TECHNICIANS	6	6	100
CHIROPODISTS	6	5	83
SPEECH THERAPISTS	6	4	66
TOTAL	**110**	**93**	**AVERAGE 85%**

Fig. 15.13. Consolidating Reports

also enabled a common approach to data collection and only two types of input documents were designed for the new system. A simplification of the data recording process leads to improvements in the quality and accuracy of the information recorded. Minor modifications to the standard forms were made to meet the individual requirements of each service. Further, as Stages 1 and 3 showed, health visitors, school nurses, community midwives and other professionals working in the community health services, already collect data relating to their work. As this formed the basis of the data requirements for the information system specified, no extra data collection was necessary.

We were fortunate to receive the full co-operation from user groups. These included management grades, such as the director of nursing services for the community, the six assistant directors of nursing services, the senior clinical medical officers, and district heads and non-management grades such as health visitors, school nurses, community midwives, district nurses and dieticians. These formed design groups meeting regularly to decide on overall strategy as well as detailed designs.

Users were also happy to try new tools and techniques such as portable hand-held data recorders as an alternative to the redesigned forms. The portable data recorders, no bigger than hand calculators, enable direct data entry into the computer system (see Catchpole, Avison & Peart, 1987 for a discussion of this trial). This experiment was not imposed on staff - we as *facilitators* made the staff groups aware of the various ways of collecting data and the staff groups chose to try these and the redesigned forms in our prototypes.

The prototypes were designed using an application generator which generated the programs from a specification of the data (and validation procedures), creating the database (Stage 7), and screen and report formats. It also created a data dictionary and maintenance software (see Part 6 of this text). The design groups were able to view screen and report layouts as they were 'painted' on the screen and suggested changes as an iterative process. A series of menus were also designed by the user groups to provide access through the system in accordance with the recommendations made at Stage 5. A password security system was also implemented.

Two staff groups, chosen by the design group, carried out a pilot study. One nursing group (school nurses who carry out 'group session' type activities) and one para-medical group (chiropodists as they carry out 'face-to-face contact' type activities) were chosen for the pilot study because they provided a contrast to test different parts of the system. A telephone 'help line' service operated during this period to assist users. A series of review meetings were held to evaluate progress throughout the period and consider any problems that had arisen. The pilot study has now been completed and new user groups are presently using the system.

The prototype was implemented on a minicomputer and this may surprise many readers who associate health service applications with very large computer systems on mainframes. However, as Catchpole (1987) shows, about two-thirds of health service applications in the UK are developed on either microcomputers and minicomputers.

Obviously, this was a large application and the description presented has only given a 'flavour' of its scope. An assessment of the prototype is included in Chapters 16 and 17.

PART SIX

MULTIVIEW STAGE 5:

DESIGNING TECHNICAL ASPECTS

Chapter 16
Design of the Technical Aspects

16.1 DETAILED TECHNICAL DESIGN

So far, we have looked at the information system requirements from various angles in order to decide exactly what is needed. Now we have to create a technical solution which can do all that is required. This will be fitted into the clerical procedures that were settled in the socio-technical and human-computer interaction stages of design. Whether we have bought a package, tried out a prototype or gone straight into detailed design, we still have to carry out a form of technical design.

The inputs to this stage are the entity model from Stage 2, the computer tasks from Stage 3, and the technical requirements for the Human-Computer Interface (Stage 4). After working through the first stages of Multiview, the technical requirements have been formulated with social and technical objectives in mind together with consideration of an appropriate human interface. In this stage, therefore a technical view can be taken so that the analyst can concentrate on **efficient** design and the production of the information systems specification. Many technical criteria are considered and the analysis and technical decisions made should take into account all the previous analysis and design stages. The interaction of the design activities are shown in Figure 16.1 to produce the final major computer processes of the technical specification:

- Applications
- Information Retrieval
- Database
- Database Maintenance
- Control
- Recovery
- Monitoring.

These processes attempt to cover everything that has to be taken into account by the computer system and the people operating it. These components or processes may be implemented in different ways and in different combinations. For example, the information retrieval area may be just another aspect of a database management system and this may also include many necessary functions for control and recovery. This logical separation is necessary because each one of them needs to be catered for, even though the physical implementation of the system may combine some of these aspects

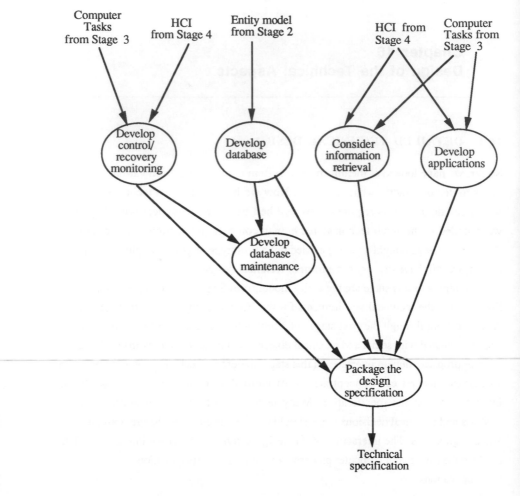

Fig. 16.1. The overall process of technical design

(or indeed separate some of these into distinct modules).

Further, no language is specified here for the formulation of the technical specification as a detailed consideration of this aspect is inappropriate for this text. The appropriate languages range from the English-like languages found in structured approaches, for example, structured English and pseudo code, through to languages based on mathematical constructs (see Avison & Fitzgerald (1988) for a discussion of the various types of language). Figure 16.2 shows a structured English specification relating to a report used in the health information system giving details of those people who have been referred by various consultants. As can be seen, it has a logical structure that is similar to that of a computer program, though it is easier to follow than conventional programming languages.

STRUCTURED ENGLISH SPECIFICATION	System: CHIS

Name
CONTACTS-LOCATION REPORT

Description

LOGIC OUTLINE

---

produce report-headings

REPEAT {for each staff group}

  access staff group record
  print staff group

  REPEAT {for each staff team within group}

    access staff team record
    print staff team

    REPEAT {for each staff member within team}

      access staff member record

      REPEAT {access all contacts for that record}

        access contact record
        cumulate by locations specified

      UNTIL all contacts accessed

    UNTIL all staff members accessed

    REPEAT {for each location identified}

      print report-line

    UNTIL all locations printed

    print staff team totals

  UNTIL all staff teams accessed

  print staff group totals

UNTIL all staff groups accessed

Keywords: IF....THEN....ELSE....SO....
           REPEAT....UNTIL
           CASE......OF....[conds:stmts]....OTHERWISE....ENDCASE

Fig. 16.2. Structured English specification

As we have seen, there are several parts to the technical subsystem and this chapter is not an attempt to cover them in detail because each of these parts could occupy a book in its own right. Furthermore it is not usually the analyst's role to deal with any of them in detail, only to provide the interface between the user and the technical designer, as they are often the main province of the technical designers and the programming team.

16.2   THE APPLICATION

The application subsystem is concerned with the technical solution formed from the user requirements. The output from this phase will be the various messages to the users (such as soft copy and hard copy reports) and the updated database with the new information gleaned from the application processing. The processes are the routines on which the programs are based.

Events are recorded as transactions. In other words, transactions are the input messages that record events in the real world. These events could include, for example, depending on the application area, an order being placed for goods, patients admitted or students enrolled. The applications subsystem would traditionally be looked at as the 'programs to be written', but today, as we have seen, many applications are handled by software packages.

As far as the user is concerned, the application subsystem contains all the things that the system was supposed to do (except for information retrieval, which is treated separately). All the functions from the function hierarchy chart that were to be computerised would be part of the application subsystem.

As we saw in the previous chapter, in the community health case we created the applications subsystem using an applications generator. In the district health authority case, a number of forms were completed as input documents to the system (effectively a statement of requirements in a very formalised way) and this was processed by the applications generator package to produce the required programs (producing code in the standard computer programming language, Cobol).

In order to design the applications, we already had the following information from the earlier design stages, although some of these had to be fleshed out in more detail as a result of the prototyping stage:

- *The tasks that had to be done* (from the function chart); for example, school nurses' timetabling and daily diary sheets, chiropodists' work allocation, and the detailed functions within each.
- *The data that had to be collected during each transaction* (from the entity/event model); for example, the doctor's name and address is collected during school-child

referral and the details of each patient are collected when registering patients.

- *The type of input method* (from the socio-technical design stage); for example, data recording on hand-held data recorders or on paper forms.

- *The sort of computer system that would be used* (from the socio-technical design stage); for example, in the community health prototype, a minicomputer system capable of processing batches of data coming from the health workers (including direct input from the data recorders) and with on-line enquiry facilities.

- *The nature of the dialogues that would have to take place and the style that would be appropriate to each* (from the human-computer interaction); for example, menu mode for application selection and forms mode for data entry and for retrieval of individual items.

16.3   INFORMATION RETRIEVAL

This is different from the applications subsystem in that the database is unchanged after the enquiry has taken place. Information retrieval is the primary purpose of many computer systems, for example, those available in libraries for borrower enquiries and on-line databases, such as Prestel in the UK, The Source in the US and Minitel in France, which are available for public enquiries.

There are, in general, two ways of performing information retrieval. The first of these are the predefinable reports which are generated as a matter of routine within the information system. Many systems have a report generator which permits users to specify the reports that they require themselves without too much technical coding.

Most systems now also give the user opportunities to make enquiries directly using a conveniently located computer terminal or a microcomputer with compact disk or hard disk containing the information. These enquiries may be standard ones within the organisation for which a special routine has already been written. Alternatively, they could be one-off enquiries set up using the query language or natural language interface provided. A query language permits the user to formulate enquiries using a formal vocabulary and syntax, but without requiring the level of detail normally associated with coding computer programs.

A query in the community health prototype might look like:

PRINT ALL VISITS WHERE DATE=31.05.90 AND CHIROPODIST=JONES

This would produce a list of visits that this particular chiropodist had to make on that day. A language like this is very suitable for people who regularly use a computer as part of their job. Such a language is not too difficult to learn, and usually a few half-

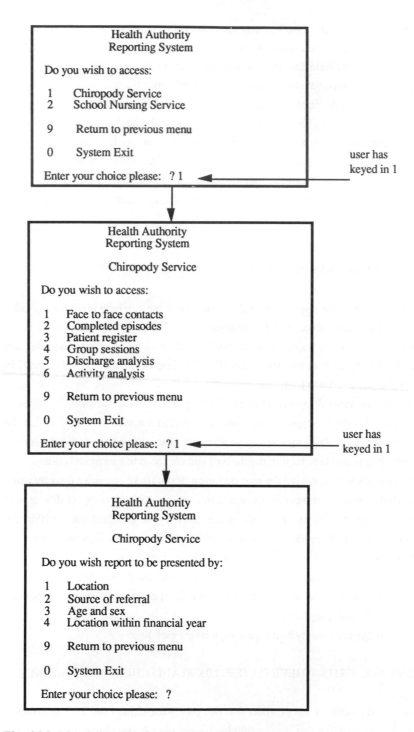

Fig. 16.3. Menu structure for reporting system

day training sessions are sufficient. Provided that users know what information is available in the database, they can obtain it in a flexible manner.

Where an information retrieval system is to be used by occasional users it needs to be much easier to operate. The most common way of offering this ease of access is through a menu. In the community health case study both dialogues and menus were used, depending on the user.

Figure 16.3 shows part of one menu structure. On the top level the user is asked whether the reports required relate to the Chiropody Service or the School Nursing Service. The user has keyed in '1' to bring down the second level menu for the Chiropody Service. This menu lists six types of report, and again the user has keyed in '1' to request a report on face to face contacts. The next level menu suggests alternative ways in which the report can be displayed. The user has keyed in '1' to ask for the report to be given in sequence of location. That particular report (shown as Figure 16.4) will then be displayed on the screen. If the user had keyed in '3', then the report shown as Figure 16.5 would be displayed and if the user had keyed in '2', then the report shown as Figure 16.6 would be provided. If, on the other hand, the user had keyed in '3' in the second level menu, control would lead straight to the display of the patient register (Figure 16.7) as there is no lower level menu for that.

The information needed to design the information retrieval system comes from the entity model, where all the information has been spelled out, from the socio-technical system, where we decided who was going to need access to the system, and from human-computer interaction design, where we decided what level and type of dialogue was required for each of these people.

In the community health prototype, the information retrieval required was of two kinds:

* regular reporting to health visitors, school nurses, and so on, and
* one-off queries as they arise, for example, progress checks on an individual patient.

Many of the reports could be determined in advance from known or predictable requirements, but there would undoubtedly be new ones needed to cope with new situations. The Government bodies involved, such as the DHSS, tend to require reports of a kind demanded by the Government Minister responsible. These are sometimes unpredictable because they depend on the particular political climate of the time. Usually they can be supplied from the existing database by a process of selecting and sorting. This is not always the case. For example, a request from one particular source required the health authority to give information on the ethnic background of patients which was, as a matter of principle, not kept in the system. So as to fulfil the request, a voluntary questionnaire was completed by patients which we hoped would satisfy requirements.

```
                    Health Authority Information System

                  Community Health Reporting System        Date  31/03/87

  Report K01            Face to Face Contacts by Location     Page 001

                                              Total Number
          Location                            of Contacts        %
  _____

  Chiropodists

      Farnley Street

          Rackman                                 29            22
          Graneham                                10             8
          Whitworth                               17            13
          Hurlingham                              39            30
          Tulsa                                   13            10
          Seven                                    4             3
          Totterham                               13            10
          Warmington                               5             4

      Farnley Street                  Total      130           100

  Chiropodists                        Total      130           100
```

Fig. 16.4. Report - Face to face contacts by location

```
                    Health Authority Information System

                  Community Health Reporting System        Date  31/03/87

  Report K03          Face to Face Contacts by Age and Sex       Page 001

                  Total Male         Total Female        Total No of
      Age         Contacts     %     Contacts      %     all Contacts    %
  _____

  Chiropodists

      Basin Street

          0 -  4       1        0         0        0         1          0
          5 - 16       1        0         7        1         8          1
         17 - 54       1        0        14        3        15          3
         55 - 64       4        1        27        5        31          6
         65 - 74      58       11       149       27       207         38
         75 - 84      54       10       172       32       226         42
         85 -         13        2        44        8        57         10

      Basin Street  Total   132      24       413       76       545        100

  Chiropodists    Total   132      24       413       76       545        100
```

Fig. 16.5. Report - Face to face contacts by age and sex

Source of Referral		Total Number of Contacts	%
Health Authority Information System			
Community Health Reporting System		Date 31/03/87	
Report K02	Face to Face Contacts by Source of Referral		Page 001

Source of Referral		Total Number of Contacts	%
Chiropodists			
Farnley Street			
Other		72	55
Self Referral or Relative		54	42
G.P		4	3
Farnley Street	Total	130	100
Basin Street			
Self Referral or Relative		451	84
G.P		33	6
Other		34	6
Community nurses etc		24	4
Clinical medical officer		1	0
Consultant		2	0
Basin Street	Total	545	100
Chiropodists	Total	675	100

Fig. 16.6. Report - Face to face contacts by source of referral

We did not attempt to define all possible reports although we did attempt to predict some of the entities and attributes that might be important in reports. This was carried out by studying the politics of health and the sorts of questions that Ministers, health authorities, and employers would be likely to ask us.

For the one-off enquiries, we tried to predict the sorts of questions that were going to be asked. These were all collected in the questions used to test the information model (see Section 9.8). Some of the questions could be answered in reports and others by setting up particular enquiries.

Report K013

Health Authority Information System

Community Health Reporting System   Date 31/03/87

Alphabetic Patient Register Sub-section   Page 001

Patient Identifier	Name of Patient	Address	Age	GP / School	Remarks
09/06/1975/M/M/AND/0	ANDREWS MARTIN ROBERT	44 GILLING STREET FERNLAND	11	DR. JAMES WHEELERS ROAD	PHYSICALLY HANDICAPPED
24/03/1972/M/M/BEL/0	BELL RAYMOND	1 LIME ROAD GREEN SEA	12	DR. JONES PEACHTREE BD	
22/02/1982/M/W/BEN/0	BENWELL GEORGE	54 RIBBLE ROAD GREEN SEA	16	DR. FITT SALTER STREET	
29/01/1975/M/R/BLE/0	BLEND PETER ERNEST	14 ELMFIELD CRESC GREEN SEA	6	DR. JONES PEACHTREE BD	PHYSICALLY HANDICAPPED
21/02/1972/M/D/CLA/0	CLARKE WAYNE	22 SEVEN STREET HIGHLAND	8	DR. WINFIELD HAYLING ROAD	
	DIXON ROY DAVID	56 EVERTON ROAD FERNLAND	13	DR. JONES SALTER STREET	

Fig. 16.7. Report - Alphabetic patient register

16.4   THE DATABASE

An information system is built around a database of some sort. 'Database' has a particular technical meaning for a computer person, but for the user it just means a collection of information, and Multiview uses the term in this more general sense. When setting up the technical area, decisions are made about the best way of implementing the requirements. However, when the choice of a database management system or less sophisticated package is made, all that concerns the users is that the technical choice enables the requirements to be met.

In this part of the design phase, we are concerned with setting up the skeleton or plan of the database rather than with getting any data into it. That will be covered in Section 16.5. There is a distinction in a computer system between database design and data entry. This is not as clear in a paper system where data is often written on pieces of paper and put in a suitable filing cabinet, with the files then re-arranged as necessary. In database design we are discussing the computer equivalent of 'drawing the layout of all the forms that have to be filled in and labelling all the drawers in the filing cabinet'.

The database has to contain all the data required to support the applications and information retrieval. The information needed to design the database comes from the entity model, along with the attributes that have been specified for each entity, that is, the results of the analysis of entities (Chapter 9).

Whether all the relationships in the entity model can be represented directly within the database will depend on the sophistication of the database management system chosen. For example, when describing entity modelling, we explained the difficulty that was often encountered in representing many-to-many relationships. Thus, during the technical design stage, decisions have to be taken about the level of sophistication required of the database management system to be installed, and about what steps should be taken to get round its limitations.

In the community health case, the database was set up using the applications generator package which facilitated the entry of database descriptions for the entities and attributes and the setting up of the relationships. This solution avoided many of the technicalities normally associated with setting up a database. The system did impose some restrictions on database design, for example, a maximum number of data items per file and a maximum record length, but none of these restrictions proved a problem in the application.

16.5   DATABASE MAINTENANCE

Database maintenance refers to all activities that have to take place in order to keep the data up-to-date and correct. This is concerned with transactions: amendments, deletions and insertions of the applications structure of the data. The responses will give proof that the data has been stored. Procedures need to be provided to:

- Insert new records
- Amend existing records
- Delete old records
- Produce proof lists.

Many of the insertions, amendments and deletions will be carried out as part of some application. In the community health case, the patient registration application will delete the corresponding referral record and create a new patient record. Similarly the receipt of visit data regarding a recent visit by a health visitor to his or her client will cause an amendment to the patient record so that it includes the additional information about the progress of the patient. The amendment may be achieved technically by wiping out the old record and creating a new one, or by writing the changed record back into the same place. This will depend on particular technical decisions that will have been taken, though it is in the domain of the technical analyst.

The raw data for inserting, amending or deleting records in the database was either input directly from the data recorders or keyed in from completed forms. The hand-held data recorders are small, battery-powered devices which can be programmed to collect data and store it in memory, and later be 'electronically drained' directly into the main computer.

Proof lists, frequently referred to as logs or journals, are kept to record details of the changes that have been made. These enable the systems administrators to keep track of what has happened and make sure that all changes are valid. Selective proof lists, being small and easily managed, are often more effective than complete lists. Proof lists are related to the control and recovery subsystems which are needed to prevent errors remaining in the system.

16.6   CONTROL

Control is an important aspect of any application, but has particular importance in the health service environment because inaccurate information could lead to incorrect treatment - or worse - and there are privacy implications as the system will contain personal data. There are many aspects of control in a computer system which must be considered if the system is going to prove useful. In this section we are concerned with the controls that are built into the system and its operation. We know what the system is supposed to be doing, we need to build features into the system that ensure that these requirements are being fulfilled.

The control subsystem helps to detect, locate and correct errors. These may be caused by:

- People putting erroneous information into the system
- Programmers who have left mistakes in the coding
- Operators who have run programs incorrectly
- Machines which have malfunctions.

There are different sorts of control features that can be applied to each of these. The most useful sorts of control are those which prevent the errors occurring in the first place. The controls will be built into all parts of the system: clerical procedures, application programs, information retrieval, database design, and maintenance. They form part of the completed system. Further, good design will prevent many errors occurring (an appropriate coding system, for example) and good training and education schemes, as well as a good working atmosphere, will encourage diligence.

When a mistake is found by the control system, an error message should be output which will identify the error and state what action is to be taken. Obviously the nature of the message and the action to be taken will vary according to the kind of error that has been identified. Some messages will be immediate, for example, when a program detects an input error, this can be 'flashed' to the user immediately, along with instructions on how to correct the input. When a program error is suspected, this would be notified to the programmers who would then run tests and re-check the code.

16.6.1 Controls on Data Entry

Part of the information that needs to be collected during detailed systems analysis concerns the ways in which invalid, incorrect, or 'suspicious' data can be identified. Here are some of the checks that can be applied:

- *Is the item of the specified data type?* For example, a patient number must be numeric.
- *Is the item within specified boundaries?* For example, largest and smallest acceptable value for numeric items (frequently called a range check), such as the month being greater than zero but less than 13.
- *Is there a limit on the actual values that may be used?* For example, if there are four items on a menu, only the numbers 1, 2, 3, or 4 are acceptable.
- *Can the item have a self checking mechanism?* For example, a check digit.
- *Can the item be cross-checked?* For example, the patient referral date must always be less than the patient date of death, individual amounts must always add up to the batch total given, and entries must be input in the correct sequence.
- *Is the data complete, have any items been missed out?*
- *Can the operator be asked to check the item?* For example, when entering a patient

number, the record with that patient name could be displayed to see whether this was the correct patient.

* *Can 'artificial intelligence' techniques be included?* For example, detect whether an item is 'reasonable', based on other data.

16.6.2 Controls on program errors

It is the ambition of the software engineer to produce code that can be proved to be totally correct to its specification. It is presently impossible to 'prove' the correctness of programs, at least of the size and complexity likely to be of interest to readers of this text, although better application generators (ones that have 'stood the test of time') are likely to produce more reliable code in a quicker time. One of the problems is that the better we get at coding, the more sophisticated the programs we want, or else the quicker and cheaper we want them. This means that much programming is carried out at the limits of competence. Combined with the problem of creating an absolutely rigorous specification, perfect code is by no means guaranteed.

Of course there is no substitute for thorough testing of programs, but to test every conceivable combination of inputs and circumstances would be impractical. It has been estimated that to test a banking system in this way would take several million years.

Because of a lack of experience with the system, the user sometimes finds errors occurring in acceptance testing that could be due to operator errors rather than program errors. A good liaison with the computer staff can help to determine the reason and get over any early difficulties.

16.6.3 Operator Error

We use the word operator as distinct from user to indicate that we are not talking about data entry mistakes, but about mistakes in operating the system. The most common of these, at least on small machines, is failure to take backup copies of files, and loading the wrong version of a file or database. In order to avoid these errors, it is essential that disciplined operating procedures are specified and followed.

16.6.4 Machine malfunctions

When users are faced with an obvious or suspected machine failure, the engineers should be contacted. This means that an appropriate servicing arrangement should have been made in advance with the supplier or an agency.

16.6.5 Errors in the database

These can occur through any of the malfunctions listed above. They can be very damaging if they are not detected, because users could go on accessing erroneous information and making decisions based on it. What is more, the error is likely to cause other information to be recorded erroneously. Even when the original mistakes have been found, it may be difficult to undo those mistakes caused as a result.

This underlines the significance of the problem, but it does not tell us how to solve it. There are various techniques available to the person looking after the database (the database administrator), which can be used to recover from corruption of the database when machine failure occurs. There are also ways in which transactions can be logged as they occur so that the effects of the transactions on the database can be undone if necessary. This is known as winding back the database. The system is 'wound back' (or 'rolled back') to where the mistake occurred, then corrected and the rest of the transactions re-processed.

The user must also check the accuracy of data and in most countries there is a legal obligation to check any records which are about individuals. People are entitled to see copies of any information about them that is stored in a computer and to dispute any errors that they believe it contains.

16.7 RECOVERY

The computer based system *will* break down due to software and hardware failures. Here, specification takes into account preparing for the failures and recovering from failures when they have been corrected. The recovery subsystem is related to the control subsystem as it tells users what to do when a mistake has been discovered. If a user makes a detectable mistake during data entry then the control system should set the recovery system to correct the mistake. Recovery from database errors can also be built into the control procedures.

As we have stressed, it is always more difficult to recover from a mistake than it is to do the thing properly in the first place. It is also more difficult to build recovery procedures into a program or instruction manual because it is difficult to predict all the kinds of mistakes that people can make. Perhaps the best way of getting things right is to make sure that people understand what the computer has done with their data. They may then be able to work out for themselves exactly what has to be done to correct it. This implies a degree of user education which few companies seem willing to pay for. A compromise solution is to build recovery routines for common mistakes into the programs and procedures, and then train a few 'trouble-shooters' who have freer access to data and procedures and can therefore correct any unusual errors.

16.8 MONITORING

For proper management of a system it is necessary to know what the system is doing, who is using it, how much time it is operating, and so on. It is very easy for the small system user to see for himself what is happening if he takes the trouble to observe. However, for a large machine, or even for a number of small machines, it is necessary to create a monitoring system.

For a central computer which is shared by several users, the operating system must log the time that the user is connected to the machine. It will also log the time that the user is using the resources of the computer's central processing unit (CPU) and the amount of disk space that is being used. Even if the users are not billed separately, it is prudent to have good information about the relative cost of various activities on the computer as this helps in general costing and budgeting.

Monitoring of activity is closely related to the control function, as part of the system preventing unauthorised activity. It is possible to monitor the following:

- Who accessed what programs and files and at what time
- How much log-on and CPU time each user consumed
- How long different programs were running
- How many different errors were reported
- Whether people have been following backup and security procedures properly
- What the relative usage of different parts of the computer system were.

16.9 SUMMARY

So far we have been concerned with the analysis and design of requirements. Now we have to move towards the definition of a specific information system which can implement those requirements. The human aspects have been defined during the socio-technical and human-computer interaction stages; the last part is the technical solution. We have identified seven different facets to this technical solution which are inter-woven. They are (see also Figure 2.7):

- The application, concerned with performing the functions, specified in the function chart, which have been computerised.
- Information retrieval, which is for responding to enquiries about data stored in the information system.
- The database in which all the data is organised.
- Database maintenance, which permits updates to the data and provides the information necessary to check for data errors.
- Control, which checks for user, program, operator and machine errors, and alerts

the system to their presence,

- Recovery, which allows the system to be repaired after an error has been detected.
- Monitoring, which keeps track of all system activities for management purposes.

16.10 EXERCISES

1   For a database management system with which you are familiar, find out which of
the seven parts of the technical solution are catered for.

2   Distinguish between aspects of the application and those of information retrieval for
a library information system.

Chapter 17
Acceptance, Maintenance and Development

17.1 MEETING USER REQUIREMENTS?

When the system builder presents the system for acceptance testing, the analyst and user have to ask the question: "Does the system meet the requirements?" More accurately, they have to ask the following questions, because as we have shown, there are several different sorts of requirements:

- Does the system actually work, or are there 'bugs' in the programs or incompatibilities in the hardware?
- Does it handle the whole of the information model? Are all the entities and functions in there?
- Does it achieve the stated socio-technical objectives?
- Are the people using the system happy with their interaction with the computer (human-computer interaction)?
- Most importantly, is it supporting the human activity system?

It is not reasonable to ask all these questions at once because the answer would be "yes, no, maybe, not quite". So what strategy should be adopted for tackling the system validation that is required?

It is clear that if the technical parts of the system are not working, then it will never have a chance to show whether it would have solved the human activity problems or not. We shall therefore start with the technical system and work outwards.

17.2 THE TECHNICAL SOLUTION

This is the aspect of systems testing that has been given most thought among computer specialists. It is the job of the technical analyst and the software engineer to ensure that the technical subsystem is fully functional. There should not be any bugs in the programs, the hardware should all be connected up properly, it should perform according to the specification, and so on. For a large or novel system these can be very difficult things to test and even harder to put right. However, they are not the concern of this book as they are the concern of technical specialists.

The software engineer should do all these things, but the user or analyst working on behalf of the user needs to design tests which make sure that the system does what the technical specification says it should do. For this purpose, therefore, the technical specification should not be couched in technical jargon. It should say things like:

Store 10,000 records

Process 100 transactions per hour.

A technical specification written out in this manner can be tested equally well on a commercially available package as it can on a custom-built system. We shall give some guidelines to systems testing from the user's point of view.

Testing takes time, effort and organisation. It therefore requires some resolve. It is very tempting to say "trust the experts", hoping that they will have delivered just what was wanted. This attitude has caused great user dissatisfaction with computer systems in the past, and it is only recently that a healthy sceptism has prevailed. The instinct is to 'prove' that it works. It should be to find out in which respects it may be deficient.

Before starting on user testing, it is useful to ask the system builders to demonstrate their systems testing procedures and results. Get them to train the users and operating staff and to be present in the early user test runs. When people start to use an unfamiliar system, it is often difficult to know whether a fault is a system malfunction, an operator error, or caused by poor documentation. Of course some testing will have to be carried out without the technical support team, but this should start only after some familiarity has been gained on the system.

It is reasonable to assume that the system has been tested on some sample data. To be sure that the test is realistic it is necessary to test the system on live data as well. Knowing what ought to be coming out of the system when processing familiar data helps the user to gain confidence in using the system and to recognise whether the new system performs satisfactorily. It also helps the user to see what it is going to be like working with the new system. In fact, these tests are testing the socio-technical system as much as the technical subsystem.

In the community health case, we opted for two different trial groups, the chiropodists and the school nurses. Most of these users felt obliged to 'play with it for a while', but none made much progress until one of the technical team was assigned to each group for systems testing. This person acted as the **facilitator**. This served two purposes:

- It provided training that was directly related to the job in hand. Most computer user training tends to be about how to operate a system and not how to perform the job that you want it to do.
- It meant that if a problem did emerge, it could be sorted out.

The facilitator carried out the training of the operator, whose tasks included controlling data entry, report extraction and distribution, and the handling of security procedures. The opportunity was also taken to help users get over their initial difficulties with an unfamiliar technology. This was frequently carried out on a small group basis. Following training and use (for approximately four months) came user evaluation. For example, the use of the portable data recorders was evaluated alongside an equivalent paper method for data collection. Training was provided and feedback on the two methods was provided by an informal interview, group discussion and a questionnaire. The recorder was found to be easy to use and slightly faster, and on the whole was preferred. Further discussion of the evaluation process in the community health case study is given in Section 17.6.

As we discussed in Chapter 16, we have identified seven technical aspects:

- Applications
- Information retrieval
- Database
- Database maintenance
- Control
- Recovery
- Monitoring.

The identification of these aspects guides testing, as the system needs to be looked at from each point in turn. The obvious place for most people to start is the applications, that is, asking whether the system is doing what is required. In doing this testing, it is likely that some testing of the control system will come 'naturally' at the same time. However, it is also necessary to test the control system more systematically later.

In testing a system it is natural to deal with many aspects at one time, although it is more thorough to organise testing so that it looks specifically at each area in turn. These are the major questions that should be asked:

- Does it perform all the applications required, and can it cope with the speed and volumes required?
- Is it possible to output all the information that is wanted and when it is wanted?
- Is the data organised effectively in the database, and is it possible to fit in all the data that may ever need to be recorded?
- Are there satisfactory arrangements for inserting, amending and deleting records and of producing proof lists giving details of the data that is stored, along with suitable data protection measures?
- Is the system picking up errors by users, programs, operators, and by equipment malfunction, and are the right people being informed?
- Is it possible to recover easily from errors that have been detected?
- Is it known what systems activities have been taking place?

To answer these questions it is necessary to look at the detailed requirements and to build the tests to match. The acceptance criteria needs to be established because no system or testing procedure is going to be perfect. It is necessary to determine a point when the system will be accepted.

17.3   TESTING THE HUMAN-COMPUTER INTERACTION

For a small system, testing the human-computer interaction consists of ensuring that the operator can cope with the system. The application package may be bought on a 'take it or leave it' basis. Some packages may provide the ability to 'tune' the system to the particular requirements of the users. With a tailor-made system it may also be possible to improve the user interface by building additional interface layers on top of the function programs.

There are two main questions to be asked:

- Does the system support all the dialogues that are necessary for the users to perform the required functions?
- Are each of these dialogues in a form that is suited to the particular style of the type of user involved?

The first question will be posed as the system is run under test conditions. In order to test whether the system performs an application correctly, it is necessary to run through the relevant dialogues. The dialogues relating to the control and recovery subsystems are likely to be more difficult to test, and they are often given less thought by the system builders. These dialogues must be tested as well.

The suitability of the style of interaction is tested in more subtle ways. There are various degrees of unsuitability which might lead to:

- User rejection
- User irritation
- Slow operation
- Excessive errors.

User rejection may be in the extreme form of industrial action, although this is more likely to be a rejection of the socio-technical system. A more common form of user rejection is seen when people avoid using the computer. Managers may take decisions without the aid of the decision support system set up for them; they may continue to use conventional message delivery systems instead of electronic mail; or they may expect their subordinates to perform all the computer interaction for them. Subordinate staff are likely to have less opportunity to reject the system directly, but may be put off or skimp computer tasks or seek transfer to other jobs or duties. Only by using the monitoring system is it possible to see whether staff are using the computer system in the way that was expected. Even if a problem has been detected, it takes further detective work to find out why this is the case and whether action needs to be taken.

User irritation is difficult to quantify. Again, it may have as much to do with the socio-technical system as the human-computer interaction. General irritation may be focussed on the computer interaction when that is not actually the cause, and vice versa. For some people change itself is irritating, particularly if they do not expect to see any direct improvements in their working lives as a result of the new system. Time and training usually overcomes this problem.

Where large numbers of staff are being trained to use the system, the trainers will soon sense whether significant members of staff are unhappy about the human-computer interaction and are likely to be able to alert appropriate computer staff to the need for changes.

Slow operation can be caused by poor response times. These may have to be endured, but if they are slowing down the rate at which work is processed then it may be cost-effective to increase computer power or alter the technical operation in some other way so as to improve response times. The analyst can work out what the benefit of the improved response time would be, but the technical people will have to say what it would cost.

Slow operation may also be caused by inappropriate organisation of computer dialogues. Time may be wasted by unnecessary keying-in or waiting for screenfulls of instructions to be displayed which the user does not need. An expert user should, for example, be able to suppress help displays which might be needed by a novice. Time can also be wasted by taking a long route through menus to reach the desired function.

The final problem with the style of human-computer interaction concerns excessive error rates. We all make errors when using a computer keyboard. There may be typographical (keying-in) errors or logical errors which occur because we try to do the wrong thing. A certain level of error is unavoidable. The actual percentage of mistakes will vary between skilled and unskilled operators. Problems arise when unskilled operators become demoralised by their inability to complete work correctly, or when skilled operators are making more mistakes than necessary and therefore wasting valuable time and increasing the risks of errors getting into the system.

Mistakes can arise when an uncomfortable combination of key strokes has to be entered. For example UK Postal Codes are difficult to type because the letters (but not the numbers) need to be typed in upper case (requiring the shift key to be depressed). It is easy to make a mistake by pressing the shift key at the wrong time. Some keyboards have a capitals lock key which might be used. Mistakes can also be made where the characters to be typed do not follow the user's logic. An example of this occurs in using many packages and programming languages where it is necessary to use quotation marks or punctuation marks which do not follow the rules of natural language.

Some of the problems with human-computer interaction can be picked up during the acceptance testing. Others may only become apparent as the monitoring system picks up excessive errors, there are unexpectedly slow speeds or people complain about the system. This then becomes a question relating to systems maintenance.

17.4 TESTING THE SOCIO-TECHNICAL SOLUTION

This testing relates to the way in which the computer system is assimilated into the working lives of staff. It is not possible to arrange test runs to detect problems in the same way that is possible of the technical subsystem. However, responsibility has to be taken for ensuring that the system is being operated effectively and that people are working well with it. Problems to look out for include:

- Excessive loading on some staff whilst others are relatively idle, or excessive peaks and troughs in the work required from individual users
- Bottlenecks where too many people need to use the system at the same time
- Difficulties encountered by users who have not had appropriate training
- Work being delayed because people are waiting for computer output
- People complaining that they are spending too much time at the workstation.

As with human-computer interaction, it may be possible to pick up some of these points during initial acceptance testing, but others will become apparent later and the system should be improved during maintenance.

17.5 TESTING THE ANALYSIS

So far in this chapter we have been looking at ways in which we can test whether the system that has been supplied meets the requirements which have been defined as a result of the analysis and design. Multiview starts with an analysis of the human activity system and of the functions, events and activities at the information analysis phase. In the socio-technical stage we are concerned with both analysis and design. The human-computer interaction and the technical stages are primarily design exercises, though supported by detailed analysis where necessary. We have to test the system against the design for those stages with a design element. Once the system has been tested against all the aspects of the design, assuming that the system is fit for the purpose it was designed for, then the contractual obligations of the supplier have been met.

The contractual relationships between problem owner, problem solver, and system supplier will determine the way in which one can evaluate the extent to which the system actually solves the problem. There are various possible relationships:

- The problem owner has gone directly to a supplier who is then responsible for both analysis and system creation,
- The problem owner has employed an analyst to help create the statement of requirements, that is, the design, and they have gone to a supplier for system creation,
- The problem owner is being served by the data processing department of his own company, or
- One of the above, along with the use of outside consultants for part of the work.

For the first of these, where an outsider has carried out both the analysis and design, it is reasonable to test the analysis before 'paying up'. The problem owner should be able to say: "You said that the system would alleviate such and such a problem in my business and it has". But there are plenty of unfortunate businesses which have gone to system suppliers because they are having problems with, for example, ordering or invoicing, and have finished up in a worse position than before. This is because the system did not improve the fundamental problem (Part One of Multiview was not carried out effectively).

If the stages of analysis and design are broken down as we have suggested in this book, then the user ought to be able to see before the hardware has been ordered or the programs written, whether the analysis is acceptable. The difficulty occurs where a company is supplying both analysis and design and may be tempted to sell an existing package. It is possible here to skimp on the analysis relating to whether that package is best for the application. Contracts should stipulate that the reports on the analysis work done should be accepted before design decisions are made.

The second relationship is where the analysis has been done in-house or by a contract analyst and then the system creation work is put out to tender. Here there are two quite different contractual arrangements. The chosen supplier must prove that his system meets the design requirements. The analyst has separately to account for the usefulness of his analysis in solving problems. This is a potentially difficult situation because analyst and supplier can blame each other for any problems in the new system. This situation also occurs between hardware and software suppliers. The best protection against this is a well-written report at each of the stages of analysis and design so that it is clear at each stage what has been agreed and who is responsible for carrying it out.

In the third situation, probably the most common in large organisations, all analysis, design and system creation is undertaken by a central data processing (computer or management services) department. Each organisation will have its own ways of managing the analysis, design, implementation and acceptance stages. This is part of the relationship that must always exist between a service department and the rest of the organisation that it serves. It is likely that acceptance of a particular project will be only one stage in the continuing development of computer services.

As we have mentioned, the presence of outside consultants for any part of the work may complicate any of the three options. It is essential that their role is agreed in writing and that they produce reports, which have to be accepted internally, for each stage of their work.

17.6 TESTING USER REACTION IN THE HEALTH AUTHORITY CASE

Two staff groups, chosen by the design group, carried out a pilot study. One nursing group (school nurses who carry out 'group session' type activities) and one para-medical group (chiropodists as they carry out 'face-to-face contact' type activities) were chosen for the pilot study because they provided a contrast to test different parts of the system. The pilot study lasted for about four months. A telephone 'help line' service operated during this period to assist users. A series of review meetings were held to evaluate progress throughout the period and consider any problems that had arisen.

One of the most critical issues in information systems management concerns how to assess the information systems in an organisation. Assessment or evaluation is an act of placing a value on an information system. This can take place from a number of different points of view, for example, those of the owners of a system, the users, or the system designers.

The owners of a system are most likely to be interested in economic assessment criteria and less interested in technical or operational aspects. They will be concerned with effects at an institutional level such as the way the organisation does business and how interactions with other organisations occur. System users will be interested in operational aspects and perhaps impact on work quality at an operational level. System designers may be concerned with the impact of an information system on the computing resources of the organisation.

We wished to assess the pilot system from the point of view of *effectiveness,* that is, the proportion by which the system meets organisational objectives and goals, and *efficiency*, that is, a measure of the 'mechanical' aspects of the system such as the accuracy, timeliness and speed of access to information. We also wished to review the training and design process, essentially a review of the participative and prototyping approach to information systems development that we chose. We wished to solicit opinions about the system from the senior managers as well as user groups and individual users. The methods used to assess the system were questionnaires with follow-up interviews and group discussions.

Readers should be aware of the difficulties in assessing information systems. Hawgood and Land (1986) describe three fundamental difficulties. Firstly, effectiveness is a subjective concept and different people will have different views on the effectiveness of a system. Secondly, information systems are immensely diverse in the functions that they carry out and in the objectives that they seek to meet. Thirdly, an evaluation should really take place by comparing the running of the organisation with and without the aid of the computer-based information system. In reality, this comparison is not usually possible.

Despite these drawbacks there is an important need to quantify the benefits of an information system and perform evaluation. A multi-disciplinary approach is needed to do this because evaluation can take place from a technical, economic, organisational or societal perspective.

It was decided to evaluate the prototype by soliciting opinions from the system owners, who are senior managers in the organisation, and system users, who operate, provide data or make use of information from the system. It is also possible for users to be owners of the system. System owners will evaluate the effectiveness of the system, and system users will evaluate the efficiency aspects.

Where possible, comparison of the prototype was made relative to the previous equivalent manual system which was replaced by the prototype, and both of these comparisons were related to theoretical objectives, goals and needs which were identified by the design group during application of the methodology. Costs and benefits associated with the old and new systems were identified, and then qualitative and quantitative items were evaluated covering such issues as services to clients, value added features, changes in the decision making process, and so on.

The questionnaires had four sections: effectiveness (objectives fulfilled, problems addressed, needs addressed, costs and achieved benefits, impact on work and clients, and impact on decision-making and control); efficiency of the system (attributes of the information produced, aspects of using the information system, value placed on information generated, data collection methods, working practices of staff, and the personal aspirations of staff); the design process (in terms of perceived 'success' of the implementation, contribution made by 'participation' procedures, and personal benefits and gains of staff); and finally the training process.

We wish to highlight some conclusions from this survey derived from comments made by management and the professionals working in the area. The respondents considered that the system has helped people to perform their work tasks more effectively, drawing attention to what is actually being done, and has resulted in staff deciding to change their working practices. The system has improved the handling of case loads, improving timetabling and utilisation of clinical time. More up-to-date, accurate and easily accessible information will help in both short and long term service planning. Respondents also suggested a number of enhancements which could be added to the system such as an *ad hoc* search option and a patient register giving details of other professions and agencies working with the client. On the negative side, respondents did point out that, at least in the short term, data collection was slower. On working practices, comments such as "it was satisfying to see what work had been done at the end of the month", "I have been made more aware of what I have been doing" and "I have realised what a large amount of time is spent travelling and walking to homes and schools" are revealing.

We have included four of the fourteen tables derived from responses which lend themselves to statistical analysis, though we do not claim objectivity in our assessment procedures. Figure 17.1 displays the comments of school nurses regarding the degree to which the old and new systems met their information objectives (expressed as percentages). The old system fared badly partly because some of the objectives did not apply. However, it is readily apparent that the data collected for the old system led to few information gains. Figure 17.2 shows the comparative attributes of the two systems as perceived by all users of the prototype system. The new system seems to fare better on all attributes. Figure 17.3 looks at the value of the information provided using a scale of extremes for each value type. Figure 17.4 looks at the various views of the users concerning the use of the new system. This is the most revealing because it is critical of the new system. It highlights in particular the time necessary to use the new system, though on follow-up interviews this was seen as a 'once-and-for-all' investment of time.

As for the method of implementation, one school nurse commented: "...as it is the community health professionals who have to use the system, we are in the best place to help design it; we know what information is important and relevant for recording ...." and another: "I have been made aware of the difficulties in the system design process" and another: "I have improved my knowledge of computer systems, and found this experience both interesting and beneficial". Many of the participants argued that they had enjoyed being involved, and the authors feel that the present expansion of the prototype to all the community professionals and future enhancements can be implemented successfully with the continued participation of those involved. As one school nurse recorded, "the system has been a success because we are all still using it after the pilot (study) has been completed".

INFORMATION OBJECTIVE	OLD SYSTEM SCORE (%)	NEW SYSTEM SCORE (%)
TO MEET THE KÖRNER OBJECTIVES	0	80
TO AVOID THE STORAGE OF DUPLICATE INFORMATION	0	90
TO PROVIDE ON-LINE ACCESS TO BASIC PATIENT DETAILS AND RECENT CONTACTS	30	90
TO SAVE TIME IN ACCESSING INFORMATION	10	100
TO PROVIDE AN UP-TO-DATE PATIENT REGISTER	0	100
TO DECREASE TIME SPENT BY STAFF ON FORM FILLING	10	90
TO REMOVE THE NEED TO MANUALLY AGGREGATE STATISTICS	0	100
TO PROVIDE MORE MEANINGFUL STATISTICS TO STAFF AND MANAGEMENT	20	100
TO PROVIDE BETTER INFORMATION FOR STRATEGIC MANPOWER AND SERVICE PLANNING; EDUCATION; EPIDEMIOLOGY AND DEMOGRAPHY	10	80
TO PROVIDE A SCHEDULING SYSTEM FOR WORKLOAD	20	50
TO PROVIDE A BETTER CONTROLLED STOCK SYSTEM FROM WORKLOAD	30	50

Fig. 17.1. Comparing old and new systems - information objectives

ATTRIBUTE	OLD SYSTEM SCORE (%)	NEW SYSTEM SCORE (%)
ACCURACY OF INFORMATION	40	84
TIMELINESS OF INFORMATION	27	63
APPROPRIATENESS TO YOUR NEEDS	39	74
RELIABILITY OF INFORMATION	43	87
COMPLETENESS OF INFORMATION	36	85
SPEED OF ACCESS TO INFORMATION	43	67

Fig. 17.2. Comparing old and new systems - attributes

VIEWS ON THE VALUE OF INFORMATION -2 -1 0 +1 +2	AVERAGE
TRIVIAL ____*____*____*X____ SOPHISTICATED	+1.19
USELESS ____*____*____*_X__ USEFUL	+1.50
UNIMPORTANT ____*____*____*_X__ IMPORTANT	+1.50
BORING ____*____*____*X____ INTERESTING	+1.13
VALUELESS ____*____*____*_X__ VALUABLE	+1.44
MEANINGLESS ____*____*____*_X__ MEANINGFUL	+1.38
UNCLEAR ____*____*____*_X__ CLEAR	+1.25

Fig.17.3. Assessing the value of the new system

VIEWS ON USING THE NEW SYSTEM -2 -1 0 +1 +2	AVERAGE
DIFFICULT TO LEARN ____*____*____*_X___ EASY TO LEARN	+1.38
DIFFICULT TO USE ____*____*____*_X___ EASY TO USE	+1.25
TROUBLESOME ____*___X*____*____ FEW PROBLEMS	- 0.13
TIME CONSUMING ____*_X__*____*____ TIME SAVING	- 0.81
IMPOSING ____*___X*____*____ UNIMPOSING	- 0.19
	+1.06

Fig.17.4. User views of the new system

There are dangers in any type of evaluation and any method should be cross-referenced using results from another method. User reactions described above may not represent the situation accurately (Silverman, 1989). The reaction of a football manager when the team wins or loses provides an illustration. These small events in a football season bring about extreme and opposite reactions when judging the team. Similarly, user reactions may be determined by the most recent experience with the system.

17.7   KEEPING THE SYSTEM WORKING

It is well understood by large systems users that maintenance of the hardware has to be catered for. There are various arrangements (and in consequence prices) depending on how quickly repairs and replacements are to be carried out. Some microcomputer users are taken by surprise when faced by hardware problems and the difficulties of getting speedy repairs or replacement of defective items.

Early work on systems analysis tended to concentrate on implementing the system and regarded this as the end of the story. But a system cannot remain entirely suitable for a number of years. Parts of it will need to be changed, though a completely new system is likely to be unnecessary for some time. The maintenance and development of existing systems is therefore important.

There are three aspects to systems maintenance, although they often blur into one another:

- Correction of bugs discovered after acceptance
- Alteration of system details as requirements change or are better understood
- Extension of the system to cover new applications or additional users.

The first of these does not call for any design work because it is a case of making sure that the system is performing according to the existing design. Bugs do occur after acceptance, as completely rigorous testing is prohibitively expensive if not actually impossible. Taking out a maintenance agreement on the software can therefore prove a valuable investment. The annual cost may be similar to that of a hardware agreement - about 10%-15% of the original price. Software maintenance is not as well defined and regulated as hardware maintenance.

No information processing system remains constant. There are always changes in the details of the requirements even if the basic requirements stay the same. The analysis and design should have taken some potential changes into account in future analysis so that the system has some flexibility built into it. However, there are a number of ways in which details or requirements might change:

- People realise that there are better ways of doing things than the ones that have been built into the design
- Problems are encountered that had not been anticipated in the design
- The organisation continues its natural development
- Changes are forced by outside agencies, for example, by legal requirements.

None of these calls for a new analysis of the human activity or socio-technical systems, although the changes should be checked back against these. It is possible that additional entities and functions will need to be added to the information model. Commonly these changes call for re-writing the details of some of the functions and for adding or changing attributes of the entities.

Where systems creation was carried out by an outside firm, then it will be necessary to cost out the proposed changes, including the necessary re-testing of the system. Where the changes are to be carried out by the data processing department, then it may be necessary to put in a formal request for changes to be made to the information system.

The third type of system maintenance is concerned with the addition of new facilities. This reflects the fact that the normal way of getting a job computerised is by building it into the existing system. Thus, maintenance blurs into the next round of system development.

We have already pointed out that incremental systems development is the safest and easiest to cope with. The only caveat is that, whenever a system grows, the point has to be detected when it grows beyond recognition. Information systems have to be subject to the same occasional scrutiny as the rest of the organisation: "What should we be doing and how should we be doing it?"

17.8 CONTINUING CHANGE

If we assume that information systems are to continue to develop, then the question becomes one of the strategy that is adopted to manage that development. There are a number of alternatives, some of which may not be made consciously. The one which accords most closely with human nature is to assume that everyone is happy enough unless they are willing to keep up a pressure for change. There is some justification for this approach. It is easy to complain, much more difficult to come up with a better idea, especially one that will justify the effort of implementing it. It does mean, however, that users who shout loudest often get most from computing.

Perhaps the most common change strategy is some version of the users' queue. Users who want some alteration to their computing service fill in a formal request. This goes to the data processing manager, a computer users' committee or some other official monitoring body. Then choices are made about which changes can be implemented. Priorities are then set and resources allocated. The assumption is that individual users are the best judges of their own requirements.

This method of handling changes does cause an applications backlog as requests pile up faster than the computer people can deal with them. This has led to calls for more flexible program design, more efficient coding techniques, and languages that are user oriented rather than machine oriented. All these should lead to programs being changed more quickly and more effectively so that new bugs do not appear in the system. Faster requirements analysis would also seem to be the logical concomitant of faster program development, otherwise the backlog will be transferred from programmers to analysts.

Although this method of managing changes to the system may seem to be fair and reasonable, this may not work out in practice. Some of the 'changes' that are requested turn out to be things that the users were, or should have been, requesting all along. These may have been revealed at the systems testing stage when the users 'see' the system for the first time and discover that things obvious to them were not communicated to the analysts. This argues for more stringent requirements analysis and, more importantly, the setting up of a prototype, as this is the only specification that the users can genuinely state meets their requirements.

Prototyping and continuing development require an on-going relationship between users, analysts and system creators. It also requires that the whole Multiview framework is taken into account with each of the changes so that the system is still meeting its real objectives.

Some of the requests for changes will have to be initiated as a result of a re-analysis of the human activity system. The assumption here is that the system owners must look at the overall system and decide where it ought to be going and then get the information system set up to help them get there.

17.9   SUMMARY

Once the system has been created, it is necessary to set up acceptance criteria. These state the tests that the system has to pass in order to prove that it meets the requirements of the design. No system will ever be completely bug free, but it should be shown to be acceptably reliable.

The acceptance criteria should cover all the aspects of design: the socio-technical design, the human-computer interaction, and the seven parts of the technical subsystem. There is also the separate question of whether the analysis and design actually solves the problems of the organisation. This is a longer term exercise.

Once the system has been accepted, there are three types of maintenance that have to be carried out. There will be bugs to fix, there will be changes of detail, and there will be additions. It may well be appropriate to take out a maintenance contract on the software as well as the hardware. Changes of detail will call for small changes in the design, but do not require re-analysis. Extensions and additions will require at least a fast run through the whole of Multiview.

The normal systems life cycle should take account of the fact that the project will be implemented in phases and that it will need to develop in response to changes in the organisation or its environment. There will also be changes required in the system as the people involved think of better ways of handling things or as better equipment is brought out. There needs to be a strategy which takes account of this continuous need for changes. In particular, there should be regular reviews of the organisational needs and whether the information system is serving those needs.

17.10 EXERCISES

1 Do you think that the method used to establish the views of the user was appropriate in the community health case study?

Chapter 18
Case Study 6: The Academic Department

This case study concerns the development of an information system for an academic department of a university. The case study is used here to bring together all aspects of Multiview. Further details of the application can be found in Avison (1989 and 1990a). The project has the long term aim of fulfilling the information requirements of staff and students of the department. It should also integrate with other systems of the university. There is also a university steering group deciding on the university's strategy for management information systems over a period of ten years. One of the authors of this text is also a member of that group. The departmental information system (DIS) will integrate with this system, but the whole application will take many years to develop fully.

The department has grown considerably over the last few years, and it is of the size where communications become more difficult and the sheer weight of administrative work makes control a particular problem. But it is essential to meet target dates, such as those stated in conference 'calls for papers' or research council 'calls for proposals', and to meet examination schedules. It is also necessary to control activities in the department, such as the selection, purchase, maintenance and use of equipment.

As the early draft of the rich picture shows (Figure 18.1), there are a number of areas that warrant investigation in the problem situation. It is interesting that the emphasis in the diagram has been placed on the courses offered by the department. Figure 18.2 gives an alternative view of the department and emphasises the role of the head of department and senior tutor. The various intermediate rich pictures were later merged to form one which was generally acceptable. Rich pictures were also drawn for a number of areas of concern in the department, and these areas have been identified as:

- *Admissions*: The admissions process must handle enquiries, visits, student and staff presentations, ensure an adequate supply of booklets, and so on. A DIS should provide useful information such as the correlation between student visits and admissions, and statistics on the qualifications of applicants.

- *Lecturer/course/student*: This subsystem needs to provide up-to-date class lists, syllabuses, reading lists and tutor lists, draw up and provide printed timetables and monitor student assessment of courses. The fact that this information is held for the community will help to ensure that the latest versions are always readily available, and there is no confusion about which *is* the latest version.

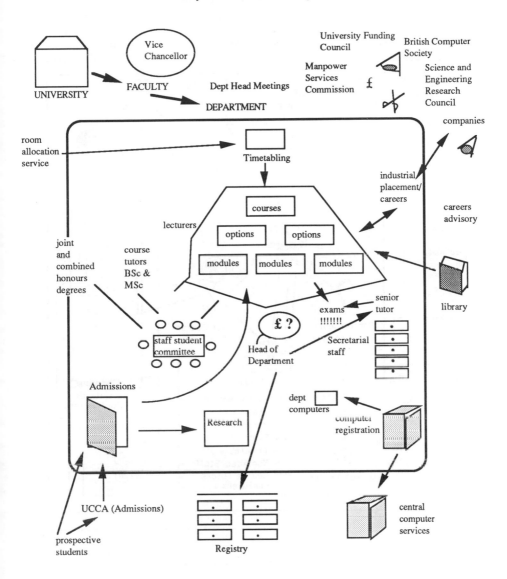

Fig. 18.1. Rich picture of academic department

- *Examinations*: Keeping track of progress in following the examination schedule through the processes of examination paper design, writing questions, typing and checking, sending to external examiners, and holding boards of examiners meetings, is complex, and failure to keep to timetables causes many problems. This subsystem is likely to inter-relate with the electronic notice-board and departmental diary subsystems.

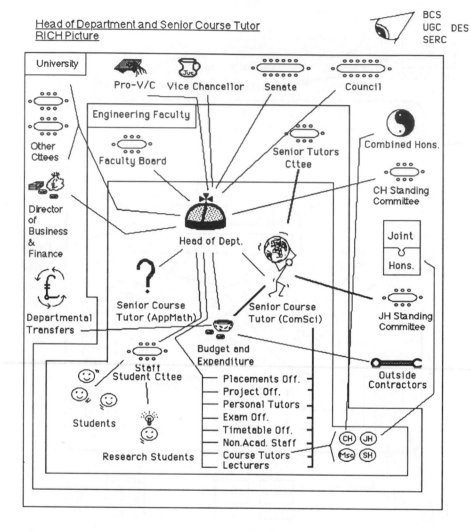

Fig. 18.2. Rich picture - concerns of head of department and senior tutor

- *Notice board*: An electronic notice board and diary can be used to hold details of department meetings, such as seminars, committee and staff meetings, and give dates related to calls for papers and research proposals. This would help to ease the process of arranging meetings when people are free.

- *Industrial Placements and Careers*: It is important to keep details of industrial placements (about half of the undergraduates opt for a 'sandwich' year). This has been further complicated recently by a number of foreign exchanges which have been financed by European programmes such as ERASMUS. The information held will include a record of visits and company names and contacts. It would also be very useful to follow the careers of graduates. Present records depend on the willingness of graduates to provide this information (which usually comes with a request for a reference) and it would be helpful to formalise this process.

- *Research*: Many calls for research proposals require detailed information about the proposed project, research staff, equipment, finance required, and so on. Completing each application individually takes much time, but the process could be speeded up considerably with a general departmental database. The details of previous research applications held in the DIS would also be useful as much of this material may be common to a number of applications.

- *Library*: The departmental library holds books, journals, technical reports, student project reports, dissertations and theses, and the library subsystem will hold details of stock, borrowings recorded, and will link to the university library and its computerised information system (GEAC). The present paper system often fails to identify easily the whereabouts of some material. The system should also manage an exchange scheme which exists between universities. The DIS could provide a satisfactory solution, for a full-time librarian for the department is not feasible at present.

- *Equipment*: Details of equipment need to be held on the database and this will include their 'owners', place held, serial numbers, costs, and maintenance record. It is true that these details, like many others discussed, *are* held presently, in this case by the computer officer given this responsibility. What is lacking is the ability to link with other aspects of the departmental system, so that, for example, equipment loaned can be tied in with coursework and project timetables, so as to make the best overall use of available equipment.

- *Computer registration*: This subsystem would register students who have rights of access to particular computer systems, and allocate paper usage and disk space. Registration and de-registration could be achieved automatically by 'liaising' with the student records on the database. Only special requests, such as those for extra disk space or for use of a new machine to carry out a project, should need significant intervention.

- *Accounting*: This subsystem could detail the financial incomings and outgoings of the department, keeping track of funds for conferences and travel, equipment, stationery, fees for seminars, and so on.

- *Decision support system*: This system would facilitate access to particular individual subsystems to deal with *ad hoc* queries and also facilitate (to appropriate users) the provision of information which might necessitate source data coming from a number of subsystems.

The overall system is to produce standard reports for regular output, provide statistical analyses, and handle ad-hoc queries.

The project has mainly been carried out by students. Each group of students has tended either to concentrate on one of the above areas (either starting from scratch or carrying on from where another group finished) or to help other groups in that year by updating the overall models (such as the entity model as new entities were discovered) and providing standards for menu layouts and other screen designs.

The entity model, shown as Figure 18.3, shows the scale of the overall project. The number of entity types approaches one hundred. Each group working on a particular area used a subset of this diagram. Figure 18.4 shows the entity model for the area 'students and courses'.

Different groups of students have been working on prototypes and the project has been progressing over a period of four years. Many of the diagrams presented in this chapter have been taken from student reports over this period. A computer officer has been appointed full-time whose role is to convert these prototypes into an integrated operational system.

The details of the entities found on Figure 18.4 are shown below. In retrospect, the attribute names should have been more helpful. We were limited to eight characters on one of the database management systems used.

Entity :   CANDIDATE
Description :   Person that applies to the department for place on a course

Attribute	Description	Example
FCADDR1	Candidate address line one	24, High Street....
FCADDR2	Candidate address line two	
FCADDR3	Candidate address line three	
FCAPDAT	Application date	12/04/93
FCAPNUM	Application number	89456937
FCNAME	Name of applicant	Davy, John.
FCSEX	Sex of applicant	M
FCTEL	Contact telephone number	0855-756453 EXTN 2234

Entity :   COMPANY
Description :   General entity referring to either industrial placement or 'first-job' organisation.

Attribute	Description	Example
FCOADD1	First line of company address	162, Baker St.
FCOADD2	Second line of company address	London,
FCOADD3	Third line of company address	W1
FCOCNAM	Name of company contact	Nigel James
FCOINFO1	First line of other details	Pay around average
FCOINFO2	Second line of other details	
FCOINFO3	Third line of other details	
FCOINFO4	Fourth line of other details	
FCOINFO5	Fifth line of other details	
FCONAME	Company Name	Cobil Oil Co. Ltd.
FCOTELE	Telephone number	01-936-8245

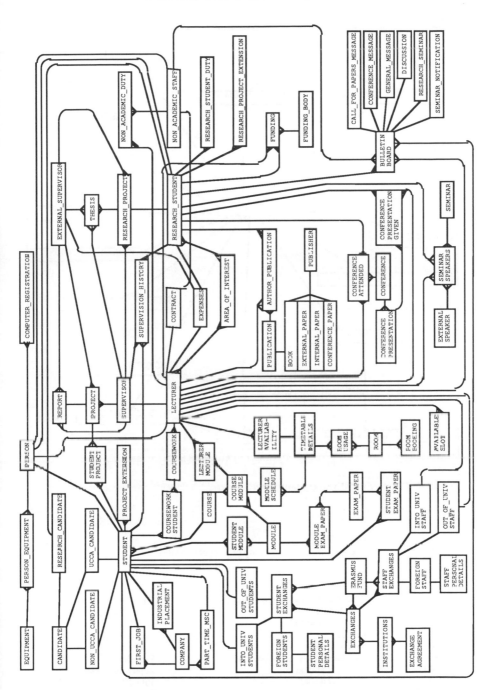

Fig. 18.3. Entity model of the academic department

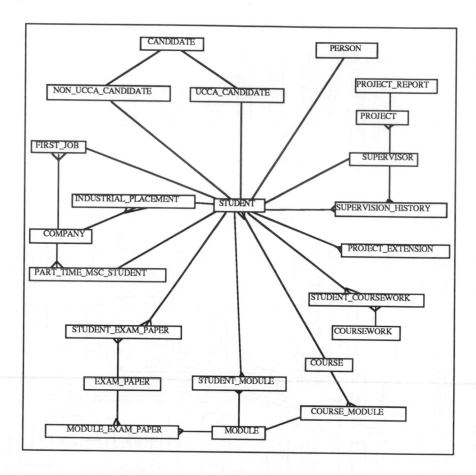

Fig.18.4. Entity model for students and courses

Entity : Description :	COURSE A university course made up of a set of modules	
Attribute	Description	Example
FCADMRE	Course admission requirements	BBC at 'A' level
FCTITLE	Course title	BSc. Computing Sc..
FCCODE	Unique course code	G500
FCOBJ	Course Objectives	Learn to ....
FCPROF	Course Profile	4 Years......
FCASSES	Part-time, full-time or both info	Full-time
FCSDATE	Course start-date	September 1986
FCEDATE	Course end-date	July 1990
FCTUTOR	Course tutor	P.C. Smith

Entity :   COURSE_MODULE
Description :   Links COURSE and MODULE

Attribute	Description	Example
FCMASSES	Method of assessment	50% Exam....
FCMCCODE	Course code for that module	G500
FCMMCODE	Module code	CS310
FCMTEACH	Teaching method	Practical Sessions..
FCMTIME	How much time does the course involve	22 hours

Entity :   COURSEWORK
Description :   Piece of assessed work as part of a module

Attribute	Description	Example
FCWTITL	Title of the coursework	A Study...
FCWCCOD	Course code of work	G500
FCWMCOD	Module code of work	CS350
FCWABS	General description of work	Discuss...........
FCWREQ	Detailed requirements	Write a ....
FCWLDAT	Submission date	25/01/90
FCWSREQ	Submission requirements	Submit to......

Entity :   EXAM_PAPER
Description :   A single exam paper, from one or more modules

Attribute	Description	Example
FEPTITL	Full title of paper	Digital Systems....
FEPNUM	Unique paper identifier	
FEPDUR	Length of exam	3 Hours
FEPEQN	Equipment needed for exam	Calculator

Entity :   FIRST_JOB
Description :   First employment after leaving the department

Attribute	Description	Example
FFJCOMP	Company name	Joe Bloggs Ltd.
FFJID	Unique student ID number	861115703
FFJSAL	First job starting salary	£13,000
FFJTITL	First job title	Service Analyst

Entity :   INDUSTRIAL_PLACEMENT
Description :   Employment as part of a course

Attribute	Description	Example
FIPCOMP	Company name	Joe Bloggs Ltd.
FIPLOC	Location of placement	Reading
FIPDATE	Placement start date	01/08/88
FIPID	Unique student ID number	861115703
FIPTITL	Job title	Network Operator

Entity :   MODULE
Description :   Subject taken as part of a course

Attribute	Description	Example
FMCODE	Module code	CS310
FMTITL	Title of Module	Intro to Struc...
FMPREREQ	Pre-requisites to starting module	CS234/ ...
FMSYL	Syllabus of module	Intro......
FMOBJ	Module objectives	To study....
FMREAD	Indicative reading list for course	NASHELSKY...

Entity :   MODULE_EXAM_PAPER
Description :   One of the modules in an exam paper

Attribute	Description	Example
FMEPCODE	Module code	CS310
FMEPDUR	Time allocated to this module in paper	1.5 hours
FMEPNUM	Exam paper number	3

Entity :   NON_UCCA_CANDIDATE
Description :   Course application not via UCCA

Attribute	Description	Example
FNUCAPNUM	Application number	00768
FNUCOUR	Course code applied for	G500
FNUCINTD	Interviewed ?	Yes
FNUCINDAT	Interview date	05/03/89
FNUCOFF	Type of offer made	Unconditional
FNUCRES	Candidates response	Accept

Entity :   PART_TIME_MSC
Description :   Job held by the part time MSc student

Attribute	Description	Example
FPTCNAM	Name of company worked for	Tesco
FPTID	Unique ID number	853441226
FPTEL	Work telephone number	021-765-8765
FPTTITL	Job title	Store manager

Entity :   PROJECT
Description :   Details of project undertaken by department member

Attribute	Description	Example
FNRPID	Unique student ID number	861115703
FNRPNUM	Project number	765
FNRPTITL	Project title	A Study into...

Entity :   PERSON
Description :   Any member of the department, student, academic etc

Attribute	Description	Example
FPSNAME	Surname	Taylor
FPFNAME	First name	Jessica
FPONAME	Other names, not first or surname	Sally
FPID	Student unique ID number	861115703
FPDOB	Date of Birth	19/08/70
FPHAD1	Home address lines	15, Queen St.,
FPHAD2		
FPHAD3		
FPHAD4		
FPSEX	Sex	Female
FPSPDET1	Special details lines	Suffers from...
FPSPDET1		
FPSTAT	Status of student	Placement
FPINT1	Interests/hobbies lines	Football
FPINT2		Archery
FPUAD1	University address lines	Flat 3, ...
FPUAD2		
FPUAD3		
FPUAD4		
FPUTEL	University telephone number	021-359-3452
FPNKIN	Name of next of kin	Bloggs, J.
FPKAD1	Next of kin address lines	
FPKAD2		
FPKAD3		
FPKAD4		
FPKHTEL	Next of kin home telephone number.	01-892-2607
FPKWTEL	Next of kin work telephone number.	01-983-4982

Entity :   PROJECT_EXTENSION
Description :   Details an application to extend a project deadline

Attribute	Description	Example
FPEXACC	Accepted or rejected ?	ACCEPTED
FPEXDAT	Date extension was applied for	12/06/88
FPEXEND	New submission date	24/07/88
FPEXID	Student ID number	892324265
FPEXNUM	Number of extensions (incl. this ext)	2

Entity :   PROJECT_REPORT / REPORT / THESIS
Description :   Written account of project work

Attribute	Description	Example
FRASID	ID of project supervisor	861115703
FRDATE	Date that the report was produced	13/11/90
FREXMO	Name of the external examiner	Walter, H, Scott
FRID	Author's dept. ID number	795646556
FRRES	Level achieved (Pass or Fail)	P
FRTITL	Title of the report	A Comparison of ..

Entity :   STUDENT
Description :   A department member taking a course

Attribute	Description	Example
FSAL1G	'A' Level Grade (First 'A' level)	B
FSAL1T	'A' Level Title (First 'A' level)	Psychology
FSAL2G	'A' Level Grade (Second 'A' level)	C
FSAL2T	'A' Level Title (Second 'A' level)	English
FSAL3G	'A' Level Grade (Third 'A' level)	B
FSAL3T	'A' Level Title (Third 'A' level)	Latin
FSAL4G	'A' Level Grade (Fourth 'A' level)	A
FSAL4T	'A' Level Title (Fourth 'A' level)	French
FSAL5G	'A' Level Grade (Fifth 'A' level)	C
FSAL5T	'A' Level Title (Fifth 'A' level)	Mathematics
FSALEVP	Total 'A' level points score	21
FSAPNUM	Unique application number	000678
FSCOUR	Course code	G500
FSGCOL	O'level or GCSE	GCSE
FSID	Unique student ID number	861115703
FSLEDES	Last educational establishment	King's School Oxford
FSOLCOMP	O'level Computer Science Grade	C
FSOLENGL	O'level English Grade	D
FSOLMATH	O'level Maths Grade	E
FSOTQUAL	Any other qualifications ?	City & Guilds in....
FSSTAT	Student course status	BSc
FSTUT	Personal Tutor	P. C. Smith
FSUCCA	UCCA candidate or not	UCCA
FSYDEP	Estimated year of leaving	1990
FSYENT	Year of entry	1986

Entity :   STUDENT_COURSEWORK
Description :   Links the STUDENT and COURSEWORK entities

Attribute	Description	Example
FCSID	Unique student ID number	861115703
FCSTITL	Official title of coursework	MSL Compiler

Entity :   STUDENT_EXAM_PAPER
Description :   Links STUDENT and EXAM_PAPER entities
                 i.e. A student taking a paper

Attribute	Description	Example
FSEPID	Unique student ID number	86111570
FSEPNUM	Exam unique ID number	000634
FSEPOCC	Number of attempts	4

Entity :   STUDENT_MODULE
Description :   A student taking a module as part of a course

Attribute	Description	Example
FSMCODE	Module code	CS310
FSMID	Student unique ID number	861115703
FSMTERM	Term module taken	3
FSMKEY	Virtual key of FSMID/MODULE	

Entity : Description :	SUPERVISION_HISTORY Record of periods of project supervision	
Attribute	Description	Example
FSHEDATE	Date supervision ended	12/01/89
FSHSDATE	Date supervision started	11/06/88
FSHSTID	Unique student ID number	861115703
FSHSUID	Unique supervisor ID number	795635643

Entity : Description :	SUPERVISOR Person that supervises a project or assesses coursework	
Attribute	Description	Example
FSUID	Supervisor ID number	664563423
FSUPOD	Position in the dept.	Admissions Officer
FSUPORG	Position within research group	Convenor

Entity : Description :	UCCA_CANDIDATE Application via UCCA	
Attribute	Description	Example
FUCOUR	Course applied for	G500
FUCAPNUM	UCCA application number	674764764
FUCAST	Aston position on UCCA form	3
FUCINTD	Interviewed ?	No
FUCINDAT	Interview date	12/11/87
FUCOFF	Offer made to applicant	Conditional
FUCRES	Candidates response	Reject

In developing the information system, the co-operation of colleagues was and still is required, and the prospective carrot of an information system to help administrative work, although neither guaranteed nor short-term, proved tempting to academic and non-academic staff alike. Colleagues agreed to help both the academic staff leading the project and the students requiring advice when investigating the application area. Such co-operation was agreed informally, through discussions, and formally, in a departmental staff meeting.

This promise of help has been fulfilled. One colleague even 'played' a non-helpful role - something that was not agreed beforehand, but happened 'naturally' - and this proved useful to students who could experience and react to this situation. This colleague had developed his own system which worked and he did not want the application to be duplicated in the DIS. This is not an unsatisfactory situation, unless he leaves the department.

In general, those colleagues teaching information systems and other teachers of computer science, administrative staff, and technicians have proved willing to be interviewed, participate in the prototype development, use the prototypes, comment on the design, attend formal presentations, and help in the assessment process.

The students take the course as an option on the final year BSc Computing Science. They have already had courses in information systems and databases. Warnings of hard work and many difficulties ahead reduce their number so that about half the students take the option. Nevertheless, the course has gained popularity over the years. Groups meet frequently to ensure that their efforts integrate successfully. Students on the course tend to be highly motivated.

Students on the 'action learning' course have gained experience in:

- Interviewing techniques;
- Group work and inter-group work;
- Project control;
- Presenting seminars;
- Training users;
- Report writing and other documentation techniques;
- Understanding roles, such as that of the database administrator;
- Using and evaluating contrasting methodologies, techniques and tools used in information systems work; and
- Producing part of a working information system.

We have always been impressed by the enthusiasm that students exercise in such work. One group which adopted Multiview decided to use a more sophisticated functional model diagram technique than that described in the text. These students used standard function diagrams early in their work, but as they gathered more information and there were *pointers to design,* they modified these diagrams to show, for example, in what ways each sub-process was connected with the others and what data was passing between them. The basic function diagrams described earlier only show "that there is a link". The technique can be seen in deMarco (1979) and a number of other methodologies use them. These charts are usually described as **structure charts** or **diagrams**.

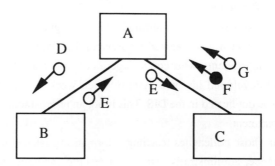

Fig.18.5. Structure diagram

The structure chart is a series of boxes (representing processes or modules) and connecting lines (representing links to subordinate processes) which are arranged in a hierarchy. The basic diagram is shown as Figure 18.5. This structure chart shows that:

- Module A can call module B and also module C. No sequencing for these calls nor whether they actually occur is implied by the diagraming notation. When the subordinate process terminates, control goes back to the calling process.
- When A calls B, it sends data of type D to B. When B terminates, it returns data of type E to A. Similarly, A communicates with C using data of types E and G.
- When C terminates, it sends a flag of type F to A. A flag is used as a flow of control data.

Figures 18.6 to 18.10 show the set of structure charts for the processing of UCCA applications. These are applicants for undergraduate courses who apply through the standard channels. Figures 18.11 to 18.13 show the data flow diagrams that were constructed representing this processing.

Groups were asked to produce reports contrasting the use of different techniques and automatic aids in given situations. As well as using different application packages, they used more general tools, such as application generators and documentation tools (including those that help draw data flow diagrams and 'normalize' data-sets), and also tools designed to support particular information systems development methodologies. Some groups followed different methodologies, but many chose Multiview as the basis of their approach.

All this enables an understanding of what to look for in exercising choice. In assessing their work, analysis based on these comparative studies is rewarded as much as 'results'. Mistakes are not rewarded, but marks are awarded to those students who recognize their mistakes in retrospect and suggest better alternatives.

Students are also able to look at some of the wider implications of information systems work, such as the effect of the Law (for example, the Data Protection Act) and the ways people react (for example, to requests for co-operation, to different interviewing methods, and to change in general). Students made recommendations for the departmental information system concerning the roles of the database administrator (DBA) and security levels for the DBA, academic staff, non-academic staff, research students and students taking formal courses.

Figure 18.14 shows some of the documentation standards that students have suggested for group work. It would be difficult to impose such standards without a spirit of cooperation. It is often more satisfactory for people to devise standards for themselves rather than having them imposed, even if they may not be as 'ideal' as some.

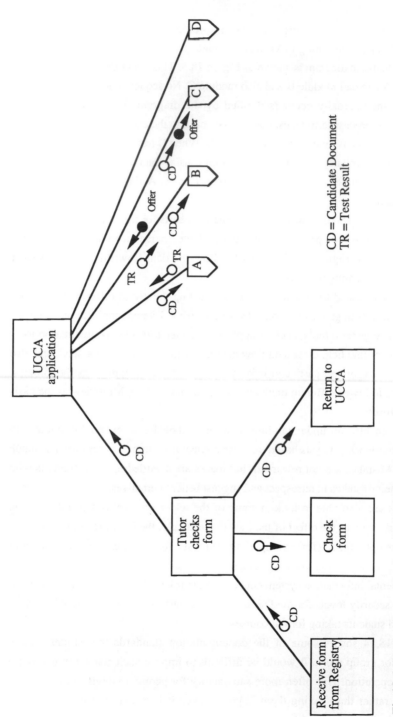

Fig.18.6. Top level structure chart for UCCA application

CD = Candidate Document
TR = Test Result

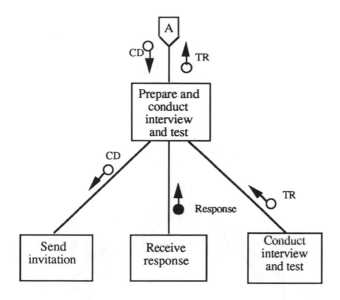

Fig. 18.7. Structure diagram for interviewing and testing applicants

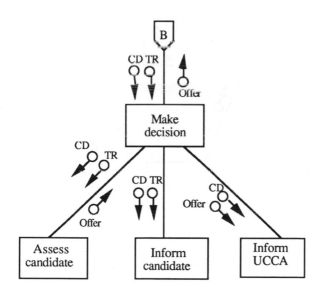

Fig. 18.8. Structure diagram for making a decision and informing applicants

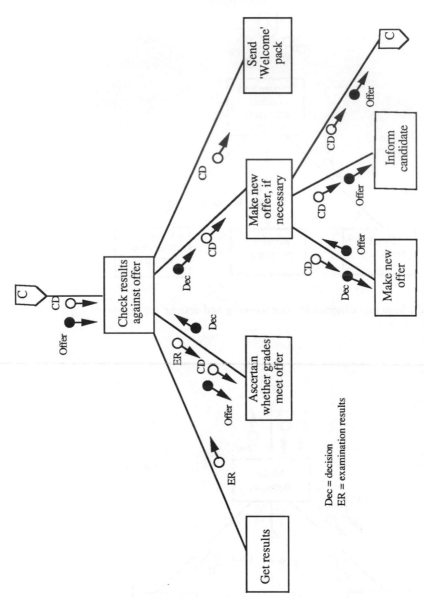

Fig.18.9. Structure diagram for examination results processing

Dec = decision
ER = examination results

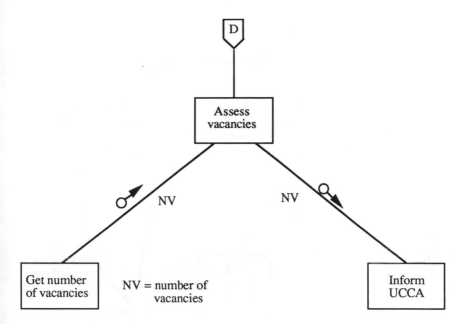

Fig. 18.10. Structure diagram for course vacancies

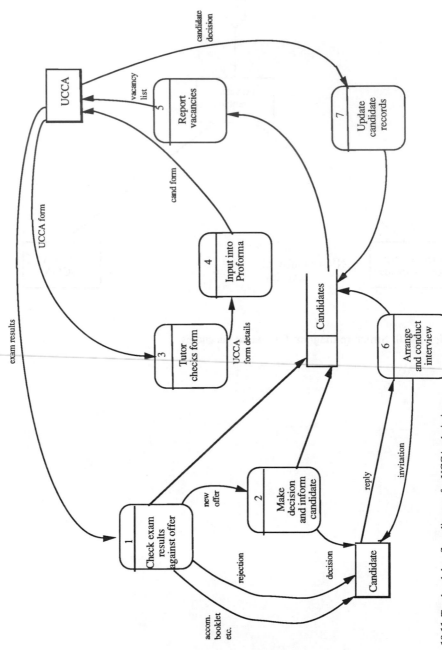

Fig. 18.11. Top level data flow diagram for UCCA admissions

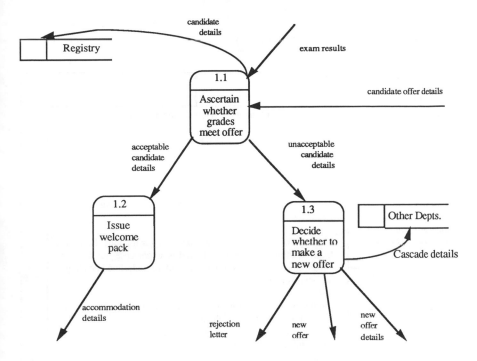

Fig.18.12. Data flow diagram second level (process 1)

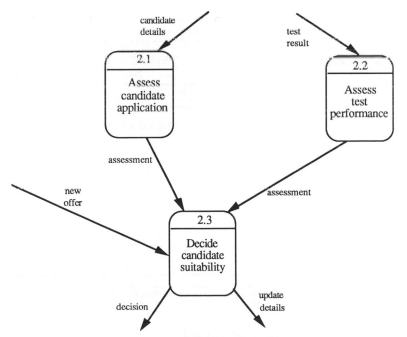

Fig.18.13. Data flow diagram second level (process 2)

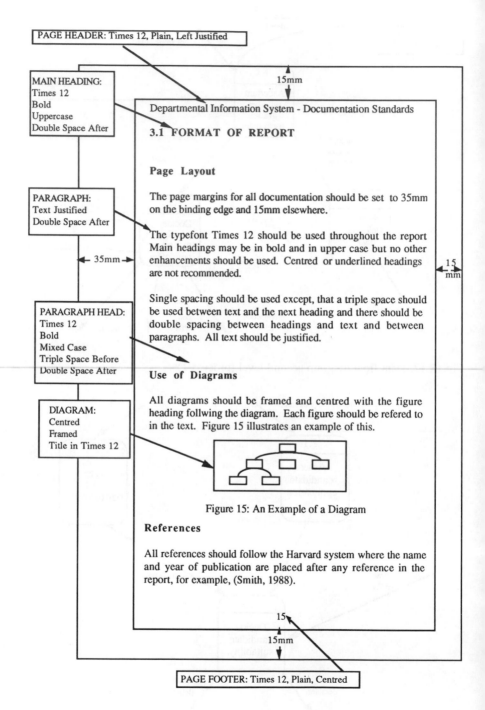

PAGE HEADER: Times 12, Plain, Left Justified

15mm

MAIN HEADING:
Times 12
Bold
Uppercase
Double Space After

Departmental Information System - Documentation Standards

3.1 FORMAT OF REPORT

Page Layout

The page margins for all documentation should be set to 35mm on the binding edge and 15mm elsewhere.

PARAGRAPH:
Text Justified
Double Space After

The typefont Times 12 should be used throughout the report Main headings may be in bold and in upper case but no other enhancements should be used. Centred or underlined headings are not recommended.

◄ 35mm ►

Single spacing should be used except, that a triple space should be used between text and the next heading and there should be double spacing between headings and text and between paragraphs. All text should be justified.

15 mm

PARAGRAPH HEAD:
Times 12
Bold
Mixed Case
Triple Space Before
Double Space After

Use of Diagrams

DIAGRAM:
Centred
Framed
Title in Times 12

All diagrams should be framed and centred with the figure heading follwing the diagram. Each figure should be refered to in the text. Figure 15 illustrates an example of this.

Figure 15: An Example of a Diagram

References

All references should follow the Harvard system where the name and year of publication are placed after any reference in the report, for example, (Smith, 1988).

15

15mm

PAGE FOOTER: Times 12, Plain, Centred

Fig.18.14. Suggested documentation standards

General consensus between student groups working on the project is required for much of the planning and development stages. Agreement on the establishment of the goals of the overall system and common standards, such as naming conventions and screen designs, is essential. However, groups of students worked reasonably independently when modelling 'their' part of the department, mapping this onto a database and developing the prototypes.

The prototype has been designed for different types of user:

- Database administrator
- Head of Department
- Senior tutor
- Admissions officer
- Course tutor
- Timetabling officer
- Examinations officer
- Careers/job placements officer
- Project supervisor
- Lecturer
- Member of non-academic staff
- Research student
- Student.

A user data model is provided for each of these user views. This allows the same data to be seen by different users in different ways; simplifies the user's perception; provides a certain amount of logical data independence when restructuring the database; and provides automatic security for personal data, as some data will not be available in a particular view. With the exception of the database administrator's view, which is the complete database, all these views are subsets of the data held in the DIS database.

An example user view is shown as Figure 18.15. It shows the data model for the admissions officers. There are three sub-views, those for the admissions officers for undergraduate courses, postgraduate courses and research students. The user model links to those parts of the database relating to the candidates, the courses (or research programmes), funding, and lecturer or supervisor. The admissions officer will be restricted to those aspects of the database, though if that person wears other 'hats' such as course tutor, then access to those parts of the database will also be permitted.

ADMISSIONS OFFICER USER DATA MODEL		
UCCA ADMISSIONS	**MSc ADMISSIONS**	**RESEARCH ADMISSIONS**
CANDIDATE DETAILS	CANDIDATE DETAILS	CANDIDATE DETAILS
Candidate UCCA-Candidate	Candidate Non-UCCA-Candidate	Candidate Research-Candidate
STUDENT DETAILS	STUDENT DETAILS	RESEARCH STUDENT
Student Person	Student Person	Research Student Person
COURSE DETAILS	COURSE DETAILS	PROJECT DETAILS
Course	Course	Research Project Research Programme
FUNDING DETAILS	FUNDING DETAILS	FUNDING DETAILS
Funding Funding body	Funding Funding body	Funding Funding body
SUPERVISOR DETAILS Supervisor Person Area-of-interest Lecturer	SUPERVISOR DETAILS Supervisor Person Area-of-interest Lecturer	SUPERVISOR DETAILS Supervisor Person Area-of-interest Lecturer

Fig. 18.15. Admissions officers' user data model

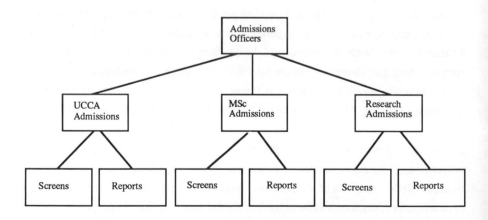

Fig. 18.16. Menu structure for admissions officers

```
┌────────────────────────────────────────────────────────────┐
│                                                              │
│  15 July 1989                            Screen ID 17        │
│          DEPARTMENT OF COMPUTER SCIENCE AND                  │
│                APPLIED MATHEMATICS                           │
│                                                              │
│       DEPARTMENTAL INFORMATION  SYSTEM                       │
│                                                              │
│    Admissions Officer Applications Menu                      │
│                                                              │
│    Select from the following:                                │
│                                                              │
│    1  UCCA Admissions Officer: Admission Details             │
│                                                              │
│    2  MSc Admissions Officer: Admission Details              │
│                                                              │
│    3  Research Admissions Officer: Admission Details         │
│                                                              │
│                                                              │
│                                                              │
│    H  Help                                                   │
│                                                              │
│    R  Return to previous menu                                │
│                                                              │
│    Q  Quit                                                   │
│                                                              │
│                                                              │
│    Enter your selection _                                    │
│                                                              │
└────────────────────────────────────────────────────────────┘
```

Fig. 18.17. The first-level menu for admissions officers

The applications are menu-driven, and the user chooses the preferred option through a series of menus, which can be by-passed by the experienced user. The basic menu structure is shown as Figure 18.16. Figure 18.17 shows the first-level menu for admissions officers and is therefore the top box of Figure 18.16. The first three selections will lead to a second level menu being set up for the appropriate admissions officer, which will involve a choice of screens or reports. Choosing option 1 in the first-level menu will lead to the display of the screen with the ID 18 (Figure 18.18). Assuming that the user wishes to print out reports concerning candidate details, option 2 will provide the various list of reports (Figure 18.19). Option 7, described as a 'statistics breakdown', gives information such as this year's figures compared to last year's, the proportion of female to male students, the proportion of home to overseas applicants, the average GCE 'A' level grade, the percentage of offers against the total number of applicants, and the percentage of offers which are accepted. Another option is Standard Table Two (option 9). This is presented as Figure 18.20. The option and report name is rather unhelpful, but it is the choice of the present admissions tutor and can, in any case, be changed easily.

```
┌─────────────────────────────────────────────────────────┐
│ 15 July 1989                                Screen ID 18 │
│          DEPARTMENT OF COMPUTER SCIENCE AND              │
│                 APPLIED MATHEMATICS                      │
│                                                          │
│          DEPARTMENTAL INFORMATION SYSTEM                 │
│                                                          │
│     UCCA Admissions Officer Applications Menu            │
│                                                          │
│     Select from the following:                           │
│                                                          │
│     1 Candidate Details - screens                        │
│     2 Candidate Details - reports                        │
│                                                          │
│     3 Student Details - screens                          │
│     4 Student Details - reports                          │
│                                                          │
│     5 Course Details - screens                           │
│     6 Course Details - reports                           │
│                                                          │
│     7 Supervisor Details - screens                       │
│     8 Supervisor Details - reports                       │
│                                                          │
│     H  Help                                              │
│                                                          │
│     R  Return to previous menu                           │
│                                                          │
│     Q  Quit                                              │
│                                                          │
│     Enter your selection _                               │
└─────────────────────────────────────────────────────────┘
```

Fig. 18.18. A second-level menu for admissions officers

```
┌─────────────────────────────────────────────────────────┐
│ 15 July 1989                                Screen ID21  │
│          DEPARTMENT OF COMPUTER SCIENCE AND              │
│                 APPLIED MATHEMATICS                      │
│                                                          │
│          DEPARTMENTAL INFORMATION SYSTEM                 │
│                                                          │
│     UCCA Admissions Officer: Candidate Reports           │
│                                                          │
│     Select from the following:                           │
│                                                          │
│         1 Overseas candidates list                       │
│         2 EEC candidates list                            │
│         3 Disabled candidates list                       │
│         4 Acknowledgement letters                        │
│         5 Offer letters                                  │
│         6 Address labels                                 │
│         7 Statistics breakdown                           │
│         8 Standard table one                             │
│         9 Standard table two                             │
│                                                          │
│     H  Help                                              │
│                                                          │
│     R  Return to previous menu                           │
│                                                          │
│     Q  Quit                                              │
│                                                          │
│     Enter your selection _                               │
└─────────────────────────────────────────────────────────┘
```

Fig. 18.19. A third-level menu for admissions officers

STANDARD TABLE TWO

WEEKLY BREAKDOWN OF UCCA ADMISSIONS PROCEDURE

Week	Ends	Rec	Unc	Con	Rej	Pen	PAc	FAc	Enr
1	07/01/90	1		1				1	
2	14/01/90	1		1				1	
3	21/01/90	3	1	1	1		1	1	1
4	28/01/90	3	1	1	1		1	1	1
5	04/02/90	3	1	1	1		1	1	1
6	11/02/90	3	1	1	1		1	1	1
7	18/02/90	3	1	1	1		1	1	1
8	25/03/90	4	2	1	1		1	2	1
9	04/03/90	4	2	1	1		1	2	1
10	11/03/90	4	2	1	1		1	2	1
11	18/03/90	4	2	1	1		1	2	1
12	25/03/90	7	2	2	1	2	1	2	1

Rec = Applications received   Unc = Number of Unconditional Offers
Con = Number of Conditional Offers   Rej = Number of Rejections
Pen = Number of Pending Offers   PAc = Number of Provisional Acceptances
FAc = Number of Firm Acceptances   Enr = Number of Candidates Enrolled

(These figures are cumulative.)

Fig. 18.20. Standard table two

The soft copy form for inputting and updating basic student information is shown as Figure 18.21. It shows the screen for adding, updating and deleting data relating to students (option 3 of the menu in Figure 18.18). The menu for the actions in this case is placed at the bottom of the screen. The user has to key-in the first letter of the options: thus A for Add, and so on. This screen is designed for experienced users. They will be used to completing these forms and do not need detailed prompting (though there is an option 'help' which shows the user what to do if required).

The data dictionary is used to describe every component of the database; locate the data areas; verify that requested modifications to the descriptions are permitted; co-ordinate restructuring tasks that must be performed on the database; control all access to the database; catalogue back-ups; and keep track of users and programs that access the database.

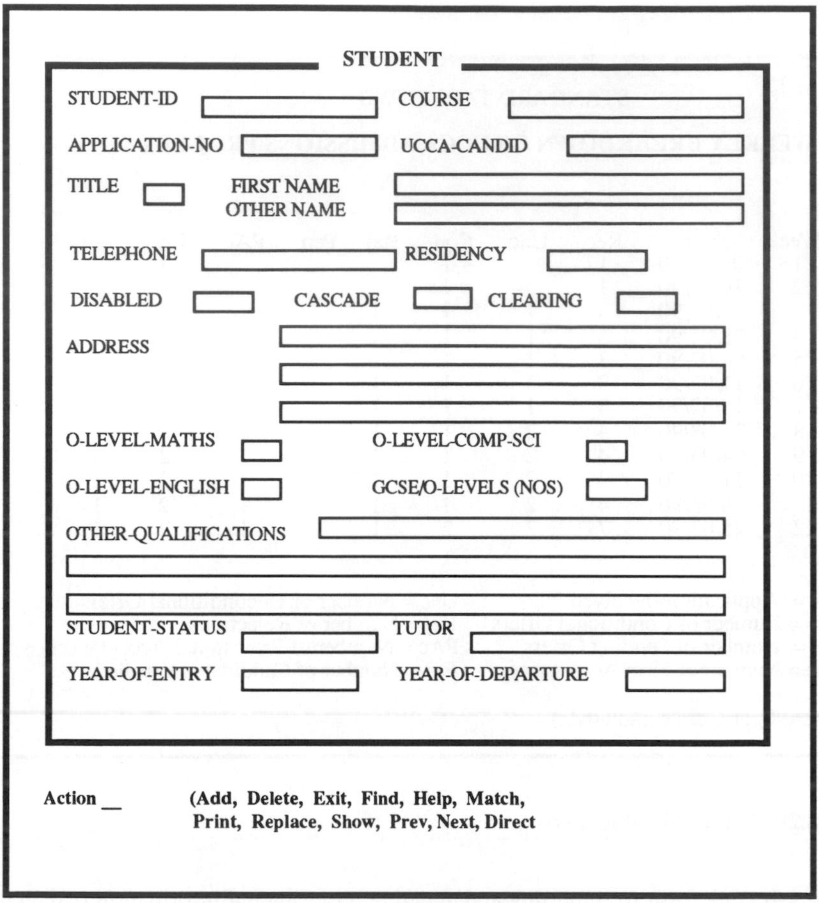

Fig. 18.21. VDU form for adding, updating or changing data relating to students

Security in the DIS is important, particularly as the database will contain personal information, and the system has a number of security features. Only registered users can create or use a file. Users are assigned an ID and password and will be registered with certain 'signon' privileges (for example, to read, create, change or delete a file) and a priority that defines the way in which they can use the system. At the user data model level, privileges that can be granted to an individual user include exclusive use of a file; the right to 'unhold' a record held by another user; rights to hold, delete, modify or add a record; and rights to modify the value of an individual data element. **Privacy** directly relates user access permission with the access constraints assigned to record types, view types and data elements. Privacy codes are assigned to record types and elements, and view types and elements. Tests compare these codes with user read and write codes, which are assigned by the database administrator to a particular user when he or she is authorised to use a model. When a database is shared by a number of users, it is also essential to maintain the **integrity** of the data. Again, it is not appropriate here to discuss this in detail, but the system provides a wide range of validity checks and integrity constraints.

The role of the computer officer includes:

- Setting up that part of the database to be implemented next
- Ensuring that the subsystem to be implemented fulfils the requirements of the particular users
- Performing a training role
- Fine-tuning aspects of the system already implemented to ensure that it continues to meet changing usage and demand of the users
- Ensuring the human-computer interface is suitable for the various types of users
- Ensuring that security and privacy requirements are met
- Evaluating software packages and hardware as they become available, and
- Co-ordinating the departmental information system with the development of the university management information system.

Tutorial systems have been designed for each user type, improving help facilities, and making the menus and screens more appropriate - in general making the system more usable (Eason, 1984). Usability in this context means making the DIS as easy to use as possible and ensuring that each user interface is appropriate to each of the thirteen different user groups. Users can now enter the system by typing 'DIS' and thereby going straight to the top menu (assuming that the user has the required access rights), whereas early versions required the user to follow a complex set of commands.

Wherever possible, the interface design needs to be flexible, even within a user group, as a naive user can quickly migrate to casual expert through to being an experienced professional. The extra facilities required to enable inexperienced users to navigate their way round a system will be time-wasting and irritating to professional users.

Although the prototype, which has been developed on a large computer using a large and complex software package, has shown that it is possible to set up a DIS using a database which will fulfil many of the information needs of staff and students and ease the administrative load on staff, there are many question marks in the prototype relating to ease of use, ease of learning, flexibility and speed of developing applications. We are constantly looking at other possible directions, such as the provision of an icon interface on a microcomputer which is linked to the mainframe. Here all accesses relating to data will be intercepted by the interface software:

- Receiving data requests from the user
- Processing those requests

- Transferring the requests to the mainframe system, executing the request and transferring the results back to the user, and
- Displaying the results in a suitable screen format.

The most likely direction is to implement the database on the mainframe and also link this with the microcomputer version of the database management system which will be implemented on the departmental network of microcomputers. This has a number of advantages:

- The use of the familiar icon interface, which the users prefer
- The availability of a number of tools which will speed up the development of some applications, in particular reports and screens
- Connections with the departmental network and the University local area network
- Easy transfer of information to other microcomputer packages for viewing in a number of ways, including graphically, and for data manipulation.

Figure 18.22 shows a screen used as part of a prototype system for student feedback. The use of buttons (for the various options) and icons (for help and return), gives a screen which seems to us a considerable improvement on the conventional menus of Figures 18.17 and 18.18. The input document shown as Figure 18.23 for recording students' general comments, also seems an improvement on the type of form illustrated as Figure 18.21. The up and down arrows for each window allow the user to extend the amount of text held beyond the actual window size. Thus the user could 'scroll' up (using the up arrow) to go to the top of the message or downwards using the down arrow.

One final comment. The experience with conventional database systems has shown that they are inappropriate to many aspects of this application, and their inappropriateness, by implication, extends to many applications. Conventional databases assume that all information can be classified and retrieved in tabular (relational) form. This limits the use of the database to a specific range of types of application and users. Some information may not suit this tabular representation, it may be better represented graphically or in image form. Information related to the DIS might be in the form of hand-written and annotated application forms or photographs. Further, some users may find tables an inconvenient and difficult-to-understand way of representing their information. In the long term, we need to develop multi-media databases, with their user interface much more flexible. This process has already started as the students' photographs are scanned and are included for display in each student's computer record (Figure 18.24).

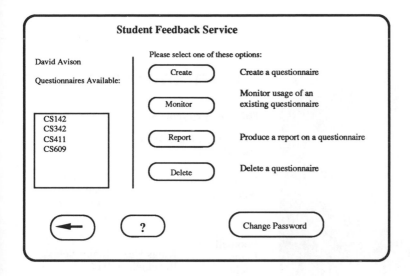

Fig. 18.22. The student feedback prototype - analysing student questionnaires

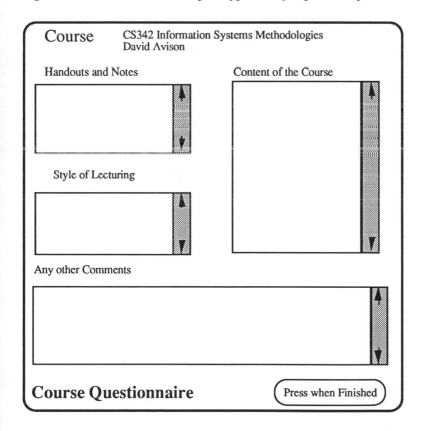

Fig. 18.23. Student feedback prototype - recording students' general comments

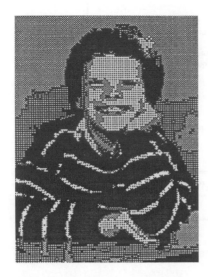

IDONTGOTO UNIVERSITY

Thomas François Avison   CS905642

BSc Computing Science
entered 1990   2 August 1979

18 Old Forest Road   French A
Wilderland   Maths C
                                             Computer B

Football
Piano   Kings Heath Junior School
Violin   Birmingham B14

Fig. 18.24. Student record with photograph

PART SEVEN

MULTIVIEW:
CONCLUSION

Chapter 19
Theory and Practice

19.1 LESSONS FROM THE FIELD WORK

In this final chapter we will firstly draw conclusions on the way Multiview worked out for us in the cases that we have described in the text. This discussion includes reflections on the experience of developing Multiview as well as attempting to draw lessons from the experience of using it.

Lesson 1 - A methodology takes time to learn
The initial formulation of the methodology, which is described in Wood-Harper (1982), took some years to develop through practice and field work. In fact, for the professional association case study the methodology was not formulated as such, it developed from experience gained in the field work. In the polytechnic distance learning unit case study, the internal systems analyst involved took some time to understand the methodology and therefore to use it in the application. Further, as the academic department case showed, although the methodology was described fully - at least to the lecturer's satisfaction - previously in a classroom situation, it was evident that the participants only fully understood it following use of the methodology in an action learning situation, in other words using the methodology 'for real'. Experiences of teaching and learning Multiview can be found in Wood-Harper and Flynn (1983), Antill and Wood-Harper (1984), Wood-Harper (1985 and 1989), Avison (1989 and 1990a).

Lesson 2- The Waterfall model is inappropriate
This methodology, as evidenced by our field work, does not, in practice, exhibit the step-by-step, top-down nature of the waterfall model (Agresti, 1986), sometimes referred to as the life cycle. None of the cases have exactly followed the methodology as espoused in Chapter 2. The users of the methodology will almost certainly find that they will carry out a series of iterations which are not shown in the classical model.

Further, in the real-world cases undertaken, some phases of the methodology were omitted and others were carried out in a different sequence from that expected. For example, in the professional association case study normalisation was not applied to the entities and in many of the cases the various matrices were omitted, and in the distance learning unit case some of the decisions relating to the technical subsystem were made very early in the project. In the academic case, on the other hand, elements were added to the methodology, for example, in the use of the structure diagrams.

Lesson 3 - The methodology is not a 'guarantor of truth'
Images within the views of the methodology are interpreted and selected depending on the context. For example, in the professional association case and the academic department case, the social options of the socio-technical phase were either omitted or not fully explored. The appropriateness of the use of some of the techniques also varied. For example, the comparative value of rich pictures, data flow diagrams and entity models varied greatly in their use for the freight import agency and computer consultancy company cases.

Lesson 4 - The political dimension is important
The manipulation of power, that is, the political dimension, is important in real-world situations. This transcends the rationale of any methodology. Most of the case studies show decisions being made which were influenced by considerations beyond those that are implied by the Multiview methodology. For example, in the professional association case, the secretary had her own motivation for the study beyond those of the association. At the early stages of applying the methodology, it was not possible to interview most members of the committee, which would be necessary to carry out a full analysis of the human activity system.

Lesson 5 - Responsible participation is contingent
A high level of responsible participation, *where appropriate,* is a positive ingredient of successful information systems development. For example, in the distance learning unit case in particular, the active participation of managers enhanced the methodology in use, and in the district health authority case, the active participation of the various health workers proved very helpful. Indeed in the community health case, the pilot groups adopted the hand-held data recorders readily and we feel that the trial would have been less successful had such a decision been imposed on the groups. In the professional association case, however, there was no responsible participation by the committee and staff members of the organisation. In the university academic department case, one key user refused to cooperate fully. One possible interpretation of this behaviour is that the particular user wanted to develop his own system. The department information system therefore 'invaded' his territory. In other case studies, some potential users were

identified as being apprehensive about the proposed information system and did not cooperate fully. This contradicts the arguments of 'pure' Multiview, presented in Part Two of the book, in which it is assumed that it is always possible to use responsible participation in information systems development.

Lesson 6 - In certain situations the methodology gives insufficient guidance
The methodology did not give sufficient guidance for all aspects of all the cases. For example, it was difficult to identify the interest groups in the professional association case and the distance learning unit case (though in the latter example the rich picture contains references to many of them). In using some of the techniques, particularly in a complex situation, further guidance was needed. The students developing the academic department information system found that the descriptions of some techniques given were inadequate, and they had to delve further in the reference manuals. In some instances they exposed weaknesses in the lecture material given previously.

Lesson 7 - the methodology is interpreted by users/analysts
The users/analysts affect the perception of the situation and they interpret the methodology. As the university academic department, the freight import agency and the computer consulting cases showed, the variety of interpretations reflected the variety of backgrounds and experiences of the analysts involved. The academic background of students, for instance, whether they were studying for an accountancy or computer science degree, influenced their choices. This effect is highlighted in professional analysts and users, where cultures, education, background, and so on, will greatly effect the interpretation of the methodology itself and the way it is used.

19.2 CONCLUSIONS FROM THIS EXPERIENCE

The following broad conclusions are implied from the lessons above (which come from the field work experience) and the literature. These arise from learning about the intellectual framework as seen in Figure 19.1. This framework depicts that the Multiview methodology transfers the relevant 'thinking about the content of the situation' to the 'content of the situation'.

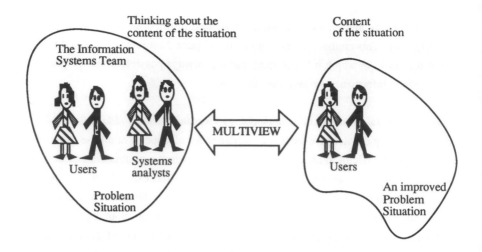

Fig. 19.1. A framework for defining an information system

Conclusion 1- The Multiview methodology is in a continuing state of development
This conclusion is not an attack on Multiview in isolation - all information systems development methodologies have limitations. Information Systems is a comparatively new discipline, the diversity of approaches is caused to some extent by the background and cultures of their authors and none is all-inclusive. The methodologies address a moving target in that the technology, along with tools and techniques supporting it, develop relentlessly. We therefore regard Multiview as defined in this text as part of a process of improving information systems practice. In a previous paper (Avison and Wood-Harper, 1986) we argue that Multiview is an *exploration* in the development of information systems rather than a methodology, because the latter term implies a formal, fixed and inflexible approach.

Readers of Wood-Harper *et al* (1985) will see many changes and the two authors of this text have had differing experiences when using Multiview. Although there is always a 'family resemblance' in each version of the methodology, we have modified our 'agreed methodology in 1985' on the basis of experiences since that time. Our experiences have been different, because no situation is the same as any other. We expect the methodology to develop further in the future. For example, we are following work of Land (1982a and 1985) to improve the process of identifying the stakeholders in a problem situation; of Land & Kennedy-McGregor (1987) in classifying information; and of Bjørn-Andersen & Davis (1985) and Symons & Walsham (1988) and others on the evaluation of information systems.

Conclusion 2- Defining an information system is contingent

Defining an information system is contingent on the methodology, the situation and the information systems development team. In some of the case studies not all of the stages of Multiview were used because of the situation (in one case there was no computer system developed). In other cases, the different analysts (for example, students in the academic department case) interpreted the 'same situation' differently. In any situation where an information system might be appropriate, there are factors such as culture, language and education which have to be taken into consideration. Sometimes the political and social climate is such that participation is difficult to achieve. In other situations particular tools and techniques are not appropriate to the problem situation. The systems analyst has to choose from a 'tool-box' those tools and techniques appropriate for each situation (Benyon & Skidmore, 1987), but within the framework of Multiview (Avison, Fitzgerald & Wood-Harper, 1988). The use of an information system methodology in practice is a hermeneutic process in which the situation is 'read' by the problem solvers (Argyris, Putman & Smith, 1985).

Conclusion 3 - Defining an information system can be considered as a social process

The process of going from 'thinking about the content of the information situation' by the information systems development team to the 'perceived content of the situation (including users)' illustrated in Figure 19.1, can be examined within different social theories relevant to information systems definition. For example, the first dimension comprises assumptions about the nature of defining an information system ranging from objective to subjective. The second dimension relates to the assumptions about the degree of change to the information situation ranging from regulation to radical. These dimensions yield four quadrants or paradigms in which the following assumptions can be located:

*   *Ontological* beliefs about the nature of reality;
*   *Information situation* beliefs about the behaviour of humans in the information situation;
*   *Epistemological* beliefs about how knowledge is acquired; and
*   *Methodological* beliefs in the appropriate devices, acquiring knowledge about and intervening in the information situation.

The four paradigms are:

*   *Functionalist* (objective-regulation);
*   *Interpretative* (subjective-regulation);
*   *Radical humanist* (subjective-radical); and
*   *Radical structuralist* (objective-radical).

The assumptions can be located in the paradigms as shown in Figure 19.2.

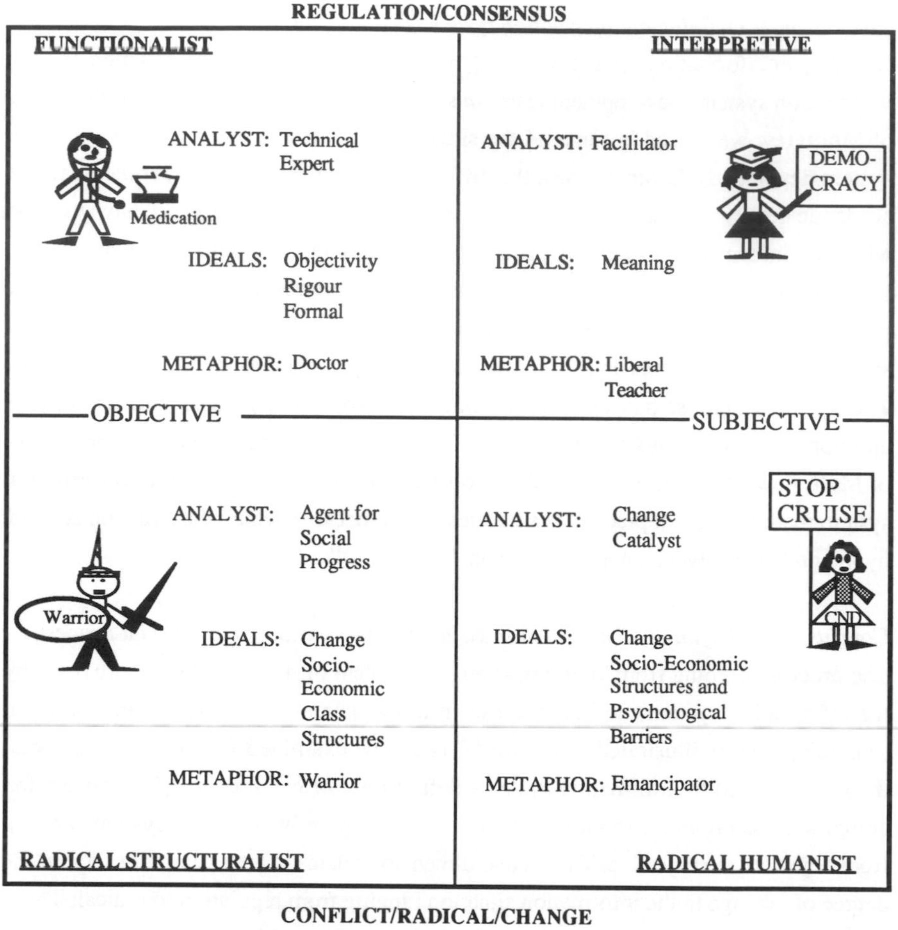

REGULATION/CONSENSUS

FUNCTIONALIST	INTERPRETIVE
ANALYST: Technical Expert	ANALYST: Facilitator
Medication	
IDEALS: Objectivity Rigour Formal	IDEALS: Meaning
METAPHOR: Doctor	METAPHOR: Liberal Teacher

————OBJECTIVE ———————————————————— SUBJECTIVE————

	STOP CRUISE
ANALYST: Agent for Social Progress	ANALYST: Change Catalyst
Warrior	CND
IDEALS: Change Socio-Economic Class Structures	IDEALS: Change Socio-Economic Structures and Psychological Barriers
METAPHOR: Warrior	METAPHOR: Emancipator
RADICAL STRUCTURALIST	RADICAL HUMANIST

CONFLICT/RADICAL/CHANGE

Fig. 19.2 Roles, ideals and metaphors assumed when defining an information system

In the functionalist perspective, the information system consists of interactions which function independently of outside manipulation. The analyst assumes that he can readily understand the situation, indeed there is an assumption of rational behaviour by the actors which makes understanding easier. The systems are well controlled, can be well understood and can be formally defined.

In the interpretive perspective, it is assumed that the analyst is subjective and interprets the problem situation. He hopes that it will be possible to understand the intentions of the actors in the situation. Participation and involvement will be the best way to obtain detailed information about the problem situation, and later to be able to predict and control the situation.

In the radical structuralist view, the situation will appear to have a formal existence but require radical change due to, for example, contradictory and conflicting elements. The systems analyst regards himself as an agent for change and social progress, emancipating people from their socio-economic structures.

Finally, in the radical humanist view, the situation is seen as external and complex. There is an emphasis on participation to enable a rapport between the actors and lead to emancipation at all levels, for example, socio-economic and psychological.

As can be seen from Figure 19.2, the view taken of the role and the effect of the systems analyst on the problem situation will depend on the perspective: it might be as a 'technical expert' imposing good practices on the situation; or as 'facilitator' helping the users achieve their goals; or as an 'agent for social progress' imposing radical change on the situation; or finally as change analyst, encouraging the users to effect major change. In the diagram we have used metaphors of doctor, teacher, warrior and emancipator to express these activities. The idea of using metaphors in information systems is discussed in Madsen (1987).

A full discussion of research methods in information systems as a whole, including further discussion of the issues discussed in this Chapter, will be given in Wood-Harper & Avison (1991).

Bibliography

Agresti, W. N. (1986) *New Paradigms for Software Development,* IEE Computer Society Press.

Andersen, E., Kensing, F., Lundin, J., Mathiassen, L., Munk-Madsen, A., Rasbech, M. & Sørgaard, P. (1990) *Professional Systems Development,* Prentice-Hall, Hemel Hempstead.

Antill, L. & Wood-Harper, A.T (1984) The Who's doing What for Whom Design Stage, *SOFT,* 2, 2.

Argyris, C., Putman, C. R. & Smith, D. (1986) *Action Science,* Jossey-Bass, San Francisco.

Avison, D. E. (1985) *Information Systems Development: A Data Base Approach,* Blackwell Scientific Publications, Oxford.

Avison, D. E. & Wood-Harper, A. T. (1986) Multiview - An Exploration in Information Systems Development, *Australian Computer Journal,* 18, 4, pp174-179.

Avison, D. E. & Catchpole, C. P. (1987) Information Systems for the Community Health Services, *Medical Informatics,* 13, 2.

Avison, D. E. & Fitzgerald, G. (1988) *Information Systems Development: Methodologies, Techniques and Tools,* Blackwell Scientific Publications, Oxford.

Avison, D. E., Fitzgerald, G. & Wood-Harper, A. T. (1988) Information Systems Development: A Tool-kit is not Enough, *Computer Journal,* 31, 4.

Avison, D. E. (1989) Action Learning for Information Systems Teaching, *International Journal of Information Management,* 9,1.

Avison, D. E. (1990a) A Departmental Information System, *International Journal of Information Management,* 10, 2.

Avison, D. E. (1990b) *Mastering Business Microcomputing,* 2nd ed, Macmillan, Basingstoke.

Bemelmans, T. M. A. (ed.) (1985) *Beyond Productivity: Information Systems Development for Organisational Effectiveness,* North Holland.

Benyon, D. & Skidmore, S. (1987) Towards a tool-kit for the systems analyst, *Computer Journal,* 30, 1, pp2-7.

Bjørn-Andersen, N. & Davis, G. B. (1988) *Proceedings of IFIP WG 8.2 Conference on Information Systems Assessment,* North Holland, Amsterdam.

Boland, R. & Hirschheim, R. A. (1987) *Critical Issues in Information Systems Research,* Wiley, Chichester.

Buckingham, R. A., Hirschheim, R. A., Land, F. F. & Tully, C. J. (1987) *Information Systems Education: Recommendations and Implementation,* CUP, Cambridge.

Burns, R. N. & Dennis, A. R. (1985) Selecting the Appropriate Application Development Methodology, *Data Base,* 17, 1, pp 19-24.

Capper, L. (1985) *The Use of Analysis and Design Methodologies in the Working Environment: An Experimental Approach,* In: Bemelmans (1985), pp37-48.

Catchpole, C. P. (1985) Survey of the Applications of Computers in the Community Health Services, *Public Health,* 99, 6, pp356-363.

Catchpole, C. P. (1987) *Information Systems Design for the Community Health Services,* PhD Thesis, Aston University, Birmingham.

Catchpole, C. P., Avison, D. E. & Peart, S. (1987) A Tale of Two Systems, *Nursing Times,* 83, 34, pp57-58.

Checkland, P. B. and Griffin, R. (1970) Management Information Systems: A Systems View, *Journal of Systems Engineering,* 1, 2.

Checkland, P. B. (1981) *Systems Thinking, Systems Practice,* John Wiley, Chichester.

Checkland, P. B. (1984) *Rethinking a Systems Approach,* In: Tomlinson & Kiss (1984).

Checkland, P. B. (1985) *Systems Theory and Information Systems,* In: Bemelmans, (1985).

Daniels, A & Yeats, D. A. (1972) *Basic Training in Systems Analysis,* 2nd ed, Pitman, London.

Date, C. J. (1986) An Introduction to Database Systems, 4th ed, Addison Wesley, Cambridge.

Davenport, R. A. (1978) Data Analysis for Data Base Design, *Australian Computer Journal,* 10.

Davis, G. B. (1974) *Management Information Systems: Conceptual Foundations, Structure and Development* McGraw-Hill, New York.

Davis, G. B. (1982) Strategies for Information Requirements Determination, *IBM Systems Journal,* 21, 2, pp 4-30.

Davis, G. B. (1983) The Domain of Information Systems, *MISRC,* 83-07.

Davis, G. B. & Olsen, M. H. (1985) *Management Information Systems: Conceptual Foundations, Structure and Development,* 2nd ed, McGraw Hill, New York.

DeMarco, T. (1979) *Structured Analysis and System Specification,* Prentice-Hall, Englewood Cliffs.

Downs, E., Clare, P. & Coe, I. (1988) *Structured Systems Analysis and Design Method: Application and Context,* Prentice Hall, Hemel Hempstead.

Eason, K. D. (1984) Towards the Experimental Study of Usability, *Behaviour and Information Technology*, 2, 2.

Episkopou, D. M. & Wood-Harper, A. T. (1984) *The Multi-view Methodology - Applications and Implications*, In: Bemelmans (1985).

Episkopou, D. M. & Wood-Harper, A. T. (1986) Towards a Framework to Choose Appropriate IS Approaches, *Computer Journal*, 29, 3.

Fok, L. M., Kumar, K. & Wood-Harper, A. T. (1987) *Methodologies for Socio-Technical Systems (STS) Development: A Comparative Review,* 8th International Conference of Information Systems, Pittsburg.

Galliers, R. (1987) *Information Analysis: Selected Readings*, Addison Wesley, Sydney.

Gane, C. P. & Sarson, T. (1979) *Structured Systems Analysis: Tools and Techniques*, Prentice-Hall, Englewood Cliffs.

Hawgood, J. & Land, F, F. (1986) A Multivalent Approach to Information System Assessment, In: Bjørn-Andersen & Davis (1988).

Herzberg, F. (1966) *Work and the Nature of Man*, Staple Press, New York.

Iivari, J. (1987) *A Methodology for IS Development as an Organisational Change: a Pragmatic Contingency Approach*, In: Klein & Kumar (1987).

Keen, P. G. W. & Scott Morton, M. S. (1978) *Decision Support Systems,* Addison-Wesley, Cambridge.

Klein, H. K. & Kumar, K. (1987) *Information Systems Development for Human Progress in Organisations,* North Holland, Amsterdam.

Kling, R, K. (1987) *Defining the Boundaries of Computing Across Complex Organisations,* In: Boland & Hirschheim (1987).

Körner, E. (1982) *First Report to the Secretary of State on Health Service Information,* Körner Steering Group, DHSS/NHS, London.

Körner, E. (1984a) *Fourth Report to the Secretary of State on Health Service Information,* Körner Steering Group, DHSS/NHS, London.

Körner, E. (1984b) *Fifth Report to the Secretary of State on Health Service Information,* Körner Steering Group, DHSS/NHS, London.

Land, F. F. (1982a) *Adapting to Changing User Requirements*, In: Galliers (1987).

Land, F. F. (1982b) Notes on Participation, *Computer Journal*, 25, 2.

Land, F. F. & Hirschheim, R. (1983) Participative Systems Design: Rationale, Tools and Techniques, *Journal of Applied Systems Analysis*, 10.

Land, F. F. (1985) Is an Information Theory Enough?, *Computer Journal*, 28, 3.

Land, F. F. & Somogyi, E. (1986) Software Engineering: The Relationship between a Formal System and its Environment, *Journal of Information Technology*, 1, 1.

Land, F. F. & Kennedy-McGregor, M. (1987) *Information and Information Systems: Concepts and Perspectives,* In: Galliers (1987).

Lyytinen, K. (1987) *A Taxonomic Perspective of Information Systems Development: Theoretical Constructs and Recommendations,* In: Boland & Hirschheim (1987).

Macdonald, I. G. & Palmer, I.R. (1982) Systems Development in a Shared Data Environment, the D2S2 Methodology, In: Olle, T. W., Sol, H. G. & Verrjin-Stuart, A. A. (eds) *Information Systems Design Methodologies: A Comparative Review,* North Holland, Amsterdam.

Madsen, K. H. (1987) *Breakthrough by Breakdown: Metaphors and Structured Domains,* In: Klein & Kumar (1987).

Markus, L. M. (1984) *Information Systems in Organisations: Bugs and Features,* Pitman, Marshfield.

Martin. J. & McClure. C. (1984) *Structured Techniques for Computing,* Savant Research Institute, Carnforth.

Mumford, E. & Weir, M. (1979) *Computer Systems in Work Design - The ETHICS Method,* Associated Business Press, London.

Mumford, E. (1981) Participative Systems Design: Structure and Method, *Systems, Objectives and Solutions,* 1.

Mumford, E. (1983a) *Designing Human Systems,* Manchester Business School, Manchester.

Mumford, E. (1983b) *Designing Participatively,* Manchester Business School, Manchester.

Mumford, E. (1985) Defining Systems Requirements to meet Business Needs: A Case Study Example, *Computer Journal,* 28, 2.

Page-Jones, M. (1980) *The Practical Guide to Structured Systems Design,* Yourdon, New York.

Pettigrew, A. M. (1983) Contextualist Research: A Natural Way to Link Theory and Practise, In: *Proceedings of the Conference on Conducting Research with Theory and Practice in Mind,* Center for Effective Organisations, University of Southern California, November 1983.

Rock-Evans, R. (1981) *Data Analysis,* IPC Press, London.

Shave, M. J. R. (1981) Entities, Functions and Binary Relations: Steps to a Conceptual Schema, *Computer Journal,* 24, 1.

Silverman, D. (1990) Six Rules of Qualitative Research: A Post-Romantic Argument, *Symbolic Interaction,* 12, 2.

Symons, V. & Walsham, G. (1988) The Evaluation of Information Systems: A Critique, *Journal of Applied Systems Analysis,* 15.

Tomlinson, R. (1984) *Rethinking the Process of Systems Analysis and Operational Research: from Practice to Precept - and Back Again*, In: Tomlinson & Kiss (1984).

Tomlinson, R. & Kiss, I. (eds) (1984), *Rethinking the Process of Operational Research and Systems Analysis*, Pergamon, Oxford.

Trist, E. (1981) *The Evolution of Socio-Technical Systems*, Ministry of Labour, Ontario.

Veryard, R. (1984) *Pragmatic Data Analysis*, Blackwell Scientific Publications, Oxford.

Waters, S. J. (1979a) *Systems Specifications*, NCC, Manchester.

Waters, S. J. (1979b) Towards Comprehensive Specifications, *Computer Journal*, 22, 3.

Wilson, B. (1984) *Systems: Concepts, Methodologies and Applications,* Wiley, Chichester.

Wood-Harper, A, T. (1982) An Analysis and Design Methodology for Information Systems in Small Organisations, In: Bjørn-Andersen, N. (ed) *Towards Tools for Transition Systems Design Methodologies*, IFIP WG8.2 Report, Copenhagen.

Wood-Harper, A. T. & Fitzgerald, G. (1982) A Taxonomy of Current Approaches to Systems Analysis, *Computer Journal*, 25, 1.

Wood-Harper, A. T. & Flynn, D. J. (1983) Action Learning for Teaching Information Systems, *Computer Journal*, 26, 1.

Wood-Harper, A. T. (1985) Information Research Methods: Using Action Research, In: Fitzgerald, G., Hirschheim, R., Mumford, E. & Wood-Harper, A. T. (eds), *Research Methods in Information Systems*, North Holland, Amsterdam.

Wood-Harper, A. T., Antill, L. & Avison, D. E. (1985) *Information Systems Definition: the Multiview Approach,* Blackwell Scientific Publications, Oxford.

Wood-Harper, A. T. (1989) *Comparison of Information Systems Definition Methodologies: Action Research Multiview Perspective*, PhD Thesis, University of East Anglia, Norwich.

Wood-Harper, A. T. & Avison, D. E. (1991), *Enquiry into Information Systems Development: the Research Arena,* Blackwell Scientific Publications, Oxford.

Yourdon, E. (1989) *Modern Structured Analysis*, Prentice-Hall, Englewood Cliffs.

Index

Items in italic refer to names of cited authors (see also Bibliography); page numbers in bold indicate principal references.